The
Comfortable
House

This book was set in Palatino by Achorn
Graphics and printed and bound by
Halliday Lithograph, in the United States
of America.

**Library of Congress Cataloging-in-
Publication Data**
Gowans, Alan
   The comfortable house : North American
suburban architecture, 1890–1930

   Bibliography: p.
   Includes index.
   1. Suburban homes—United States. 2.
Suburban homes—Canada. I. Title.
NA7571.G68   1986   728.3′7′0973   86-2987
ISBN 0-262-07095-2

This book was commissioned by *The Old-
House Journal,* in whose pages a survey of
post-Victorian domestic architecture entitled "The Comfortable House" appeared
in 1982.

The Comfortable House

North American Suburban Architecture 1890–1930

Alan Gowans

Bibliography by Lamia Doumato

The MIT Press
Cambridge, Massachusetts
London, England

It is true that even in our republican land the average does not mean the noblest, either among men or buildings. But it means that which is *collectively* most prominent. The general effect of a modern town depends less upon its monumental structures than upon the aggregate of its dwellings, humble in comparison though these individually may be. So there is no architectural branch in which success is more desirable than in the domestic branch.

Mariana Griswold Van Rensselaer, "Recent Architecture in America. V. City Dwellings," *Century Magazine* 31 (November 1885–April 1886): 548.

Twenty years ago, the historian who wanted to write about nineteenth-century houses had to confront two prejudices. One of them regarded domestic architecture as too insignificant a topic for art-historical investigation; the other reflected a widespread aversion to the forms of nineteenth-century "Victorian" architecture as a whole. . . . Prejudice against the nineteenth century has almost entirely disappeared among responsible critics. . . . Yet . . . the other prejudice [has] . . . turned itself right around. The single-family houses that are most historically significant through the period . . . now seem not too common but somewhat too esoteric to be studied without apology. . . . products of a blindly complacent and unduly favored minority. . . . Should we not rather be studying the nineteenth-century city as a whole, in all its urbanistic complication, its tenements, social mixtures, gas houses, trolly lines, and colonial dependencies? The answer, if there is one, has to be that we must study both at once.

Vincent Scully, "American Houses: Thomas Jefferson to Frank Lloyd Wright," in E. Kaufmann (ed.), *The Rise of an American Architecture* (New York, Praeger, 1970), 163.

Contents

Acknowledgments

I wish to thank Clem Labine and Patricia Poore of *The Old-House Journal* for their early support and encouragement of this project. The first draft of this book was written in the summer of 1982 at the Center for Advanced Study in the Visual Arts at the National Gallery of Art in Washington, and my warm thanks are due to CASVA's Dean, Henry Millon, and the staff of the NGA library for so generously making special space and facilities available to me. Also I want to acknowledge the great assistance rendered by the staff of the University of Victoria library, where the book was completed, and especially the Interlibrary Loan department. A special word of appreciation to John Crosby Freeman, director of the American Life Foundation, both for initial encouragement and for help in the difficult task of working with such *fliegende Blätter* as this kind of study involves; not only have ALF's reprints been invaluable, but it was also in great part thanks to his efforts, when on the faculty of the University of Victoria, that UVic's library has such good holdings in North American architecture. Last but not least, my best thanks to the staff of The MIT Press for all their help, encouragement, and talent.

Introduction

Just because you may wish to build a home with little money, you are not obliged to put up with an architectural crime. A few years ago, if a person were subject only to the mercy of a local contractor or a near-architect of the small town, he very probably would have been inflicted with some such dire calamity. But today, thanks to the wave of thought which is sweeping over these great United States—the psychological influence that is demanding better, more cheerful and therefore more livable homes, one may have something aesthetic, something nice, and expend no more in the obtaining than his father spent for that bald-faced old "house."[1]

The Comfortable House originated in an attempt to make coherent the profusion of styles represented in suburban houses built in the period 1890–1930, when, thanks to partial or total prefabrication, more houses were erected than in the nation's entire previous history and when combinations of forms and ornament were distinct from both the more familiar Picturesque stylings of the preceding period and from the more consistent Academic and popular/commercial styling of houses in the 1930s and succeeding decades.

Styles in the 1890–1930 years cannot be identified by one or two dominant features (here a pointed window, there a pinnacle, and it's Gothic Revival; here a round arch, there a bracket, and it's Italianate; pylons make it Egyptian, mansards make it Second Empire, and so on), and Academic insistence on drawing from a single stylistic format had little effect at the popular level until the 1920s. Styles got so fragmented, in fact, that it is necessary to briefly recapitulate the entire history of North American architectural styles in order to keep the 1890–1930 period in perspective and especially to see if and how its styles differed in social function from those of earlier times.

Social function—how styles *worked*, in and for society, and what they were made to *do*—is critical. Determining social function involves asking crass questions like: Why did builders think some features worth paying for but not others? Why, if economy was their most advertised virtue, did they think it worthwhile to retain so many

ornamental stylistic tags? Obviously, to make their houses saleable: purchasers found houses styled one way more attractive than another and certainly preferable to unornamented ones. And why should that have been? Because, obviously, purchasers had certain preconceived ideas about how a house should look, what it should symbolize or signal (subliminally, consciously, whatever)—that is, how it should work for them, what it should do for them, what kind of statement it should make about them. And what produced these preconceptions? With that we are forced to reckon with the whole climate of mind of those times, with the Comfortable House in its cultural context.

In American cultural history the years 1890–1930 could be described as the immediately post-frontier age. Without necessarily buying the whole package of ideas proposed by the Frederick Jackson Turner school, one can easily recognize many qualities in suburban houses of those years which derive from attitudes shaped by that frontier over the preceding three hundred years—and still, indeed, active. For though *we* may perceive retrospectively that the frontier was vanishing by 1890, few were the contemporaries who did so.

Belief in endlessly abundant raw materials and endlessly abundant land continued through those years; it informed both the confident assumption that suburbs could go on expanding forever without inflating land prices and the proud assertions of quality made by so many catalog writers. "We'll pay $1 for every knot you can find in our wood" was Aladdin's consistent boast from the company's first 1906 catalog into the 1920s—a claim including summer cottages and barracks as well as bungalows![2] It also fueled that confidence in national progress and personal upward mobility which an ever-expanding frontier had imprinted upon the American character. Houses so quickly built and so relatively easy to exchange or abandon implied and helped make possible the social and geographic mobility which from earliest times seemed so distinctively American. P. A. Bruce's *Economic History of Virginia in the Seventeenth Century*[3] makes manifest that what we consider a typically twentieth-century American landscape spectacle—ruined frame farmhouses with abandoned fields all around—is in fact something that goes back to the beginning of American history. The people who deserted those homes did so, more often than not, in hope of better things rather than in despair or disillusion. What we take to be the breakdown of the extended family, which makes grandpa a voice on the end of long-distance telephone calls rather than the hoary *pater familias* of popular legend, knees wreathed in happy grandchildren, is not some modern tragedy, but a logical consequence of people being free to better themselves in life by moving out of some sterile circle. So the flimsy, impermanent buildings of the seventeenth and eighteenth centuries, still complained of by Jefferson in *Notes . . . on Virginia* (irrationally, for a doctrinaire democrat) were succeeded by the balloon-frame house of the nineteenth century; the ready-cut or mail-order house; the one-room-wide, one-story-high box house of the early twentieth century; and, finally, the mobile home of our own times. What J. B. Jackson has written so perceptively of the latter expresses the dominant characteristic of all these American houses:

The temporary dwelling . . . . has always offered, though for a brief time only, a kind of freedom we often undervalue: the freedom from burdensome emotional ties with the environment, freedom from communal responsibilities, freedom from the tyranny of the traditional home and its possessions; the freedom from belonging to a tight-knit social order; and above all, the freedom to move on to somewhere else.[4]

The Comfortable House reflected as well the role that land speculators played in peopling this continent. Less euphorically, perhaps, the mass-produced, prefabricated house epitomized that jack-of-all-trades strain of amateurishness in American life inculcated and maintained by the frontier's tendency to dilute population density and encourage self-sufficiency.

Such beliefs—or better, perhaps, assumptions taken for self-evident—did not derive from the frontier alone,

of course; there may be an element of coincidence in the Comfortable House's appearance and flourishing just as the frontier vanished. Yet for whatever reason, the 1890–1930 years have a coherent ideological identity within the broad stream of American culture. Above all they represent a climactic confidence in those social and political institutions established at the Revolution: in this country, every person can indeed become personally independent, just as the nation had.

Hence the term "Comfortable House." Has there ever been an era when houses were *un*comfortable? Well, yes, as a matter of fact. Through most of human history the average house was uncomfortable by our standards; perhaps by our standards all of them were. Palaces elegant, grand, exquisite you can find; homesteads solid, sturdy, simple. But comfortable? That's a very recent *desideratum*. Even so characteristically American forms as the early nineteenth-century Classical Revival temple-house and the High Picturesque mansion of the 1860s and 1870s subordinated comfort to the making of statements about ideology and social status. Only at the end of that century was comfort taken for granted. And certainly it was only then taken to be a right that the poor as well as the rich might expect. Such expectation was more than periodic campaign rhetoric, furthermore. It was based upon confident belief that within the American system a Comfortable House for all was a realistic goal. To a greater extent than nowadays remembered, that expectation and that goal were realized.

Our appreciation of the unique achievement the Comfortable House represents has been delayed, if not derailed, by the decades of triumphant Modernism just past. To Modernist cast of thought, American suburban houses of the 1890–1930 years, on whatever level, were all impossibly vulgar, amateurish, bourgeois, and tasteless. The same applied to their Academic and popular/commercial successors. Yet the Comfortable House survived all invective because it filled a real social need for which no effective alternative was offered.[5] It still does.

1

The Comfortable
House in Its Times

Architecture is both a creation and a mirror of its times. And the times that created the Comfortable House, were, like all ages, complex. They were the best of times; they were the worst of times.

They were the best of times especially in retrospect. Confidence is what a modern would most remark about the era. All its works were stamped with this confidence, but none more than the popular domestic building, what is called here the Comfortable House of the typical suburbs, outlying city areas, and small towns.

Looking back from a time when the whole of Western civilization could be annihilated overnight, when pollution and overpopulation and miseries without end press in on every side, the years from 1890 to 1930, or at least from 1890 to 1914, seem like a golden age of security. Western civilization possessed a technology immeasurably superior to anything seen in the world before, and its component nations were expanding rapidly over the globe, confidently occupying territories with the certainty that Westernizing natives could only do them good.

American optimism in the early years of this century was but the most obvious aspect of an optimism endemic in the Western world. Its philosophical base lay in the doctrine of evolution as then interpreted. Contemplating the march from amoeba to Man, as pictured over the preceding half century, one conclusion seemed inescapable: there was in the universe some law or principle which determined that everything must get, was getting, and would continue to get, better and better. Evolution had culminated in Man, and Man was culminating—had culminated, indeed—in the modern liberal democratic states of western Europe and, above all, the United States.

Admittedly (and paradoxically), believers in the inevitability of progress could find no evidence of purpose in evolution (largely because in formulating the doctrine, any possibility of purpose had been ruled out from the start, of course!). All the more reason for satisfaction, then, that sheer blind happy chance had produced that ascent from primeval sludge to prehistoric cave, from Cheops to Caucasian professor of enlightened outlook and scientific education, which constituted the liberal view of history.

Nowhere was Western civilization's general optimism more rampant than in the United States after 1890. Two centuries before, French Enlightenment leaders had prophesied how the future was going to be, and in America that future was coming true. "We see," wrote Baron Turgot in a sketch on universal history as it looked to him in 1750,

the establishment of societies and the formation of nations which one after the other dominate other nations or obey them. Empires rise and fall; the laws and forms of government succeed one another; the arts and sciences are discovered and made more perfect. Sometimes arrested, sometimes accelerated in their progress, they pass through different climates. Interest, ambition, and vain glory perpetually change the scene of the world, inundating the earth with blood. But in the midst of these ravages man's mores become sweeter, the human mind becomes enlightened, and the isolated nations come closer to each other. Commerce and politics reunite finally all the parts of the globe and the whole mass of the human-kind, alternating between calm and agitation, good and bad, marches constantly, though slowly, toward greater perfection.[1]

Well, to be sure, as things turned out, *he* didn't see that. He saw his politics as finance minister leading France to disaster and revolution; he saw the continent plunged into bloody wars and France at last beaten, decimated, reduced to the status of a satellite of triumphant, relatively unenlightened Britain. But few in 1890 would have denied that now in America his vision was finally at long last coming true; the nation "conceived in liberty and dedicated to the proposition that all men are created equal" had survived its own cruel civil war and now seemed flourishing proof that "any nation so conceived and so dedicated can long endure." Here in America what Turgot had prophesied was coming to pass: a perfection consisting of a religious respect for personal liberty and labor; of unchallenged acceptance of the principle that rights to property are inviolate; of ever-increasing abundance of goods; of ever-increasing wealth, ever more widely shared; of ever-growing enjoyment, enlightenment, and means to happiness for all.

And America seemed to have achieved all this without sacrificing traditional Western values. Churches in the United States were crowded, and church building was a major field of architectural endeavor. And the preaching therein was optimistic—no longer the old hell-fire and salvation doctrines, but, at least in those main-line Protestant denominations to which the great majority of Americans still belonged, a Social Gospel, helping democracy put finishing touches on the perfecting of society here and now. The Western kind of purposefully enduring propertied family, planted in America at its beginnings, seemed to have survived all strains and stresses too. Not only had it survived, it had multiplied. Alongside Adamses and Carters and Lees now stood Astors and Vanderbilts and Rockefellers, not quite propertied families in the old sense to be sure, but arguably in the same tradition. A steady supply of sober, well-disciplined youths assured the perpetuation and advance of the learned professions and sciences. Divorce was rare. Families were large. The traditional working classes continued to work, and with new incentive; more and more moved into the middle class, and immigrants and blacks replaced them. Society seemed to stand solid like an elephant, permanent, enduring. Small wonder that, superficially at least, the architecture of this age seems the image of confident success.

"I count those years between 1880 and 1900," wrote Ralph Adams Cram in his 1936 autobiography,

as the most remarkable in American architectural history, for in so brief a space of time it was given a wholly new direction. Ten years before the beginning of this era it was, as I have said, the most degraded in human history; at the close, it stood in the front of all the work of the Western world, with new possibilities opening before it in the thirty years to follow on—possibilities that were to be taken advantage of to the full.[2]

Few would have disagreed; most architects then coming into practice thought theirs was to be a "golden age," knowing all about the past that needed to be known, confidently and competently dictating the future. They created images of wealth and power. Great mansions for the rich, made of rich materials—heavy oak and walnut, polished marble, gilt fittings, velvet draperies, tiled flooring. Great fairs, proclaiming successes without end, past and future. White cities of Imperial Roman columns and arcades at Chicago, San Francisco, St. Louis; churrigueresque at San Diego; Art Deco at Chicago's Century of Progress. Great skyscrapers, product and proclamation of America's fantastic growth in economic power in those post-Victorian years (by 1930 every American city of any importance had a cluster, where few had had even one in 1890), envied and copied by the Soviet Union, templed on street facade and crown, with plain shafts rising twenty, thirty, fifty stories into the air, and visible from all the far suburbs ringing the metropolis round (figures 1.1, 1.2).

And the suburbs themselves—in some ways they were the greatest declaration of wealth and power of all. How rich, how varied the interiors of even simple bungalows seemed—conscious embodiments of belief in progress and in "the reality of the world-wide movement in the direction of better things," as Gustav Stickley put it in the closing essay of *Craftsman Homes* (1901). How confidently Aladdin's catalog compared their mail-order, ready-cut houses with the greatest monuments of all the ages:

To him who says the Readi-Cut System is not possible or practicable, point to the Pyramids of Egypt, refer to Solomon's Temple as described in the Bible, or inspect the Washington Monument, or the 57-story Woolworth Building in New York City. You will find that each was prepared, erected, and completed by the Readi-Cut System (figure 1.3).

All this optimism seemed to climax in the 1920s. America's undamaged industrial plant and her un-scathed banking system towered over Europe's war-ruined economies. American power was unchallenged; American isolation (and security) regained. As people used to say with Dr. Coué, "Every day in every way I'm getting better and better." It was the decade of the Charleston and the flapper, the sheikh and the college rah-rah, bearskin coats and hiked-up skirts and roll-down stockings. A great time to be alive and living in some comfortable house in some comfortable suburb! Well, for some. For the middle class and the upper, business classes. Not particularly for workingmen. Certainly not for farmers. Or for blacks. And not really for all the middle class. Certainly not for those given to reflection and pondering on the deep causes of things. For there was much out of joint in post-Victorian America too. And ultimately the character of its suburbs, its comfortable houses, was dictated more by those deep anxieties than by the surface bubblings.

Post-Victorian America was the worst of times on the very deepest levels. For then the full implications of the laws of thermodynamics sank in. Not just among the more learned philosophers and scientists, pondering in colloquia or scholarly journals, but among ordinary educated people. Who could forget images like H. G. Wells's word-picture of the huge red dying sun and the moribund planet earth in his popular science fiction novel *Time Machine*, which appeared in 1900? In the organic world, the world of plants and animals, of Man and of History, all might be evolutionary progress. It is exactly opposite in the inorganic world, where energy flows slowly, ceaselessly, uncontrollably toward an ultimate equilibrium wherein all available energy has been exhausted. Slowly, ceaselessly, uncontrollably, that is, the universe evolves into a wasteland of frozen matter, all energy forever locked into irrecoverable form, night and stillness and death predestined, final forever. Since from that inorganic world arose all life, and to that

1.1 City Hall, Oakland, California. Completed in 1914 by the firm of Palmer, Hornbostle, and Jones. Archetypal symbol of civic confidence, consciously designed as such. Articulated in terms of human perceptions, expression of materials and structure being subordinated to that end. (IMG:NAL)

1.2 Bucharest Hotel on the Moscow River. The Soviet state in the 1930s paid American capitalism the supreme compliment of imitation, correctly perceiving its skyscrapers as prime symbols of economic accomplishment. (IMG:NAL). ''Appropriating skyscrapers for symbols of the triumphant proletariat made perfect sense. . . . Why not employ . . . a symbol of capitalism known to every Russian through newspaper pictures and movies, to proclaim how workers have now, thanks to the Party, taken over those enchanted palaces from banished landlords and cremated Czars?'' (Alan Gowans, *Learning to See*, 1981, pp. 438–39)

1.3 Twin prides of American civilization and symbols of capitalist accomplishment: Cass Gilbert's Woolworth Building of 1913 and the Aladdin Readi-Cut System of homebuilding. In its way, this advertisement from Aladdin's 1919 catalog is a counterpart to the Philadelphia Centennial of 1876 and the Philadelphia City Hall intended to go along with it—a continuing assertion that in America the progress of all the ages finds consummation.

world all life had one day to return in death, it followed that in the world of plants and animals, of Man and of History, nothing can have more than illusory significance. Not Man. Once traditional religions had talked about the soul as an eternal immortal reality, on its way back to God; but now they talked mostly about bringing the Kingdom of Heaven down to earth—an earth doomed to nothingness. Not history. Once upon a time Man was thought of as a being created noble and good by God and though fallen, struggling to regain paradise, a being with a history worthy of study, a history to be learned from. But if Man comes to be where he is as the result of blind progress up from slime, why study that history? What can be learned from filthy savages squatting in caves? For that matter, what can be learned from Aristotle or Aquinas, mere way-stations on the road to Enlightened Us, victims of childish ignorances any high-school science student could correct?

Few people thought consciously of these things. They were busy with their daily rounds—eating and talking, loving and worrying and planning for next week. Yet this nihilistic future formed a mental backdrop for anyone capable of reflecting at all. It helps explain how a heavy, gloomy book like Spengler's *Decline of the West* (1917) could become a best-seller. And there was another equally hidden—or more precisely, inexpressible—anxiety: the corrosive effects of democracy itself. Officially the country was dedicated to democratic equality. It also was dedicated to the propertied family, to the sanctity of traditional marriage. These two could not ultimately survive together. A land controlled by a few vastly wealthy and correspondingly powerful families cannot be a land of democratic equality. A marriage where women pledge to obey their husbands and to accept their leadership doesn't fit any model of democratic equality either. And when you consider that the traditional Western family was an institution concerned with perpetuating property—then the total incompatibility of liberal political and social thinking with traditional valuing of home and family must be plain too. But never say that out loud!

Such a background goes far to explain the hysteria, the overreaction to relatively minor crises, typical of this time. It explains the bitterness of the Scopes trial, between evolutionists and supporters of the traditional cosmology (whose cause was, in terms of logic and public opinion, if not in strict law, hopeless from the start). Or the Big Red Scare, when for some time large numbers of Americans appeared seriously to believe that a handful of foreign radicals could overthrow the government of the United States. Or the extravagant patriotic oratory typical of this age. Making the eagle scream on the Glorious Fourth, on Lincoln's birthday, and on other such occasions seemed to cover up a nagging suspicion that American history might not, after all, be the world's paradigm: that the glorious outcome of the Civil War was a bit equivocal (why, if it had been a grand and glorious thing for the thirteen colonies to break their allegiance to King and Country and declare their independence, was it a wicked and criminal thing for the nine Confederate states to secede from the Northern states?); that the Spanish-American war of the late 1890s was something other than a spreading of democratic freedom across the globe (annexing the Philippines and Cuba did seem a bit like empire-building in the old European sense); that there was a false note in American's entering the Great War of 1914–18. "America is privileged," Wilson had said—and the words are writ grandly today across the World War I memorial building in Nashville—"to spend her blood and her might for the principles that gave her birth and happiness and the peace she has cherished." But hadn't George Washington said something about avoiding foreign entanglements, especially getting into the European states' endless cycle of wars?

Even the sainted Revolutionary War itself had as a principal justification the opening of the continent to immigration, the breaking of Britain's mercantilist system, and now look:

Wide open and unguarded stand our gates,
And through them presses a wild motley throng—
Men from the Volga and the Tartar steppes,
Featureless figures from the Hoang-Ho,
Malayan, Scythian, Teuton, Kelt, and Slav,
Flying the Old World's poverty and scorn;
These bringing with them unknown gods and rites,
Those, tiger passions, here to stretch their claws.
In street and alley and what strange tongues are these,
Accents of menace alien to our air,
Voices that once the Tower of Babel knew!

So old-stock American Thomas Bailey Aldrich, lamenting the invidious effects of open immigration.[3] Alas, these new Americans can never match the old ones' virtue; their blood has been corrupted by untold centuries of low cunning and lower morals. It's not, it can't be, our basic democratic ideals that are causing such chaos in the country; it must be that these newcomers aren't capable of understanding how American democracy works. They think it is . . . whereas it is. . . . The voices trail off into babel, this time old American Anglo-Saxon Babel. Whence those interrelated movements toward isolationism, immigration limitation, and prohibition that climax the age—extraordinary *tours de force* in which the world's most powerful nation proposed to disengage itself from the world and history, return to its unencumbered colonial self, and simultaneously legislate sin, or at least what some sizable part of its body politic thought was sin, out of existence. Only a kind of national neurosis can explain such things.

Or can explain the hysterical note in political reformers characteristic of this age. It too has deeper roots than those which appear to nourish it. The same progressives, broadly speaking, who thought they were serving humanity by bludgeoning Tennessee yokels out of hoary, outmoded religious beliefs were themselves compensating for the loss of those beliefs by fierce (and ultimately even more irrational) dedication to the proposition that this life here and now could be made a Heaven on Earth. Utopianism of all sorts flourished in the 1890–1930 years; it was a major source of the era's hopes and, of course, its discontents.[4] The religious zeal of a dozen generations of Calvinists and Pietists and Dissenters was deflected into this great cause—by purer politics, by purer laws, by harmonious human intercourse, Heaven can be realized here and now, in our time and history, not in some supernatural realm. Hence the sudden ferocity of intolerance about slums and sweatshops and sorrows of life generally. The poor ye have always with you, said Jesus. But his nominal followers in the post-Victorian age did not agree. Poverty should be abolished. So should political chicanery. It had not existed in the past, they claimed—look at Jefferson, look at Lincoln, look at Washington. If you objected that these were politicians in their time, with their share of shady dealings, you were a defamer, a radical, a foreigner, un-American. Only in modern times has there been political corruption (a notion constituting yet another thread leading to the vast colonial revival of this age, of course!). We must and we will eradicate crooks from public life. Wilson and Teddy Roosevelt, even Harding and McKinley, rode to power on promises to restore politics to its pristine purity. (Nor was this particular hysteria to be forgotten after the post-Victorian age, one might add.)

Or can explain the hysteria over collapse of the family. Nobody could publicly or even perhaps privately admit that if democratic equality is the goal of society, then the purposeful, propertied, landed family and the kind of marriage that produced it would have to be destroyed and replaced by something more democratic, like sequential polyandry or polygamy predicated on the waxing and waning of physical attraction between two absolute legal equals. Therefore the rising divorce rate, which was statistically plain from 1850 onward, had to be blamed on something else. On birth control and its advocates, for instance—weren't they giving women freedoms they couldn't handle? On too much female education—of course they want to go off and work because they're overeducated for homemaking. On automobiles, where women learn promiscuity that makes

them chafe in the marriage bond later on. On those unspeakable foreigners like Dr. Freud, who teach, or are understood to teach, that you go crazy if you repress sexual urges, that you blow up like a steam engine with blocked valves; he and his disciples are responsible for people having no self-control any more, for home-wreckers prowling everywhere.

It was the 1890–1930 years as the worst of times that gave the Comfortable House its character. Three basic comfortable qualities were projected, or were supposed to be projected, by the post-Victorian suburban house at all levels, rich and poor, white collar and blue collar: security in the sense of defense against the world; roots in the past, especially a colonial and English past; and virtue in the sense of family stability. In sum, it projected that "unspeakable comfort" promised by Calvinist tradition to the Elect, now secularized.

Home as a Refuge and a Defense against the World

The idea of "defense" runs all through writings about "home" in the post-Victorian age. It's as if the country were under some kind of siege. Here's a typical example, from a brochure put out by the Van Sweringen Company:

Shaker Village has been under preparation for twenty years; under sale ten years. In all this time the ideals which gave the enterprise its distinctive character, have never been modified nor compromised. Throughout this Century the character and defenses of this property will not change. Notwithstanding the exceptional location, the beauty, the accessible remoteness, the climate, the greatest inducement of Shaker Village is this protection which enables planning for permanent homes.

"Here is a secure haven for the home-harried," says another, "for those ruthlessly ousted from the paths of the City's progress."

Home as an Image of Roots and as a Cultural Symbol

In the late seventeenth and early eighteenth centuries there was an idealization of English values in America brought about by closer trade ties and even more by the emergence of an upper-class elite who feared that the barbarizing environment they had to live in would lead to cultural degeneration unless constantly reinforced from the homeland.[5] Something of the sort seems to have happened forcibly in post-Victorian America. Two "barbarizing" agents were operative: the Civil War and its aftermath, and the mass immigration that began in the 1880s.

Before the Civil War, Americans considered themselves superior to Europeans. Theirs was the model Europe must sooner or later follow: a nation free of strife, a nation leading the march to democratic brotherhood. Europeans might smile at the naive temple-house images to civic virtue that Americans built in the 1820s and '30s and '40s, but who cared? Those virtues were uniquely American. Disillusionment set in only gradually. It appeared first in perversions of the ideal, such as Italianate and High Picturesque mansions of the 1850s–1870s that proclaimed, via ostentatious waste and crazy proliferation of decoration, that money is the principal virtue, and then in the creeping uneasiness that America was not so unique a nation after all. In the Gothic Revival mansions of the 1850s, culminating in the Lockwood-Matthews house in Norwalk, Connecticut (see figure 9.4), a new value was already apparent. What that house and others like it strove to manifest was neither virtue nor wealth, but Culture, that is, European culture. That unparalleled chronicler of the American mind, Mark Twain, caught the new mood in the 1870s with his *Innocents Abroad*—any old culture, however seedy, however sick, must be superior to ours. That mood grew steadily in and through post-Victorian times (and, need it be said, thrives in our time more than ever).

Inevitably there was a turning back to America's glorious past, when it was perceived as a seminal not a failed country; when people looked to it for guidance; when it was the light of the world, a "city set on a hill." So temperance advocates and their successors the prohibitionists wanted a return to what they thought of as a time of plain living, high thinking, and sober acting. Social reformers and their successors the isolationists preached a return to village folkways on a national scale. As for political reformers, Richard Hofstadter pointed out how, "beginning with the time of Bryan" (and on into the era of "normalcy" in the 1920s),

the dominant American ideal has been steadily fixed on bygone institutions and conditions. In early twentieth-century progressivism this backward-looking vision reached the dimensions of a major paradox. Such heroes of the progressive revival as Bryan, LaFollette, and Wilson proclaimed that they were trying to undo the mischief of the past forty years and re-create the old nation of limited and decentralized power, genuine competition, democratic opportunity, and enterprise.[6]

For architectural reformers, the glorious past meant above all colonial times, the age that bred the Founding Fathers, especially Washington, whose conservatism was the continuing secret of his appeal, as Barry Schwartz has so convincingly reminded us.[7] Colonial Revival impulses began after the Centennial of 1876 and are still with us, prompting supercilious wonderment from fashionable architecture spokesman George Nelson in 1952. The continuing post-World War II Colonial Revival was, Nelson declared,

a rather pathetic attempt to recreate something of the stability, security and graciousness of the bygone period when Colonial was a valid architectural expression of building techniques and community attitudes. . . . That the generation which concocted the atom bomb and shot radar impulses to the moon should choose to inhabit dwellings reminiscent of the time of Cotton Mather cannot be explained in any but emotional terms.[8]

But of course, what else? The historic art of architecture always was the art of creating visual metaphors of cherished values—Pyramids, Parthenon, Chartres, papal villas and Palladian mansions, capitols and houses of Parliament. Only in the last few generations, in infatuated obedience to some imagined dictates of *Zeitgeist,* has that been forgotten. Only in the last few generations has it been assumed that if the "spirit of our age" is epitomized by railroads, we must build everything of steel and glass; if by rockets, then we must all live in launch pads—as if the "spirit of the age" could be objectively determined and measured by anyone, as if mankind should or could shed its past completely, every so often, like a snake slipping out of its skin.

The Colonial Revival has been for a hundred years a powerful instrument for providing a sense of security, stability, and roots. Its first big promotion came with outbursts of patriotism (admittedly, inspired as compensation for a sense of futility and failure engendered by the war) at the 1876 Centennial in Philadelphia, and it was reinforced mightily by the Columbian Exposition of 1893 in Chicago.[9] Revivalists made little distinction between British colonials and American revolutionaries; they were one and the same. By the 1890s, when people like Bruce Price could write about the Founding Fathers as a "society intelligent, refined, and almost chivalric in its intercourse,"[10] these virtues began to be extended to include earlier colonials as well. The whole colonial period was soon commonly imaged in arts of all kinds as an age of paragons from beginning to end. In Federal times Washington had been pictured as a saint in process of apotheosis (on the dome of the Capitol as well as in innumerable prints); now that treatment was extended, though less literally, to all "colonials." Hence inspiration for the Jefferson memorial, for the monument at Plymouth Rock, the Astoria column, and so many more. R. T. H. Halsey, founder of the American wing at the Metropolitan Museum in New York, explained in the early 1920s to a group of Republican ladies how

[it] is our pride in ancestry that adds to the appeal which American furniture makes to some of us . . . because it represents the home furnishings of our people in the days when our country was struggling to get on its feet, of those who protected this country from enemies within just as you women in this last campaign did such convincing work to preserve us from the dominating influence of foreign ideas.[11]

That "pride in ancestry" also apparently found expression in the houses themselves, for as William Rhoads notes, though "no attempt has been made to check systematically the ancestry of Colonial Revival clients . . . it appears that the great majority of Colonial Revival houses were commissioned by Americans of old native stock."[12] If that were true, then the Colonial Revival must inevitably have led back to even deeper roots in that England which in colonial times had been idealized by the now-idealized colonial elite themselves.

England in the 1890s looked very different from England in the 1980s, or even the England of 1776. In the 1890s it was the heart of a vast empire, the greatest nation on earth, prime bearer of the White Man's burden to civilize the earth's less fortunate peoples. Many in the American elite, contemplating this great power and the distracted state of their own post-Civil War nation, secretly, and perhaps unconsciously, began wishing the Revolution had somehow never happened. Some even worked themselves into believing it had not in fact happened. Admiral Mahon's *Importance of Seapower* seemed almost to assume Britain and America had a common navy! As early as 1918 people of Mahon's and Halsey's mind were developing a theory of the American Revolution as a kind of civil war, in which the American position had actually been supported by the "better portion" of the English people. Thus the American elite could talk about their heritage of Anglo-American, or just English, culture as the sure defense against change in the *status quo* (which would of course undermine their own position) and assurance that no matter how wild immigration became, America would remain an "English country."

The effect of this sort of thinking on architecture was immediate and powerful. When Joy Wheeler Dow wrote a series of articles published in 1904 as *American Renaissance,* he contrasted the Georgian Colonial ("American Renaissance") with all other house types and styles and found it scoring 100 percent in "Anglo-Saxon home atmosphere"—clearly the only possible mode.[13] Recreating colonial English architecture would in some way seemingly manage to preserve and even recreate the vanished world of these ancestors. "We want to belong somewhere and to something, not to be entirely cut off by ourselves as stray atoms in boundless space, either chronological or geographical," Dow wrote.[14] He anticipated by three years Henry James's account, in *The American Scene,* of his feelings upon realizing that his former home in Boston had been demolished: "It was as if the bottom had fallen out of one's biography, and one plunged backward into space without meeting anything."[15] Herbert Croly summed it all up in 1914:

The quality which almost all the owners of elaborate and costly country houses particularly desire is . . . age—the quality of confirmation which a building obtains from having been lived in for some generations, until nature and human usage have served to tie it into the countryside and to an established social order.[16]

Rational arguments that past worlds cannot be recreated (for example, the theme of Daniel Boorstin's *Lost World of Thomas Jefferson*) are irrelevant to the appeal of colonial and English, or colonial/English, or "English cottage" associations in the 1890–1930 years, for that kind of appeal was not and never can be subject to rational analysis. It was always an emotional response to vague and unnamed fears. Literally speaking, one can never go back to roots. The oak can never return to an acorn, nor the Vatican to an Upper Room, nor post-Victorian America to the Thirteen Colonies. But the nostalgic wish-fulfilling attempt shaped an entire body of American domestic building in this age.

Home as an Image of Morality and Virtue and as a Symbol of the Family

Focus for all the age's varied fears, spoken and unspoken, was The Home. There children learned—or should learn—respect for tradition, for history. There they learn—or should learn—sound social values that would produce lasting marriages. The cure for all problems is a Good Home Life. The cause of all troubles is Family Breakdown. Whence the ethical symbolism of the Comfortable House.

The house, or homestead, is one of the fundamental symbolic types in all architecture. The contrast between the peasant hut/homestead and the lord's palace is a prime visual metaphor of the class-structured state. In colonial America, and throughout the first British empire, which ended at Yorktown, the homestead had always been (among other things) a symbol of successful landed family-founding.[17]

During the nineteenth century, American house symbolism underwent steady change. Since the idea of an aristocratic landed family was incompatible with the idea of a liberal egalitarian democracy, the old symbolism attaching to its mansions could not stand either, at least in theory. In practice, of course, the two long coexisted and their incompatibility gave rise to one of the favorite ideas of progressive critics—that the great mansion was somehow an image of Wickedness and Folly. Everyone has been taught to admire Louis Sullivan's scornful comments about the Vanderbilt house on Fifth Avenue—how ridiculous and monstrous it was for a modern capitalist to live in a copy of a French king's castle. Actually, in terms of social function, the Vanderbilt mansion he derides was built on time-honored principles: the house as visual metaphor of the founding of a new landed family, a new aristocracy. Clearly, Sullivan's comments are not relevant in any framework of strictly architectural or even social thinking; they are a statement of his ideological conviction that the founding of

great landed families was morally wrong, was fundamentally incompatible with the democracy he so pas-
sionately believed in. This is in line with Downing's
comments half a century before that the inordinately expensive country seats just beginning to appear were
"contrary to republican institutions . . . wholly in contradiction to the spirit of our time and people." [18]

Both strictures would apply not only to such mansions
as the Lockwood-Matthews in Norwalk of 1860 (direct
ancestor of the Vanderbilt French castles), but also to all
those garish Italianate mansions dripping with brackets
and scrolled-arch verandahs erected out of Civil War for-
tunes in every sizable American town of the period—
many of them, astonishingly to modern sensibilities,
built while the conflict still raged! Then, the old idea of a
house proclaiming the establishment of a new aristocracy was still generally enough held for people to accept
the principle: In defense of the Union, you risk your life,
I risk my money. We each get an appropriate reward.
You, your name on a monument; me, a monumental
mansion. In fact it still held in some quarters as late
as the early twentieth century. In his 1904 book Joy
Wheeler Dow argued, for instance, that by their use
(that is, by their social function) the mansions of the rich
should properly be considered American no matter what
model they had been built on: the Vanderbilt mansion
in New York (and all the others in Newport or Asheville, or wherever), despite its original inspiration in
European palaces, "had gradually grown to look to us
what it really is, i.e., good American Renaissance." [19]

But by 1900 all such arguments were beginning to
seem labored, if not positively tendentious. On all levels
they were being superseded by the idea of the house
symbolizing virtuous and patriotic life. That idea had
started to gain currency during the early republic, specifically with the temple-house of the Roman and Greek
Revivals.

The first positive formulation of this new house symbolism can be found—like so many firsts—in the writings of Andrew Jackson Downing. According to him, the
American villa and cottage should properly be understood in terms of a "republican home, built by no rob-
bery of the property of another class, maintained by no
infringement of a brother's rights." "The individual
home," he maintained, "has a great social value for a
people. There is moral influence in the country home
where the family hearth is made a central point of the
Beautiful and the Good." [20] This concept ultimately became central to the Comfortable House of post-Victorian
times. The Comfortable House is where character is
formed. Character molds the nation. No notion in the
1890–1930 years gave rise to greater quantities of poesy
and profundity, cant and declamation, idealization and
bathos, than this. Decade after decade it continued.

The Pallisers prefaced their 1887 *New Cottage Homes*
with stanzas on the theme "Blessed Are They Who Have
Homes":

I want to be home when the night comes down—
When the night comes down and the sun is hid—
And the pale, cold moon lights the glimmering town,
And is heard the shrill cricket and the katy-did,
Ah me! "There's no place like home."

I want to be home when the night comes down,
When the storm-king raves and the billows roar,
And the sign-boards creak in the rickety town,
And the mad waves dash strong ships on shore,
Ah me! What a snug place is home.

With my books, my papers, and my glowing hearth
With my wife and children around me there;
With health and love and innocent mirth
With a heart content and free from care,—
Ah me! What a heaven is home.

The 1910 Sears catalog addressed itself "to churchgoers"
and told them that

To get the most out of life as Our Creator intended it to
be, A HOME OF YOUR OWN IS AN ABSOLUTE
NECESSITY.

And Aladdin's 1919 catalog asked:

Did you ever really consider the wonderful difference in the meaning of the words house and home? A house is a structure to live in. Home—the dearest place on earth—is that structure that is part of you—made so by its association with your family, their joys and sorrows, their hopes, aspirations, and fears. It is a refuge from the trials and struggles of the outer world. It is a visible expression of yourself, your tastes and character.

Jens Pedersen announced that "the primary object" in publishing his book *Beautiful Homes and Plans* (Minneapolis, 1922) was

to aid the prospective home builder in planning and designing, and to create a desire on the part of every AMERICAN citizen to OWN HIS OWN HOME, for by so doing he is creating for himself a standing of permanency and prestige in the community in which he resides and at the same time establishing a position, financially and socially for himself and family. Furthermore, the American home of today is far superior to that of any other nation as to comforts, convenience and artistic embellishments and has contributed in producing a state of contentment and well being, conducive in a large measure to the peace and tranquility this nation has enjoyed, also in maintaining a loyal and true American spirit which emanates from the Great American Home.

"Can you not realize," implored a Van Sweringen advertising pamphlet promoting Shaker Heights in 1927,

what the influence of such homes must be upon the lives of the children living in them? Do not character and refinement depend much upon the manner in which they are housed? Yet, without neighbourhood support, is not home influence forever in jeopardy?

But it was left, as so often in the realm of 1920s lofty sentiments, for President Warren Harding to have the last word. McAdoo once described Harding's speeches as an army of words marching across the landscape in search of an idea, sometimes actually capturing one. So, at the dedication of the "Home Sweet Home" exhibit by the Home Owners Service and General Federation of Women's Clubs in June of 1923 in front of the White House, Harding effused:

The home is at last not merely the center, but truly the aim, the object, and the purpose of all human organization. We do not seek to improve society in order that from better homes we may bring forth better servants of the state, more efficient cannon fodder for its armed forces; rather we seek to make better homes in order that we may avoid the necessity for conflict and turmoil in our world. The home is the apex and the aim, the end rather than the means of our whole social system.[21]

Not a contemptible goal, however contemptibly expressed.

Frank Lloyd Wright was surely no admirer of President Harding, but the concept of home as molder of virtue is just as central to Wright's thinking. Norris Smith has shown how Wright's houses can be read as visual metaphors of Home and Family.[22] Wright himself in many writings promoted the idea that a domestic environment in which true individuality (spiritual and creative, as distinct from individualistic—a relic of fedualism, anarchic product of an anarchic economic system) could flourish was the answer to all problems of modern life and, moreover, a panacea for the problems of democracy, a salvation for the whole world. In his houses would dwell the "World Citizen" who, "because of well-founded confidence in his own strength. . . . is eager to share the work of the World. The World will be invigorated by the happiness and vitality of his own actual practice of the Democracy he preaches. The results of his Democracy would become Ideal for all the world."[23] It was a sentiment that would have been endorsed by all builders of the Comfortable Age—high architects, low spec builders, everyone in between —however differently they might interpret it in practice.

2

The Comfortable House in Its Suburban Place

Comfortable Houses from the 1890–1930 years can be found in every corner of the land. But they flourished in one place in particular—the suburbs. Countrysides by history, tradition, and circumstance produced the picturesque house and the practical house. Cities by tradition and necessity produced the standardized row house/tenement and the palatial house/apartment. Suburbs by necessity and circumstance produced the Comfortable House. By suburb I don't necessarily mean just the modern judicial definition—a separate community near a city but not incorporated within its boundaries—I mean sub-urban, less than fully urban. In the 1890–1930 years that meant, besides suburbs proper, tracts technically within city limits as well as small towns; in what follows, "suburb" should be understood in that sense.[1]

In Europe and Britain, you are either *inside* cities or *outside* them. But in the United States, in order to get either into or out of a city, you must first pass through a belt, often miles wide, of "urban sprawl." That sprawling ring of suburbs giving American cities their special character began to develop between the late 1850s and the early 1900s.

Suburbs turned American cities inside out, just as (and the parallel is not entirely coincidental) office buildings had been turned upside down by elevators over the same period. For most of history, being well-to-do had carried the privilege of living near a city's center, able to live beside or indeed in one's place of business without long, tiring, time-consuming travels back and forth from the city's outskirts.[2] Suburban living had meant a nobleman's country villa—not a base for commutation, but a retreat from care, or plague, or heat. By the 1890s (at the latest), being well-to-do offered the reverse privilege—a chance to commute to the city center from some district farther out than most, even from some nearby small town, rather than from suburbs proper, which were the domain of middle classes or even, here and there, of working-class people!

By then suburban living was nothing new; planned suburbs had appeared quite early in the century. But the basic concept behind such early examples as Llewellyn Park in New Jersey (from the 1840s and 1850s) was a kind of country village. They were not normal places for city dwellers and business people to live. By 1910 things had changed. Now planned or "developed"[3] suburbs were *the* places for solid middle-class citizens to live, and they moved out there by the thousands, leaving city cores to slums and tall office buildings, older neighborhoods to less affluent citizenry and/or small commercial enterprise. In the suburbs new building types appeared—garages and campgrounds (forerunners of the motels of the 1920s), limited access highways, shopping centers, company towns. But the most significant architectural creation of suburban living between 1890 and 1930 was the suburban house itself. It was—however rarely recognized as such—something essentially new in the world.

Censuses show that when the United States was founded, no more than 10 percent of its people lived in cities. By 1900, nearly half did. During the 1920s alone the official percentage climbed from 51.4 to 57.6. That figure would have been much higher had suburbs—parts of the urban agglomeration not legally part of the city proper—been regularly counted. For it was in the suburbs that urban growth was overwhelmingly concentrated from at least the 1890s.

Several population movements combined to fill the suburbs—migration from inner cities outward; from the countryside to inner city and then out to suburbs; from foreign countries to inner city and then, with prosperity, to suburbs. The combined result was an altered architectural pattern. Inner cities had been the location of the grandest mansions from medieval times through the middle of the nineteenth century. Just as old prints show us how merchants' homes and businesses were combined in the old medieval inner cities of Europe (in the New World you can still see, projecting from the upper gabled stories of Dutch merchants' houses in New York or Albany or New Castle on Delaware, arms with

2.1 An image of industrial success in colonial times: the Corbit house in Odessa, Delaware, from the 1770s. Symmetrical balance and ornament drawn from Roman and Renaissance palaces proclaim the owner's rise from skilled workman (tanner) to the status of gentleman. (IMG:NAL)

pulleys for hauling goods up into attics), so still in eighteenth-century America William Corbit could not only build a splendid (for the time and place) Georgian mansion in what he hoped would be the middle of a flourishing new town (Appoquinimink Creek, Delaware, later renamed Odessa), but also put it right next to the stinking tan yard whence his prosperity derived (figure 2.1). And in the 1880s, William Carson of Eureka hired a fancy architect to come up from San Francisco to design him the flashiest mansion on the northern California coast, a grand garish pile commemorating his rise to the status of Eureka's wealthiest and most successful citizen, but he sited it (as we would think, incongruously) overlooking the unsightly lumber yard on which his fortune was based (figure 2.2). But by the 1890s mansions were built in inner cities no longer. They were put in the most remote, the most rural suburbs. Skyscrapers and, especially in America's eastern seaboard cities, slums occupied their places. Inner city was now the place where

immigrant laborers and lumpen proletariat lived —in aging row houses blackened and shaken by overhead trains, sunk in the shadow of the grand office towers, whole families crowded into a few rooms. Such tenements are a necessary background for full understanding of what the Comfortable House implied—escape from squalor, escape from hopelessness.[4] To be sure, the occasional mansion survived in the inner city, aged heirs stubbornly immured within. In a few places too—Philadelphia and Baltimore are examples—some building of row houses for working-class tenants was still going on. But by the 1890s most of the well-to-do were gone from inner cities, and by 1900 the middle class was well on its way out also—away from all this, out to the suburbs. First by train. Then by trolley. Then by automobile.

Already by mid-century trains had made possible elegant suburbs like A. J. Davis's collection of medieval castles in Llewellyn Park, New Jersey. By the 1870s elevated steam lines were taking commuters to and from New York's inner suburbs. And by 1900 Los Angeles

2.2 An image of commercial success in the Gilded Age, created by conspicuous waste: the William Carson house in Eureka, California, from the 1880s. It is a monument to an age when few doubted that to be a successful entrepreneur was to benefit mankind, when, in consequence, contemplation of a flourishing business beside one's mansion gave its owner unspeakable joy, and when to dwell within sight and sound of the busy heart of a city was truly to live. (IMG:NAL)

had a full network of suburban railroads; you can see them still in those early movie comedies, where old jalopies are forever getting stuck on level crossings with locomotives roaring down upon them. But tickets were usually too expensive for the middle class to afford on a daily basis. (We can easily forget how dramatically transportation costs have fallen over two centuries; just recall how normal it was in the seventeenth and eighteenth centuries for immigrants to pay for a transatlantic passage by indenturing themselves as servants for two, five, even seven years!) Hence the early prestige of commuting by rail, which Philadelphia's "Main Line" still recalls. That prestige helped railroad commuting withstand competition from the trolley, invented by electrical engineer Frank Sprague in the 1880s, first operational in Richmond and common everywhere by 1900.

Originally intended as an improvement over horsecars in urban transportation, trolleys by 1900 were serving middle- and lower-class suburbs as well. They never supplanted trains, however, which continued to serve the well-to-do. That pattern held even when buses and subways in their turn supplanted trolleys. Still today, for that matter, it is the more affluent who commute in by train from Bryn Athyn and Cape Ann, New Canaan and Darien; the middle class who drive in from nearer suburbs; the working class who get to work by bus and subway. What the trolley did was make possible the middle class "suburban development," as distinct from the planned upper-class suburb.

A final boost to suburban expansion came with the automobile. New developments no longer needed to be near rail or trolley lines; the areas between existing suburbs could be filled in and new ones pushed further out. By 1930 the automobile had largely put the inter-urban or suburban trolley out of business; trains survived thanks to the practice of commuting by car to the railroad station and back, but already by the 1920s enough people drove the whole distance in and out of inner cities to create the morning and evening "rush." The statistics are awesome. Registration figures indicate something like two hundred thousand automobiles operating on American roads around 1910, over six million by 1919, over twenty-three million by 1929. Their proliferation presumed a comparably expanding infrastructure of the new steel-reinforced concrete roads and traffic signs of all sorts, including electric stop-and-go lights. The first primitive parking meters appeared. In twenty years, cars went from luxuries to necessities, so that the Lynds' study of "Middletown" (Muncie, Indiana)[5] indicated that in the 1920s not only were there two cars for every three families, but of sixty working-class families owning cars, twenty-one lived in houses without bathtubs! Not, of course, that the car necessarily took precedence over that other icon of the age, the Comfortable House; but by the 1920s it was mainly working-class people who remained behind in the inner city, and the car provided their means of escape.

Enough working-class people were moving to suburbs by the 1920s, however, that restrictive deeds became necessary (or so it seemed to developers) to ensure the "quality" of neighborhoods. Separate blue- and white-collar suburbs appeared, with delicately graded nuances in between according to income and ethnic background. Financing of course favored the middle (not to mention upper) classes, who had some spare cash in the bank: a common practice among banks was to refuse loans for a house until would-be suburbanites had paid off the developer who sold them their lots, and then to loan only for short terms like three to five years, demanding full payment at the end of that time. But nothing stopped the movement to the suburbs. Ethnic societies and working-class church corporations formed building and loan associations (ancestors of the present savings and loan corporations), which pooled resources and chose by lottery or some other device which lucky members got the necessary cash—better a few than none!

Farmers, too, often sold out and used the proceeds to relocate in the suburbs, commuting in like ex-urbanites. Less lucky farmers (all through the post-Victorian years farmers were squeezed by mechanization and in the 1920s were caught by mortgages and taxes based on in-flated land values of the 1917–1920 period, which collapsed in the 1920s) found themselves in the inner city, competing with all those likewise stranded there by harsh fortune: blacks, flocking in from the rural south for unskilled labor jobs; Slavs, Jews, and Italians from the great immigration waves of the 1880s, 1890s, and 1900s, blocked from the suburbs by discrimination; Appalachians, blocked by illiteracy and traditional fecklessness.

In the suburbs a new quality of life began to develop. Zoning was an early manifestation of it. A German idea originally (as what wasn't in those years—government welfare, automats, doctorates—in every field it seemed that Germany was leading the way), zoning was adopted by Americans not only because of its obvious utility (anybody could see that sooner or later unlimited private land speculation and use had to be controlled for the good of all), but also particularly because of the example of the great Columbian Exposition of 1893 in Chicago, whose glittering and nicely ordered Great White City contrasted so dramatically with the hodge-podge jungle of unzoned Chicago surrounding it. Out of that fair (very largely) grew the City Beautiful movement, and out of the City Beautiful movement grew (very largely) city planning proper, which became common by the 1910s. By the 1920s only "grandfather clauses" permitted factories or service garages to remain standing on older residential streets, reminders of the Bad Old Days.

Supplementing municipal ordinances were developers' restrictive covenants. In the mid-1920s the Van Sweringen Company could assure prospective residents of Shaker Heights outside Cleveland of "PROTECTION":

Restrictions are established against every controllable influence which can operate to the disadvantage of an exclusive home-community. Within this area are excluded all commercial, merchandising, and industrial enterprises, multiple houses and amusement devices, except in specifically prescribed locations. All plans for buildings must be submitted for approval; and grades, lot lines and locations are prescribed and controlled.

"A result," the company somewhat ingenuously promised, was "COMMUNITY SPIRIT: This is expressed, not only in general friendliness, but in such practical ways as support of Boy Scouts, Community Chests. . . . "

Of course diehards fought back; long after Los Angeles (1915) and New York (1916) had passed laws limiting building sizes and types of land use throughout the city, zoning was still being challenged in the courts as unconstitutional, not to say un-American. Finally in 1926 the Supreme Court ruled that Americans collectively had a right to protect their own property values.

So the suburbs grew until by 1930 every American city had rings of suburbs like the skins of an onion, and beyond that, usually, other rings of platted fields. From 1900 domestic building in inner cities virtually ceased, except for a few replacements and occasional new worker tenements or row houses (of course, much of what has now become inner city was outer city, even suburb, in the 1890s). Given continuing depression on the farm, for all intents and purposes residential building action meant suburban building action.

It was far from all the same kind of action. The suburbs were differentiated by wealth and social status and on occasion given special character as well. Detroit, center of the automobile industry, and Los Angeles, already a city built by and for wheels, were appropriately distinguished at the end of the 1920s by immense tracts of "garage suburbs"—fields subdivided into lots on which stood one-room structures intended one day to accommodate a car, but which temporarily (that is, for decades) accommodated families instead, with jalopy parked outside. "Garage suburbs" remind us of one fact of suburban life now easily forgotten: most purchases were cash. First you bought the lot; only when it was paid for did you put something on it, and often you wouldn't have enough to pay for your house, so you bought your garage instead and lived there until you'd accumulated enough for the house—which might be a long, long time.

At the other end of the scale were those rare totally planned communities like the Country Club District begun outside Kansas City in 1908 and built over the following fifty (!) years by the J. C. Nichols Company—a chain of subdivisions covering more than six thousand acres—and fabulous Shaker Heights outside Cleveland. Shaker Heights included not only shops, theaters, and churches but, in essence, its own metropolis as well, since the same "creators and developers," the Van Sweringens, were also responsible for much of downtown Cleveland and connected the two directly by street railway (figure 2.3). In Shaker Heights, every house had to be designed by an architect—of the generation influenced by the English country house vernacular practiced by Baillie Scott, Voysey, and Lutyens and having at their disposal a body of handicraft capable of using textures and materials to maximum effect. The result was that "the largest residence development under single control in the world" pioneered new house-to-road relationships, with curving road plans, and new large-fronted lots capable of showing off the wide house facades to best advantage. Shaker Heights segregated by wealth and (consequently) social status: certain size houses were restricted to certain areas. (A kind of segregation practiced by cemeteries also! Cemeteries in fact pioneered a good many suburban planning practices; could cemeteries like Mount Auburn be considered America's first suburbs?)

Variants were almost limitless. There were industrial suburbs on rectilinear grids laid out by major architects of the day, like McKim, Mead and White's Echota near Niagara Falls, and by mass-prefabricating mail-order builders, like Aladdin City outside Miami. There were quasi-recreational suburbs like Manhattan Beach Estates on Long Island, "Swept by Ocean Breezes [according to its brochure] . . . where the air you breathe is pure ocean ozone" (no longer, alas, since it's right on the flight path to JFK and Laguardia). There were large-scale suburbs on curvilinear street systems, direct ancestors of the mass suburbs of the 1950s, like Vandergrift, Pennsylvania, planned in 1895 by Frederick Law Olmstead for

"Sorely throb my feet, a-tramping
city pavements (Ah, the springy
sod upon an upland moor!)"

2.3 This illustration from the Van
Sweringen Company's "Peaceful
Shaker Heights" brochure of 1929,
with accompanying poesy, aptly images the concept of home as refuge
from the storms of life, especially
city life. It s worth noting, however,
that the traditional juxtaposition of
home with business, or residence
with the economic instrument that
made it possible, is maintained in
this picture—the 1920s suburb overlooks the metropolis just as the
Carson and Corbit houses overlooked the source of *their* wealth.

the Apollo Steel Company. (Paradoxically, the automobile age made such curvilinear street patterns and
cul-de-sacs popular devices for protecting suburban
dwellers from the automobile, as could be seen explicitly
in the Engineers Mutual Company plan for Rockford,
Illinois, and most strikingly of all in Fairhill Road
Village in Cleveland, whose streets were faced by built-
in garage entrances, while the houses' principal facades
overlooked ravines.)

There were exotic suburbs, especially in Colonial
Spanish styles, the *crème de la crème* being San Clemente,
Palos Verdes Estates, and Rancho Santa Fe in California;
and, in Florida, fantastic Coral Gables outside Miami.
Coral Gables already had two thousand houses by 1926
and ultimately included schools, apartments, country
clubs, and hotels (the Miami Biltmore was twenty-six
stories high), all in a "modified Mediterranean" style,
set in palm-shaded streets, ornamented with lagoons,
Mediterranean bridges, and fountains. Many workaday
rivals included "American Venice," thirty-four miles out
from Manhattan on Long Island, which, its blurbs proclaimed, "recalls the famous city of the Doges, only
more charming—and more homelike. . . . Lazy gon-
dolas! Beautiful Italian gardens! And, ever present, the
waters of the Great South Bay lapping lazily all day
upon a beach as white and fine as the soul of a little
child." On occasion older towns were made over into an
exotic suburban image; neo-Colonial Spanish Ojai and
Santa Barbara in California are outstanding examples.

Then there were more prosaic, but still far from dull,
suburbs like Montclair, New Jersey, and Jackson Heights
in Queens, both originally intended as "Wasp" en-
claves. Both had shopping sections in vaguely English
Tudor style. Montclair's big feature was a city park with
an elaborate pond complete with an island on which, in
due course, was set a grand war memorial (to World
War I; the suburb was not long-enough populated for
any other) with a life-size group created by Charles
Keck. Jackson Heights proudly (until Pruitt–Igoe, anyway!) claimed to be an ancestor of Le Corbusier's and

"green belt" planning ideas, with high-rise apartment blocks in parklike settings (but unlike Corbusian cities, with single-family dwelling sections as well). Begun in 1909, it was still expanding in the 1920s and, alas, infilled continuously thereafter so as to lose all original character (figures 2.4, 2.5).

The Los Angeles area pioneered bungalow courts, a kind of mini-suburb featuring a number of bungalows set around an oval drive, with cars and services entering at the back. The St. Francis bungalow court in Pasadena was the best-known example; Robinson's department store now stands on the site. Florida had some early examples too, most notably Bungalow Terrace in Tampa, which occupied an entire suburban block in what is now known as Hyde Park. Platted in 1916, it was laid out in four rows with a central walkway down the middle, covered by an arbor (variant of the ubiquitous pergola–bungalow combination). Curiously enough, such arrangements can be found to have origins or at least

2.4 The elegant and innovative suburb of Jackson Heights on Long Island, as it was in the 1920s. Here, the tree-lined, grassy mall that once divided 34th Avenue: Towers complex on the left, in vaguely Mediterranean style (leisure and ease); Château on the right with vaguely French Renaissance towers and dormers (palatial luxury). (New York City Landmarks Preservation Commission)

2.5 Back garden view of the Towers in Jackson Heights, looking south across 34th Avenue to the Château. Multifamily suburban buildings were the exception rather than the rule in the 1890–1930s. (New York City Landmarks Preservation Commission)

counterparts in India, like the bungalow type itself. The famous Dean's Hotel in Peshawar, which the British built as their elegant hostlery in the Punjab's summer capital, was essentially a bungalow court.

The bungalow court proved to have little future as a suburban type, inasmuch as most have disappeared. But it was rich in progeny, as it was a direct ancestor of the concept of garden apartments and workers' housing projects. Typically, it was high-style, avant-garde architects like Schindler, Gill, and Neutra who explored this latter possibility (for example, Gill's project for Mexican laborers of 1911; Neutra's well-publicized Channel Heights Housing of 1941). The avant-garde's love affair with workers' housing, with its half-unconscious ideological fueling, thus dates in America from the years when the future leaders of European Modernism were learning their ideas in far-off Berlin.

The suburb generated other new forms as well, such as the garage, the motel, the shopping center, the gas station, and above all the Comfortable House itself. Since most suburbs after 1900 were predicated on use of automobiles, garages were an essential feature. Earlier, domestic establishments for the well-to-do and upper classes included carriage houses where vehicles were kept, often with an apartment or two above for grooms and drivers, and stables for horses (figure 2.6). For considerations of both smell and social distinction, the carriage house was kept well separate from the house proper. It was conceived as a kind of barn and barns in North America were habitually put away from houses. This habit, as much as any fear of fire or even smells, explains why it took so long for the concept of a built-in garage to gain acceptance (figure 2.7)—until the 1950s, in fact, although there are isolated early examples of "A Home with Attached Garage," as in *Keith's Magazine* for February 1918: "A door at the grade level of the basement stairs opens to the garage. The wall which separates the garage from the house is built of tile and the door is fireproofed." It even took some while before garage and house were regularly built in the same style (one reason being, of course, that in the beginning and for long thereafter garages were built separately from and later than the houses themselves, often likewise ordered from catalogs; see figures 2.8 and 4.1). In Los Angeles, styling of house and garage eventually came to

Garage No. 42.

A LITTLE out of the ordinary, this garage was built to contain a certain amount of storage space in addition to housing the machine. Another door located beside that shown or a single door somewhat wider would make it possible to drive in two machines with ease and still have an abundance of room for work bench and storage. Above is space for a small apartment which might be occupied by the caretaker and his wife who would find employment about the house. The lower portion of the garage is of stucco or expanded metal and the upper part and roof are shingled. The concrete foundation is carried below the frost line. The floor is a slab of monolithic concrete.

The size is 28 ft. wide by 19 ft. wide. Estimated cost, $500.00.

2.6 Ancestry of suburban garage in villa carriage house is evident in this "American Garage in Cement and Frame" from *Keith's Attractive Garages* of ca. 1911.

2.7 Residence of James O. Inman in Burrillville, Rhode Island, ca. 1875–80. The carriage house is strictly separate from the residence, but it has been given a matching sort of gambrel roof. This practice carried directly over into mass prefabrication; Gordon-Van Tine's catalog of ca. 1905 offers a very similar carriage house (plan 44) with the admonition: "Whatever the style of the house, the stable whether in the city or the country, should be built in keeping with that style. In other words, a straight gable house should call for a straight gable barn, and a gambrel-roofed house for a gambrel-roofed barn." But always well away from the residence—if for no other reason than such carriage houses customarily provided space for horses and hay. (Gordon-Van Tine's included two cows and a chicken run, as well!)

2.8 Transition from carriage house to garage is exemplified here in Ogdensburg, New York (left). The original carriage house of ca. 1875–85 probably became a garage when the house was built in front of it ca. 1915. The choice of gambreled gables for the house was perhaps motivated by a wish to match the garage, as advised in many catalogs of the time. (IMG:NAL)

be legislated, presumably because of those "garage suburbs." Garages, it was stipulated, must be "miniatures of fine homes."[6] The evolution of garages can be followed very well in mail-order catalogs and surviving buildings (figures 2.9, 2.10).

Motels and shopping centers both appeared in the 1920s, and both were responses to the problem created by suburbs multiplying ever further from the city center, of tedious driving in and out for shopping or lodging of guests. Arthur Heineman's Milestone Motel in San Luis Obispo of 1925 is widely credited with being the first place to be called a "motor hotel"; and Country Club Plaza in Kansas City of 1927 is, according to Victor Gruen,[7] the first shopping center, although the shopping squares of Shaker Heights contend for this distinction. Motels as a type evolved from campgrounds and appeared all over the country at about the same time; California gave them their definitive form via the bungalow court. Gas stations, too, might qualify as creations of the automobile suburb, although the small Georgian mansions, classical temples, and "Snow White and the Seven Dwarfs" fairyland castles into which they soon blossomed out of their utilitarian blacksmithy origins were primarily intended to appeal to the 1920s "romance of the road" mindset. But the fine flower of all these new forms was the suburban house itself.

The suburban house was a single-family dwelling incorporating technological advances that were indeed impressive. Comfort and convenience were its hallmarks. Indoor plumbing, built-in gas and electric facilities, central heating, all that had been luxuries available only to the well-to-do just a few decades earlier, now became standard features for all. Privies and chamber pots vanished, except for young children's potty-chairs; in their place homeowners could choose among all sorts of models of porcelain toilets and bathtubs and sinks. Laundry facilities began to appear in basements.

2.9 At first sight this house from ca. 1915 on Southern Boulevard in Albany, New York, seems to represent some ingenious adaptation of an older house to the automobile age by tacking a *porte-cochère* onto its front, especially since the *porte-cochère* gives no access to the verandah. But no, such designs were quite common in building catalogs of the period. (IMG:NAL)

2.10 Aladdin's Shadow Lawn model, from 1919 catalog, shows a typical extension of the verandah to form a *porte-cochère*. Such designs recognized garages as integral parts of automobile suburbs; indeed they advertised ownership of an automobile. But the garage was no more integrated with the residence than the carriage house had been—less, in fact, since it often was built separately from the house, from other plans, and was kept discreetly out of sight.

2.11 The greatest single factor making the Comfortable House comfortable was central heating. Systems like this one advertised in Montgomery Ward's 1927 *Wardway Homes* catalog put winter comfort within the reach of all. Interestingly, it had no effect on the rigid compartmentalization of interior spaces theoretically required when rooms had separate stoves or fireplaces and needed to be sealed off. In fact, this compartmentalization was insisted upon for psychological reasons: the privacy this age considered indispensable for each family member and activity.

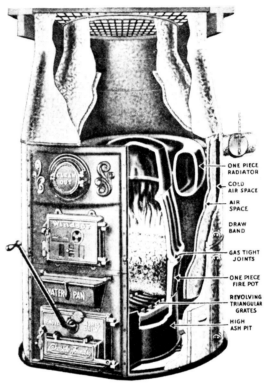

ONE PIECE RADIATOR
COLD AIR SPACE
AIR SPACE
DRAW BAND
GAS TIGHT JOINTS
ONE PIECE FIRE POT
REVOLVING TRIANGULAR GRATES
HIGH ASH PIT

Coal-fired central-heating systems almost entirely superseded the wood- or coal-burning stove (even before that old American contribution to home comfort—Franklin had promoted it as early as the 1770s—had been accepted widely elsewhere). The earliest effective central-heating system seems to have been introduced in Quebec City in 1818, but not until post-Victorian times did central heating become normal for all houses. By the 1920s alternative steam, hot air, or hot water systems were all available (figure 2.11). Central heating made much more open planning possible in theory, but in practice the great majority of new suburban houses retained the nineteenth-century system of isolated room-boxes, not so much through conservatism as in response to owners' continuing preference for individual privacy.

Whatever the post-Victorian age's outward professions, its real religion was Science. However varied understanding of "Science" might be from class to class and according to education, still its power to move minds was awesome. While on one level intellectuals were applauding "scientific" socialism as a panacea, on another advertisers who could preface arguments with "Science says" or "Science has proved" had their sale made—with predictable results for the Comfortable

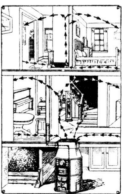

Diagram Shows Circulation of Heat from Pipeless Furnace

May, 1926.
Montgomery Ward & Co., Chicago.
Your Windsor Furnace sure is a wonder. It has rendered the best service that could be had. Any man can install it. Every room in the house is the same temperature. I used only seven and a half tons of coal this winter. My neighbor used over ten tons to heat the same size house.
Mr. Henry Huberty,
Chicago, Illinois.

Nov. 5, 1926.
Montgomery Ward & Co., Saint Paul.
I installed the Pipeless Furnace myself. Anyone can do the job in a short time. It is easy to operate and is economical on the coal pile. It gives an even heat all over the house. I can't say too much for the Windsor.
Yours truly,
Mr. Wm. Bliesnar,
Wood Lake, Minn.

June, 1926.
Montgomery Ward & Co., Kansas City.
I have bought two furnaces from you and installed them myself, which is very easy and simple to do. I think your furnace is just as good, just as easy to operate and gives just as good service as any furnace on the market, as I have bought other furnaces and paid nearly three times the price that your furnace cost me.
E. L. Ambort,
Lees Summit, Mo.

June, 1926.
Montgomery Ward & Co., Chicago.
After using the Windsor Pipeless Furnace, I can say that it is just right for the heating of my house. First, I saved $125. Second, The Windsor Pipeless Furnace is easily installed. Third, it is very economical. Fourth, the Furnace is a very quick heater and keeps rooms at an even temperature.
Yours very truly,
Arthur H. Jordan, Mexico, Maine

House. Hence its emphasis on new "scientific" labor-saving devices (electric vacuum cleaners, irons, toasters, laundry machines), on innovative materials (porcelain tile, linoleum, special stucco compounds), on screens and cemented cellar floors (Science has proved, Comrades, that flies carry germs, that damp basements cause tuberculosis), on sleeping porches (Science has proved that Fresh Air is Good for You; Sinclair Lewis's *Babbitt* opens with his hero awakening on his sleeping porch). Bathrooms and kitchens most obviously manifested the new scientific enthusiasm, of course—the one, now centrally heated, became a white, pristine, clinical temple to hygiene; the other, with its "germ-carrying" painted wood cabinets and wooden slicing boards all banished, was a porcelainized metal food-processing laboratory. Out went wood boxes and root cellars; in came electric or gas stoves and refrigerators.[8]

Other changes in houses were more the result of social shifts toward more democratic equality than of scientific dicta. As more informal life-styles reduced the need for a formal area to greet guests, entrance halls became rarer (you can trace the process very well by comparing catalogs from around 1905, 1915, and 1925, for example) and vestibules dwindled into hall closets. The social functions of both entrance hall and vestibule tended to be subsumed in middle- and lower-class catalog houses by verandahs, where families could greet guests and friends both in summer and, in the many cases where verandahs could be glassed in, winters as well.

Formal parlors, preserved throughout the nineteenth century in both farmhouse and city row house, also began to disappear. Once they had been a kind of sanctum, a shrine where families displayed (but rarely used) their best furniture, where ancestors' portraits in tintype and sepia lined walls and loaded tabletops, where souvenirs of honeymoons in Niagara Falls and excursions to Coney Island recorded family history. Now formal parlors became butts for mockery even in the hinterlands. Hear how the *Weiser [Idaho] Signal* for March 10, 1909 (p. 6) amuses its readers with a piece on "the best parlor":

What misery sits enthroned within its forbidden doors! When you make a visit you are invited within its sacred portals. The door creaks, as if protesting against the invasion. A clamy [sic] atmosphere envelops you as you enter, that makes you involuntarily shudder and wonder if the room is haunted. You sit on a hair cloth chair and clutch frantically at the arms to keep from slipping off. The ambrotypes of deceased uncles and cousins and aunts look down at you from their oval frames and scowl. The whatnot in the corner is covered with bric-a-brac intended to be ornamental, but which looks more like some play house replete with broken dishes and empty bottles, and kept in the best room in memory of some child, dead years ago. You feel in your bones that there has been no one in that room for months before and that when you go out it will once more be sealed like a tomb and left to the care of the relatives on the wall. You long for a glimpse of the sunlight out of doors.

If you could see a hat or coat lying carelessly about to denote that you were still in the land of the living, it would be a relief. You wish you could find a cat in the room and step on its tail, or run a pin into the old aunt who looks down from the wall with stony stare at least fifty years old, or kick the hair cloth chair right into the whatnot, or do anything to cause a little commotion and an appearance of life. And when, after a visit of half an hour, about as cheerful as a funeral, you leave the room, you feel as if you had been in the presence of the dead. The best parlor, where sunlight and children, and laughter, and music and fun are excluded, should give place to something more cheerful and more fitting for Christian homes.

Evidenced here is not only a change of taste, but even more a shift in social function. For the old formal parlor *had* a function: it was the rural and middle-class descendant of the formal rooms of mansion and palace, where the ancestry and stability of the great landed families were proclaimed by portraits of the founders, husband and wife, facing each other above fireplace or entrance doors (as in the Lee mansion, Stratford, Virginia, or George Mason's Gunston Hall). Its disappearance manifested how the old concept of houses as visual metaphors of the family was eroding, how indeed the whole concept of architectural symbolism generally was being lost.

But overreaching all these physical, technological, and social factors molding the Comfortable House was the concept of the suburb itself. Decade after decade the suburbs rippled outward from America's major cities. To some, especially after World War II, they looked like planless thickets, mazes, jungles. But the idea that all city–suburb complexes actually are, in the famous description of Los Angeles from *Better Homes and Gardens* of 1976, "topless, bottomless, shapeless and endless"[9] is true only if you think of city planning in terms of the Empire State Plaza in Albany or Gorky Street in Moscow. If you assume that everything that grows in a natural way must be a chaotic perpetuation of inequalities, which it is a planner's duty to eradicate, then you will be upset by Sam Bass Warner's explaining how in Boston's streetcar suburbs, "the 22,500 new dwellings of Roxbury, West Roxbury, and Dorchester," and by inference most other such suburbs, "were the product of separate decisions made by 9000 individual builders":

Some of these builders were carpenters, some real estate men, most were not professionals at all. The vast majority were either men building houses for their own occupancy or small investors who built a house nearby their own residence in order to profit from the rents of one to three tenants.[10]

And you will agree with the contention of Tunnard and Pushkarev in the mid-1960s[11] that in order to save "Man-Made America" from chaos, it was necessary to subject all these suburbs to "Control." The "Controllers," whose identity was not hard to guess, would presumably level them all and erect in their stead mile after mile of "Radiant Cities" on Corbusier's model.

Fortunately, few would agree with that position today; more fortunately still, even in the planners' heyday enough people resisted to save those suburbs. For in no way were they thickets or mazes or jungles. As often as not, they followed natural topography—roads followed trails established when lands were first settled; bridges were built where ferries had terminated; old hedgerows

and trees were surprisingly often preserved as "salable features." Unfortunately, from a doctrinaire ideological standpoint, these suburbs worked as humane and livable environments on principles of enlightened self-interest, that wicked old Adam Smithish doctrine. Just as policemen are not required on every corner to keep traffic flowing, so suburban builders were capable of ordering an environment on a few general principles understood by all: equal services for all districts; water and electricity supplied without discrimination, because it was obvious that pure water and clean streets were in everybody's interest; no interference with individual builders, because it was also obvious that requiring bathrooms and minimum room sizes and regulating the number of occupants benefited everybody; no regulation of building styles and types, because the "rural idea" of the suburb provided a common denominator for design generally. Why then such furious clamor about "chaos"? Mainly, again, because the kind of "planning without plans" that created the post-Victorian suburbs was so ideologically distasteful to avant-garde planners after World War II: it tended to produce suburbs separated from each other and internally divided along class lines. Sometimes such suburbs even looked like company towns, where class structure was deliberately spelled out by diverse styles and forms of houses.

In sum, post-Victorian suburbs were altogether too individualistic, too inegalitarian, for architectural opinion in the 1960s. But for the decades from 1890 to 1930 they were perfect—perfectly comfortable.

These post-Victorian suburbs fulfilled a social function essentially new in history. The idea of a location far enough from the city to have rural qualities—open fields nearby, good-sized garden behind, and set off from the street by a front lawn—yet close enough for people to commute to the city to earn their living was new. It required a correspondingly new concept of the house, as a dwelling intended to sit in its own plot of ground, like the rural houses of earlier America, yet also related to other houses on a street, like older urban row houses.

Practical, psychological, and traditional motives all co-alesced in the new concept. Practical, because suburban land was cheap enough to permit an individual house to sit on a lot of its own, as urban land had never been. Psychological, because such houses could be seen, and were seen, as images of sturdy independence in their apartness from their neighbors (this was true even of company towns, where popular preference for detached single-family or side-by-side duplex dwellings over-whelmed attempts to reproduce the old urban row units). Traditional, because the concept of a suburban house came out of a specifically American, as contrasted to European, historical experience.

Despite massive urbanization in the nineteenth cen-tury, Americans until well into the twentieth century still thought of their nation as rural. Even up to Coo-lidge's time, presidential candidates routinely posed on tractors in overalls. The virtues of country living were axiomatic and legendary. European workers might be content to be domiciled in barracks-like *Siedlungen,* but American workers would not put up with it, as one company after another found in planning and building its towns. And writers from the 1840s to the 1950s con-sistently talked about "the American house" as if it were always a country house. Thus Downing's book on cot-tages considers cottages proper, as small picturesque dwellings nestled in verdure; villas, as big picturesque dwellings nestled in verdure; farmhouses, as plain houses nestled in verdure. That many of the houses he and Vaux and all their followers illustrated might in fact be built on treeless streets in cities or towns or villages had almost no influence on their conception or design. The typical American house-designer throughout the nineteenth century continued to conceive of houses as individual units set in landscapes, not as one among many comparable units on streets.

And far into the twentieth century too. The reasons are complex. One is suggested by L. M. Hacker in his essay "The Anti-Capitalist Bias of American Histor-ians."[12] What could be called the Charles A. Beard tra-dition of historical writing about cities and company towns was from beginning to end saturated with a Jef-fersonian/Populist philosophy (not necessarily related to Marxism) which held as an article of faith that no big capitalist institution could ever have any moral character and, as a corollary, that anything not rural is corrupt. Another reason is cultural snobbery. As late as MOMA's big *Built in USA* show in 1953, architectural criticism and history still seemed dominated by the "monumental" single-family dwelling, the mansion rather than the homestead; domestic design was routinely discussed as if "Fallingwater" represented a norm for house siting, as if the rural house designed with little or no concern for houses on adjoining lots or for streets was still its commonest problem. And all this when American ar-chitecture had long since addressed the problem and found a solution, in the Comfortable House of the post-Victorian suburb.

Eric Johannesen has usefully pointed out in his fine study of Cleveland how in the better suburbs devel-oping after 1900,

the architecture was different from that of the earlier mansions on Euclid Avenue, formerly the city's best res-idential district. The houses were designed for a differ-ent scale of entertaining and living, and many of them partook of the character of an indigenous suburban type that was developing in the first decade of the century, having a basically horizontal look, with the long facade facing the street.[13]

But the new type was even further developed in middle- and lower-middle-class suburbs—curiously, but perhaps inevitably. Look without prejudice at typical examples of the sort of houses being built via mail-order catalogs (figures 2.12, 2.13, 2.14).

Until recently, all such structures have been routinely dismissed as representing only the incurable vulgarity and debasement of American popular/commercial cul-ture. Something of historical styles is recognizable in them, but so poor and confused—so went the argu-ment—are their quotations from older styles that, com-pared to correct Academic revivals, not to mention the

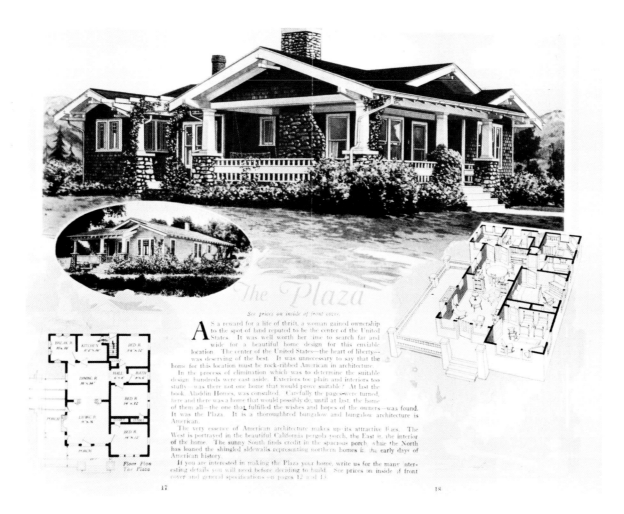

2.12 Successful mass-producible suburban house design depended upon creating illusions of a spacious lot no matter how cramped the actual one might be. On three sides at least such a house should imply yard space: front, back, sides. Comfortable House designers met this challenge in a variety of ingenious ways. For example, the Plaza model advertised in Aladdin's 1919 catalog supplemented its basic rectangle with a wraparound front porch and a back porch also accessible from the side; when the gables of these porches repeated the front gables, a full "yard facade" was created.

2.13 The Ashland model advertised in Bennett Better-Built Ready-Cut Houses catalogs of the 1920s marked its front facade by a full porch, its rear facade by a full second-floor deck, and its side facade by a wraparound sidewalk and hooded gable over the side door.

2.14 "We present here a cottage with no outstanding features," announces the blurb for Southern Architectural Design Bureau's design 436, from *One Hundred Plans Showing the Manner in Which Beauty, Comfort, Hospitality, Distinction Are Combined in Homes of the South Available for Construction Anywhere* (Shreveport, 1922; and filed by Library of Congress system next to *Stately Homes of Natchez!*). One is tempted to agree, but, upon reflection, one thing *is* remarkable about it. Even in this elemental dwelling the designer contrived signs of a surrounding spacious lot by using front and back porches and a wraparound sidewalk. It constitutes, as it were, a tiny image of independence—not "workers' housing" but "a worker's home."

revealed principles of Modernism, they rarely rise even
to the level of the ridiculous. Yet, in sober analysis, they
came closer than any other kind of design to solving one
of the times' most critical problems—how to create what
the Chicago House Wrecking Company succinctly called
"a combination of country and city home" (figure 2.15).

They did this, essentially, by creating three facades:
front (street), back, and side. As often as not, side facades faced only the adjoining house, across a driveway
or narrow alley; but no matter, because what the ad men
said was fundamentally true. These were not city
houses, because they were not wholly street oriented
like the old row houses. They were not country houses
either because they stood on smallish lots contiguous to
many others. Their street facades were not identical to
their neighbors', as in the older row houses. Furthermore, back and side facades retained something of the
individuality of country houses even when houses were
built right up to property lines. Neither city nor country
houses, they represented a really new kind of dwelling,
designed for a new, suburban kind of place.

2.15 Chicago House Wrecking
Company design 133: "A combination of country and city home,"
says the text, and says it all.

3

The Builders of Post-Victorian America

On Fifth Avenue in New York between 70th and 71st streets, facing the Frick Museum, is an unusual monument to Richard Morris Hunt, "erected 1898 by the Art Societies of New York—The Architectural League, the National Sculpture Society, Century Associates, Municipal Art Society, National Academy of Design, American Institute of Architects, American Society of Beaux-Arts Architects" (figure 3.1). About architects you could say in general what Samuel Johnson said about the Irish, "Sir, they are an honest people; they never speak well of each other." But this appears to have been a genuine tribute by professional architects and artists to a man who, more than any other, helped make architecture truly professional by finally cutting the umbilical cord to old apprentice-cum-craftsman traditions of training and who helped make architects proudly conscious of their capability, and duty, to reform the public environment and, through it, society at large.

This new feeling—a post-Victorian spirit, if you like—permeates all the enormously varied aspects of architecture in the 1890–1930 years. Among the new professional architects one might expect it, but it is just as evident among popular/commercial, vernacular, and amateur contractor builders. Not that the architectural scene in the 1890–1930 years was all harmony; far from it. Quarrels divided self-styled "Progressives" from "Beaux-Arts" architects, who also considered themselves "progressive" and refused to cede that proud title, and separated both from spec and mail-order builders. Sometimes in those years it seemed as if all-out war was being waged. Nonetheless, we now realize that those were wars fought in an atmosphere of liberal democracy; the aim was to win advantages (clients), not to destroy the enemy. That is above all what differentiates the post-Victorian age in American architecture from the modern age to come.

3.1 Detail of monument by Daniel Chester French to Richard Morris Hunt erected "by his fellow artists." Appropriately, the monument faces the city, even though technically it stands in Central Park (on the Park side of Fifth Avenue)—for Hunt above all else exemplified how to be a major architect in this period meant to be a designer of big city monuments. Works by him, McKim, White, Cass Gilbert, Carrère, and other giants of the day were meant not only to be ornaments to the city but also orderers of it, structuring the community's time, work, and play. Graffiti and posters defacing this monument suggest some present-day devaluation of such concepts, in architecture and life alike. (IMG:NAL)

The Architects

The new professional architects coming to maturity in the 1880s were more high profile than their predecessors had ever been. For one thing, there were far more of them—ten thousand "architects" were listed in the 1900 census. And they were far more highly educated—the leading ones in Europe, others in newly developing architectural schools in the United States. This made them more specialized than before, so that besides those names preserved in (and perhaps via) architectural history books, there were "regional" architects—both geographically regional ("schools" in New England, the Midwest prairie, California) and culturally, such as Charles Donagh Maginnis, who specialized in Catholic institutional buildings; George Washington Smith, who specialized in Spanish Colonial for southern California; or the Trosts in Texas, whose speciality was "Progressive" adaptations thereof.

The new architects were far more literate; they read intensively and wrote voluminously themselves. This was a great period for founding new architectural magazines and journals, and publishing articles in them was one of the main ways (besides choosing ancestors with care) that post-Victorian architects built careers. Many were accomplished authors, and some—like Ralph Adams Cram, who wrote every bit as stylishly and dogmatically as he designed, or Russell Sturgis, and even more Talbot Hamlin—were much better known to succeeding generations as writers on art and architectural history than as the distinguished architects they were in their own time.

The new architects also traveled; they knew Europe intimately and could on demand produce an "instant museum" for a client not only from books but from firsthand contacts. The eccentric American millionaire collector of the turn of the century, trotting around the world with a crowd of dealer-agent-experts like pack mules strung out behind him, buying ancestral busts and tapestries, paintings and furniture by the boatload for shipment to Newport or Los Angeles or Miami—and sometimes too buying a whole Spanish monastery or Chinese temple or English town hall to put his treasures into—as often as not had an architect or two in his entourage. They knew what they were doing; only in an age like this could an architect write:

It is probable that we shall never again have a distinctive style, but what I hope and believe we shall some day possess is something akin to a style—so flexible that it can be made to meet every practical and constructive need, so beautiful and complete as to harmonize the heretofore discordant notes of Art and Science, and to challenge comparison with the wonders of past ages, yet malleable enough to be moulded at the designer's will.

Significantly for the crosscurrents of understanding then prevailing, that was none other than Bertram Goodhue writing in Stickley's *Craftsman Magazine* in 1905.[1]

The role the country's leading architects were most conscious of was that of shapers and reformers of America's huge new cities—New York, Chicago, Boston, Philadelphia, Baltimore, Washington. They understood how cities constitute visible history, which architects have a major hand in making. As never before they understood how, as Nathan Silver so admirably put it:

The Past is important because a sense of continuity is necessary to people—the knowledge that some things have a longer than mortal existence. Cities, as the greatest works of man, provide the deepest assurance that this is so . . . by revealing and asserting the sometimes hidden mysteries of their being. Cities are places where different styles converge and mix. As a cultural manifestation, this may be a city's greatest function—its ability to present the full record of the past. Lewis Mumford put it most succinctly of all: "In the city, time becomes visible."[2]

They created what are still in many cases those cities' great identifying set pieces—monuments to transportation, government, culture, and education—and that is mainly what they are remembered for. Early in his career, Richard Morris Hunt designed many houses that are admirable achievements but that are remembered chiefly by scholars. What Hunt's contemporaries thought to be his climactic achievements were his New York mansions for W. K. Vanderbilt, Mrs. William Astor, and Elbridge T. Gerry in the 1880s and early 1890s—monuments more than homes, icons for the kind of city that New York was, for the center of a new aristocracy based upon finance capital. Hunt's Great White City concept for the Chicago fair of 1893 became a vision of what great American cities could be and should become. Likewise it was their big-city monuments that made McKim, Mead and White the premier firm of their age—Madison Square Garden, Union Club, the Morgan Library, Pennsylvania Station in New York—not their work in Echota outside Niagara Falls or their capitol in Providence or the Low house in Bristol. So with Carrère and Hastings, Cass Gilbert, John Russell Pope, Henry Bacon, Paul Cret, Henry Hornbostel (see figure 1.1)—no need to belabor the point. To be a major architect in this period meant to be a designer of big-city monuments.

To this principle Frank Lloyd Wright was a great exception. According to Norris Smith:

By 1909 Wright had built scores of houses for families of impeccable social standing and had been accorded both local and national recognition such as no architect in his thirties had received before or has received since. In 1908 the *Architectural Record* (which is published in New York, not in Chicago) had devoted an entire issue to the presentation of his first essay, together with no less than eighty-seven illustrations of his work—an issue in which even the advertisements for plumbing and heating equipment were illustrated with photographs of his buildings. In his own short bibliography Manson lists fifteen periodical references to articles by or about Wright from the years between 1900 and 1910.[3]

But it was precisely his making such a reputation from designing houses that was the remarkable thing about Wright. He had done virtually no big-city public monuments. Like a dog's walking on his hind legs, it was not so much that his house designs were universally admired as that an architect should be famed for that sort of practice at all. A sign of the times, perhaps, but something whose significance has often been overlooked because of the tendency to see Wright and the Chicago School as heroes of a great lost, legendary struggle of Progressives against Academics—legendary in the real sense of the word. How "they killed Sullivan and they nearly killed me," when Hunt and McKim got the commission for the Columbian Exposition in 1893; how Goodhue snatched the San Diego commission away from Gill, who nearly had it, and how different California architecture might have been had Goodhue not steered the Spanish Colonial Revival down an empty Academic revivalist course; how Wright lost the commission for McCormick's River Forest mansion to more conventional but socially better-connected Charles Platt, and how this disappointment led to his throwing up his Chicago practice and running off to Europe with Mrs. Cheney . . . the tales are numberless.

And then the sad finale: the wicked triumphing and trumpeting and spreading himself like a green bay tree, as described by William Rhoads:

Russell F. Whitehead, editor of the *White Pine Series of Architectural Monographs* that served as a key source for Colonial Revivalists in the late 1910s and 1920s, was happy that Sullivan and Wright (as well as the European modernists) had had little impact on American architecture by 1923. Why did they have so little success? Could it be that "our architects have not the spirit to appreciate, or the intelligence to inquire what lies behind the flat, angular and dirty-colored surfaces of the new art"? Whitehead thought not. Rather he believed "there is nothing but this surface, and . . . the whole movement is not the result of a genuine need . . . for a new method of expression, but rather born of a restless and simian desire for novelty." Originality was for Whitehead an evil to be diminished by childish name calling.[4]

The implication is that somehow philistines and reactionaries had imposed their backward taste on the country. This is hardly the case. Much closer to the truth is the fact that, as Norris Smith says, "architecture is an art of urban man; it is to him that it speaks even in its most antiurban manifestations,"[5] and in this context Wright had throughout this period little to say. Commenting on Wright's Steel Cathedral project of 1927, Smith says:

The Steel Cathedral attests to Wright's continuing bafflement and helplessness before the problem of the city. Eighteen years after his flight from Chicago he was still utterly unable to address the American city with forms that could be said to have a significant bearing upon either the life of the community or the constitution of the state; and because he could not do so, even the houses he was building lack the cogency that the best works from his Oak Park years so plainly possessed.[6]

Few of his followers had coped successfully with civic monuments either. Wright's Price Tower in Bartlesville, a design essentially worked out in the late 1920s, was a great indication of how the tall building might make a city live, visually and environmentally, rather than sterilize it like the glass boxes. But by the time it finally materialized in the fifties, the sterilizing glass box was so well on its way to total triumph that the Price Tower was no more than a melancholy reminder of what America's cities might have been. And an isolated flash of inspiration too; for as Wright demonstrated with his proposal for the Arizona State Capitol, he never seemed consistently or consciously to understand the nature of a public monument. His suggestion that capitols should be shaped with reference to their landscape and climate would imply that, because Arizona is arid and mountainous, there would be no need for its capitol to symbolize a community of laws or interest with other states of the Union whose terrain is flat and whose climate is humid. This is closer to Disneyland building than responsible public architecture. No, insofar as the city was concerned, Wright and the Progressive movement could be fairly criticized by the standards of McKim's firm: "The architectural world is too wide, it knows too much of the past to be content today with merely eccentric or purely personal solutions to great problems."[7] On such grounds Sullivan was culpable too; the general criticism of his Transportation Building at the Chicago fair as being out of keeping with the spirit of the plan is, alas, well

founded. Because they could not contribute to forming city imagery, the Progressives' wars with the Academics were lost from the start.

But then the Progressives didn't address the other great architectural problem of the day very successfully either. Although the bulk of their houses were in suburbs, they rarely tried to design genuinely suburban houses. They—and here I use Wright as an example for all the rest—too commonly treated the suburban house as if it were a country house that just happened to be located near a city (as late as the 1950s Wright was still urging the "free man" to keep as far from the wicked city as possible). There is no real street front in Wright's Prairie houses (figure 3.2), and they are not cognizant of their relation to other houses quite nearby. Wright's Robie house looked marvelous in the isolation of a drawing board or in book illustrations or even on its narrow city lot as first built. But as soon as other houses were built on lots adjoining, it jarred—an exquisite rural villa jammed alongside a lot of real suburban houses. Not to make *his* houses suburban must, in Wright's case anyway, have been a conscious decision. He was trying, in Smith's words,

to win for the free, outspoken Whitmanesque individual a new kind of membership in the urban community— one that would simultaneously make for greater personal freedom and for greater collective solidarity. Gradually he must have come to realize that what he wanted was at once to reshape the city into a closely knit "family of families" and also to declare that the free man who is true to himself can have no place in the city at all but must make his home in the openness of the natural landscape.[8]

But this is utopian. It does not address problems of improving the world, but problems that might need addressing if the world (human beings) were improved already. It therefore does little to answer the needs of the times.

Speaking in broadest terms, then, we might venture the following paradox: the complement to the splendid set pieces of Academic urban architecture was not so

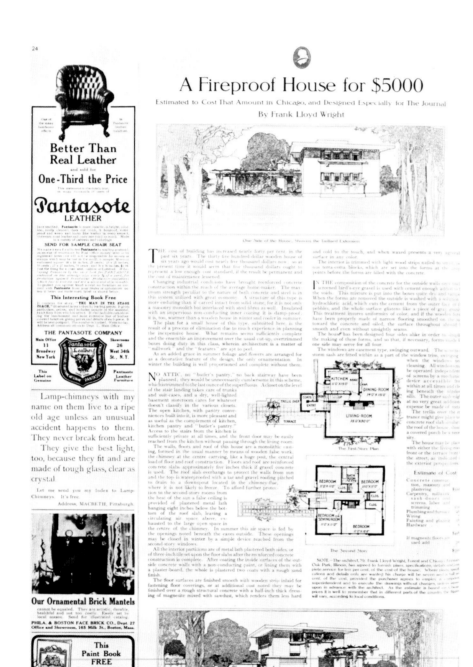

A Fireproof House for $5000

Estimated to Cost That Amount in Chicago, and Designed Especially for The Journal

By Frank Lloyd Wright

One Side of the House, Showing the Trellised Extension

The First-Story Plan

The Second Story

Another View of the House and Grounds

3.2 Even when he was supposed to be designing a suburban house for the masses, Wright could hardly bring himself to produce a suburban, as distinct from rural, house. This ''Fireproof House for $5000'' in the *Ladies Home Journal* for April 1907 could not be built on a normal suburban lot of that time; in contrast to ready-cuts it demands, rather than implies, a spacious lot. Its kind of curving entrance was more suited to one of Downing's country residences of the 1850s. It was designed, in a word, not so much to better an existing environment but for an environment better than the existing one. What a contrast in taste it makes to the ads on this same page! (Library of Congress)

much the Progressives' domestic architecture as popular/commercial builders' suburban houses. That is not to deny the existence of all sorts of fine suburban houses by Academic designers, nor all sorts of poor ones by spec builders, still less the nobility (I think that is the word) of Wright's concept of the free life in an ideal suburban setting. It's just a matter of degree. In that general sense, the counterpart to the skyscraper and monumental arch and templed library was the Comfortable House.

Near-Architects[9] and Non-Architects

Competition from amateurs is a cross professional architects have had to bear from the time their profession began emerging from apprenticeship/master status early in the nineteenth century. Vernacular builders—for example, carpenters and joiners who had learned from their fathers and grandfathers and who reproduced more or less faithfully, in time-honored ways and materials, types and proportions inherited from generations past—had always been around. The term "vernacular" was first applied to architecture in an analogy with human language by Sir George Gilbert Scott in 1857. Its meaning is flexible according to situation; but in essence, "vernacular" means an unaffected, unselfconscious, unaccented way of building, comparable to the speech of someone who has never left a given region and speaks the local accent without affectation, without pretense of a better "class" accent. In other words, it is use of architectural style without being conscious of style—unlike both high art/architecture and popular/commercial building. As vernacular builders did jobs architects seldom came near anyway, they were only occasional nuisances.

Then there were contractors, who replicated and adapted "on spec" plans taken from a wide variety of sources—books, catalogs, trade literature, newspapers, lumberyard fliers, or free combinations of them all—who were also a bearable annoyance and had also been around for a long time. What post-Victorian architects,

especially given their new professional self-esteem, felt to be a novel and unfair sort of trial, and more ominous than any earlier, was the proliferation in their time of people selling houses by mail, often advertising complete house packages, shipped by railroad, erectable by anybody. Even totally unlettered (architecturally speaking) pirates were setting up practice as house builders. Prefabricators might protest that "copyright protects each and every part of this book—type matter, illustrations, and floor plans" and warn that "use by anyone without specific permission is expressly forbidden . . . prosecuted to the full extent of the law,"[10] but how could they possibly prevent a local carpenter from copying the "wonderful money-saving devices" advertised, when every detail was described so carefully? These mail-order firms represented a formidable threat, not least because they were responsible for so huge a percentage of the houses of the time. To alarmed post-Victorian architects, they seemed to have mushroomed overnight, although what they were witnessing was the final flowering of a movement long underway, an inherent and inevitable product of the American capitalist system.

A persistent legend credits Richard Sears of Sears, Roebuck with inventing mail-order architecture. That seems to be true only insofar as he may have been first to complete a "total package" by offering financing in installments. The basic idea goes back much further, to the late 1840s, in fact, when introduction of adhesive postage stamps (1847) made mail service cheap and reliable. The popularity of Downing's 1842 *Cottage Residences* (to handle the volume of inquiries, he invited A. J. Davis and later Calvert Vaux into partnership) can be explained by this new ease of postal communication plus new conditions in the 1840s that enabled local builders to carry out plans from books without benefit of professional building apprenticeship: standardization of millwork for balloon-frame construction and a network of railroads to carry timber to sites all over the country.

By the 1850s a standardized format had been developed by successful refiners of the Downing/Davis/Vaux lead: each house was presented through elevations and floor plans, some details, advice to amateur housebuilders, and what we would call today a promotional blurb. Its principal practitioners in subsequent decades were Gervase Wheeler, Samuel Sloan, George E. Woodward, and Isaac H. Hobbs, Jr. (working for Louis Antoine Godey). Wheeler and Sloan flourished especially in the 1850s, Woodward in the 1860s (in which decade his activity could only be described as marvelous, including four books between 1865 and 1867 and a quarterly magazine), and Hobbs/Godey throughout the period 1840–70. *Godey's Lady's Book* was probably the country's most widely read monthly magazine between 1840 and 1860,[11] and as early as 1849 Godey could proudly announce:

Everywhere have we received credit for our efforts to improve the cottage architecture of our country, and we have the proud satisfaction of knowing that hundreds of cottages have been built from plans that we have published. In one place not far from us, it has been suggested to call the place Godeyville, so numerous have been the cottages put up there from our plans.[12]

As late as 1875 at least a hundred houses a year were being built or adapted from Godey plans, according to Hobbs.

Credit for the idea of supplying plans direct by mail seems due to the firm of Cleaveland and Backus Brothers, operating out of 41 Wall Street, New York. In their 1856 *Village and Farm Cottages* appears this announcement:

For the convenience of such as may wish to build after any of the designs in this work, the Authors have prepared careful, lithographed working drawings and printed specifications for each. These comprise every thing necessary to enable any competent workman fully to understand the plans. They will be forwarded, together with blank forms of contract, by mail, on receipt of a special application, and remittance, at the following rates:—For any one of the first ten designs, $3. For Numbers 11, 12, 13, and 14, $4 each. For the last ten, $5 each.

They will be pleased to answer any inquiries that may arise, and to make such suggestions relative to the execution of the designs in particular localities, as the circumstances of the case, and the information furnished, shall seem to require.[13]

Their lead was quickly followed. Particularly successful was Henry Holly, also of New York, with his *Country Seats* (1864) and especially *Modern Dwellings in Town and Country* (1878). Holly's style was a pastiche of High-Victorian picturesqueness: he took ideas from Charles Eastlake's Gothic/Stick, R. Norman Shaw's Queen Anne, and *Habitations modernes* by Eugène Emmanuel Viollet-le-Duc. Holly carried on a flourishing mail-order plans business, publicized more than marred by a lawsuit with the University of the South at Sewanee over the crumbling walls of their theology building, built from his plans but of a local stone whose compression tolerance was too low.

This suit reminds us that all these mail-order plans still had to be translated into architecture by local architects, builders, or carpenters and what disasters or misinterpretations might result. One step toward a remedy was taken by the brothers George and Charles Palliser. George Palliser emigrated from England to Newark in 1868 as a master carpenter, finding work in the burgeoning North Jersey suburbs. He became co-owner of a sash, blind, and door factory, then moved to Bridgeport, Connecticut, in 1873 as head of a company commissioned to build speculative housing for P. T. Barnum, then mayor of the town. In 1876 he published a booklet, *Model Homes for the People, A Complete Guide to the Proper and Economical Erection of Buildings*, which sold for twenty-five cents; its success was so extraordinary that in partnership with his brother he published two years later *Palliser's American Cottage Homes*, on which his reputation still rests. These two works, like those by Cleaveland and Backus Brothers and Henry Holly, published plans and elevations of existing buildings, but they went even further. Readers who found something attractive could write in with specific particulars—how much they had to spend, where the house would sit, what direction it faced. With this information, and an appropriate fee, Palliser would write to architects he kept on commission, who would prepare appropriate sketches and plans. Palliser forwarded these to the client, who was encouraged to correct or alter at will. The architect then prepared final plans complete with all details and specifications for local builders or contractors.

What Palliser provided was a kind of mail-order architect. Obviously it was much cheaper to consult by mail than by the conventional series of personal meetings between architect and client. Imitators soon appeared, like Robert W. Shoppell of New York, whose 1881 catalog claimed to eliminate time-consuming correspondence by keeping a large architectural staff on the premises to prepare every conceivable variation on standard plans that a client might need. In 1883 Shoppell brought out *How to Build, Furnish, and Decorate,* a book, as the text makes clear, providing all the services an architect might provide "at a fractional part of the charges made by architects" and, incidentally, also at a fraction of the charges made by the Pallisers. It was a declaration of war on two fronts.[14]

This provision of architectural services by mail was one of two main ways the Comfortable House of the 1890–1930 years was built. Followers of the Palliser/Shoppell lead were almost innumerable (figure 3.3). The two biggest, perhaps, were the Radford Architectural Company of Chicago (originally Riverside), Illinois, and the Gordon-Van Tine Company of Davenport, Iowa (figures 3.4, 3.5).

Radford proclaimed itself "The Largest Architectural Establishment in the World," prepared to supply complete plans and specifications for over one thousand different kinds of buildings. For only $8 and $15 they would supply what otherwise (that is, from architects or competing firms in the Pallisers' tradition) would be "$75 and $100 plans." Their catalogs were in fact small

Find Out

Why Not Learn Right Now How Much the House That You Want Will Cost?

If it is worth five minutes of your time to learn how much the materials for the house you've always wanted will cost, answer the questions asked below, and H-L-F experts will tell you. We guarantee no extras.

No Charge; No Obligation—H-L-F experts devised this new, exclusive system, in order to answer for home builders everywhere, the big question, HOW MUCH? This expert advice is free. Use it.

Complete Plans Free to You—Save costly mistakes by building from plans; they're free to H-L-F customers. Our price is for quality lumber, direct from mill. We answer right the question of HOW MUCH?

Answer These Questions; We'll Tell You Quick HOW MUCH

Width (outside measure)..........ft., ...in.; Length (outside measure)..........ft., ...in.
Do you want one-story house? .... Story-and-half house? .... Two-story house? ....
Check the rooms you want:
Living Room (......) Dining Room (......) Kitchen (......) Den (......) Library (......)
Music Room (..........) Bedrooms (how many? (..........) Bathroom (..........)
Porches (how many and what size?) (..)
Will outside be Wood? .... Brick? .... Brick Veneer? .... Concrete Blocks? ....
What sort of siding?..................Or will you use shingles?..................
What height ceilings downstairs? .... upstairs? ....
What height outside wall studs?..................
Do you prefer plaster or wall board?..................
Do you want an attic?..................

How Much

Forest Products MANUFACTURERS Direct

PLAIN HIP   GABLE   GAMBREL

Which style of roof do you prefer?

PLAIN GABLE   GABLE + GABLE DORMER   HIP + HIP DORMER

Name ....
Post Office ....
Street No.
or R. F. D...State..................
When are you going to build?..
Did you enclose 10 cents for Plan Book?..................

Hewitt-Lea-Funck Co. 405 Crary Bldg. Seattle, Wash.
Capital $1,000,000.   Not in any Trust or Combine

Big Book of Plans 10 Cents

This book will teach you more about building in ten minutes than you could learn in weeks of investigation or study. It shows pictures of real homes, arrangement of rooms, detailed, guaranteed costs. A beautifully printed book on tinted paper, in every way equal to books which architects ask a dollar for. Be sure to get this book—it costs 10 cents. Worth a thousand dimes to any home builder.

3.3 Exemplifying the diversity of "architectural services" to middle- and working-class home builders of the early twentieth century is this advertisement in *Bungalow Magazine* of May 1914.

EXECUTIVE OFFICES
OF

THE RADFORD ARCHITECTURAL COMPANY

Entire Eleventh Floor Medinah Building—CHICAGO, ILLINOIS

Largest Architectural Establishment in the World

$75.00 to $100.00 plans for only $8.00 to $15.00. Complete plans and specifications for over one thousand different kinds of buildings. Every plan and specification guaranteed.

Owners and publishers of the largest and most up-to-date collection of building plan and reference books. Every Home Builder should see our plans before building.

3.4 Offices of the Radford Architectural Company in Chicago, about 1908. Special care was taken to display the reference books on shelves, and mounted photographs of executed designs run along the office dividers. This photograph is also interesting as an early example of office interior design, not always easy to locate. Though the firm's architecture was decidedly on the old-fashioned side, its office had a quite modern look—all one free and open area, nothing private. (*Radford's Cement Houses*, 1909, pp. 168–69)

Gordon-Van Tine Co.'s Building Material Plant

At Davenport, Ia., and Vast Lumber Yards at St. Louis

Our business with Carpenters and Contractors throughout the Nation is growing with giant strides. They have come to realize the tremendous advantages offered by the Gordon-Van Tine Company's wonderful Millwork and Building Material Plant in Davenport, where everything used in a building, from shingle nails to the finest interior wood-work, can be secured in double-quick time at a fraction of retail prices.

3.5 Gordon-Van Tine advertisement from *Bungalow Magazine*, May 1914, showing plant.

books: *The Radford American Homes* (1903), *Radford's Bungalows* (1908), *Radford's Artistic Bungalows* (1908), *Radford's Artistic Homes* (1908), *Radford's Cement Homes* (1909). And beneath each plan and elevation, quite in the old-fashioned manner, they promised:

If a plan in this book pleases you, if the arrangement of the rooms is satisfactory, and if the interior is pleasing and attractive, we claim that it can be built as cheap or cheaper than if any other architect designed it. Blue prints consist of foundation plan; floor plan; front, rear, two side elevations; wall sections and all necessary interior details. Specifications consist of twenty-two pages of typewritten matter.

Full and complete working plans and specifications of this house will be furnished for $5.00. Cost of this house is from about $1,250.00 to about $1,450.00, according to the locality in which it is built.

Like Shoppell two decades earlier, Radford obviously aimed to provide the widest possible range of designs. The practical result was that among Radford's offerings were some of the most stylistically old-fashioned lines of all post-Victorian popular/commercial builders—not only distinct Gothic and temple-house survivals, but also perpetuations of High-Victorian picturesque eclecticism.

Though they featured many suburban house elevations and plans, Gordon-Van Tine, more than most post-Victorian popular/commercial builders, pitched wares at a farm clientele. Their catalogs often proclaimed: "distinctly a farmer's home and its arrangement is adapted solely to farm life"; "every farm home ought to have a good porch"; "a bargain list of complete supplies . . . for the farmer, the carpenter, the contractor or the home-builder anywhere." Their catalogs featured barns, granaries, hen and duck houses, sheds, hot-beds, cold frames. They did not supply prefabricated packaged buildings, but were moving in that direction through enormous offerings of windows, doors, porches, stairs. The handyman farmer of American tradition, by turns carpenter, stooker, barn builder, wheelwright, smith, odd-jobs man, was never far from

Gordon-Van Tine's mind; it was to that sort of person that their offerings spoke most persuasively. But the blueprints supplied customers were obviously the work of professional architects and presumably required some contractor to execute them. Gordon-Van Tine moved a step in the direction of ready-cut homes, but not all the way.

The virtually countless local companies of this sort were responsible for the local flavor that so often enlivens popular/commercial buildings of the times. Minnesota, for instance, was served by Jens Pedersen and J. W. Lindstrom. Pedersen's designs, not surprisingly, have a decidedly Scandinavian flavor; things much like them were being built in Sweden, especially in these same years, and Pedersen may very well have been importing ideas direct. Certainly the ethnic origins of so many Minnesotans could have made Pedersen's vaguely Scandinavian designs appealing, as would his consistent concern for winterizing porches and for heating systems, not shared by all mail-order builders. "J. W. Lindstrom, Architect," likewise obviously of Scandinavian descent, worked out of Minneapolis and specialized in "Duplex and Apartment Houses." His book of that name, appearing about 1920, provided designs and elevations for everything from duplexes to apartments with thirty-six units incorporated in a grand central-court plan. He also offered plans and elevations for a Christian Science church, a motion-picture theater, a two-story "general hospital building," a two-story clubhouse, several bank buildings, a block of stores, a drug store, and a public garage. Lindstrom obviously would have been very useful for a developer to have around. On his own he published *Cottages and Semi-Bungalows* in the early 1920s, and he seems also to have collaborated with M. L. Keith of Minneapolis, whose company published *Keith's Magazine on Home Building;* twelve books of diverse plans, including *Keith's Book of Bungalows* and *Keith's Attractive Homes;* forty designs for duplex houses and flats at fifty cents each; twenty-five designs for modern churches, also at fifty cents; sixteen designs for bank buildings in a booklet costing ten cents; and *Keith's Twenty Wonder Houses,* the firm's chosen *crème de la crème.* Keith's personalized service—"Your own Original Ideas Worked into a Bright, Original, Attractive Home"—seems much the same as Palliser's thirty years before.

To architectural historians generally, the best known of all mail-order plan suppliers was *The Ladies Home Journal,* which picked up and improved upon the "Modern Homes" feature in the old *Godey's Lady's Book.* The reason is, of course, that the *Ladies Home Journal* published three Prairie houses by Frank Lloyd Wright. As against that, the overwhelming majority of houses promoted in the *Journal* were Colonial Revival, and it was these that Stanford White had in mind when he wrote of editor Edward Bok, "I firmly believe that Edward Bok has more completely influenced American domestic architecture for the better than any man in his generation."[15] From the five-dollar plans published in the *Journal,* some thousands of houses were actually built.

Implicit in all architect-by-mail building schemes was the idea of architecture by mail: supplying not just mail-order architects but also mail-order buildings would eliminate the mistakes and misinterpretations of local carpenters or contractors. Let would-be home owners order the total house, have all its parts precut and numbered, put the whole into a crate transportable by rail, and let purchasers assemble it (literally) by number upon preconstructed foundations, by themselves, on their own lot.

Exactly who first hit upon the idea of mass-prefabrication of buildings is hard to ascertain, for two reasons. The principle of mass-prefabrication is persistently confused with the simple practice of prefabrication, which was certainly known in eighteenth-century America at the latest (for example, St. Paul's Church in Halifax was prefabricated in Boston and shipped to Nova Scotia for assembly in 1753). In addition, there were so many intermediate stages. Ordering ready-made parts of buildings—hardware and doors and porches and steps and cupboards and fireplaces, not to mention jig-cut balusters and scrolled ornament of all sorts—out of catalogs had been going on for a long time, beginning with cast-iron porches and railings available out of catalogs considerably before the Civil War (figure 3.6).

Earliest of the suppliers to provide books illustrating details of woodwork manufacturable by steam-powered planers, band saws, and other tools, on a scale legible to amateurs were probably Marcus Fayette Cummings and Charles Crosby Miller. Their *Designs for Street Fronts, Suburban Houses, and Cottages* of 1865 advertised

designs for all the various features which enter into the composition of buildings, both for the city and country, and these features are again given in detail, and drawn to so large a scale that anyone familiar with the construction of work cannot fail to comprehend their forms and their construction.

Cummings and Miller thus improved upon earlier books in which (according to them) details were "almost invariably drawn to so small a scale as to render comprehending their details impossible to any one except experienced architects."

The Pallisers followed this lead; thus in addition to architects by mail, one could get mechanics by mail, in the sense that any craftsman of even limited ability could in theory produce competent detailed work from these plans and drawings. But why stop there? By the 1880s both Palliser and Shoppell were including advertisements for manufactured architectural details that could be ordered whole by mail. And there were plenty of others. A big supplier of house plans by mail between ca. 1905 and ca. 1915, the Chicago House Wrecking Company, got its start in the building business (as its incongruous name suggests) by selling salvaged house parts of all kinds. They supplied lumber, millwork, mantels, hardware, structural iron, furniture, carpets and rugs, plumbing, heating, iron pipe, fencing, and roofing. But they didn't take the logical next step and supply entire houses.

WOOD HEAD BLOCKS.

DESIGNS FOR STAIRS.

2834
5¼ × 12½, $60.00 per 100

2835
5¼ × 11½, $13 00 per 100

2836
5¼ × 12, $24 00 per 100

1463

1465

BRACKETS.

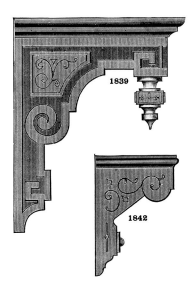

1839

1842

3.6 Excerpts from facsimile of *Combined Book of Sash, Doors, Blinds, Mouldings, Stair Work . . . Embossed Ground and Cut Glass,* Chicago, 1898 (published by American Life Foundation, Watkins Glen, New York, 1978). Sections of this *Combined Book* go back as far as W. L. Churchill's *Universal Moulding Book* of 1871. By the 1900s such offerings were routine for big mass-prefabricators of suburban houses like Gordon-Van Tine and Chicago House Wrecking Company.

That distinction seems to belong to George F. Barber, who began shipping entire dwellings of his design out of Knoxville, Tennessee, around 1889 (figure 3.7). Barber was a builder who moved to Tennessee from Illinois for his health, discovered himself unable to crack the old-boy network of long-time residents who controlled business opportunities in Knoxville, and in desperation began prefabricating buildings for shipment by rail. Before he went out of business—he retired about 1905 but his sons carried on until 1915—he had sold a great number, perhaps thousands, of houses in this way.[16]

It seems probable that the first mass prefabrication was in the form of sectional wooden houses by the E. F. Hodgson Company of Dover, Massachusetts, in 1892.[17] They were soon followed by the Pope and Cottle Company (later Prebuilt Company) of Revere, Massachusetts, which was organized in 1905. But these and other sectional suppliers (for example, Springfield [Massachusetts] Portable House Company; M. B. Kolb of New York; St. John's Portable Building Company of St. John's, Michigan; Louis Bossert of Brooklyn) seem to have begun with small structures like chicken houses, children's playhouses, servants' quarters for summer houses, and vacation cottages (figure 3.8). Such structures were, of course, obvious ancestors of barracks housing used in the First World War. But these companies were surpassed by the first company to offer full build-it-yourself-entirely services: the Aladdin Company of Bay City, Michigan. Aladdin supplied, systematically and on a large scale, complete houses that could be ordered by mail and shipped by rail for on-the-spot assembly by amateurs. Founded in 1904 by two brothers, Will and Otto Sovereign, it is still going strong under the slogan, "We build a better tomorrow by building a better today."

Aladdin's catalogs (mostly the work of O. E. Sovereign) constitute a mini-history of American domestic building and taste. They picture "the largest conveyor of finished lumber in the world" doing "the work of many men and horses" and thereby saving the house builder money by eliminating the local lumber dealer and high-

3.7 Advertisement for totally prefabricated house in vaguely Queen Anne style, by George F. Barber, 1892.

a

b

3.8 Offerings in the *Springfield Portable Houses* catalog of ca. 1906: *a.* a cottage and *b.* servants quarters. An accompanying letter testifies: "One of the greatest difficulties attendant upon summering in the country, at the seashore or in the mountains, is the lack of room for the accommodation of a sufficient number of servants . . . Our SERVANTS' QUARTERS overcome this disadvantage . . . cozy, comfortable and well ventilated . . . lend to the tenants a sense of freedom that enhances their employment and gives them a taste of bungalowing that they would otherwise not obtain." Even in these tiny places, a persistent taste for picturesqueness is manifest.

paid carpenters. By 1919 the catalogs provided well-drawn elevations, many in color; plans of all floors set out; and, most valuable to amateurs, cut-back isometrics of each floor, with indications of furniture placement. Descriptions were lucid and—by comparison with, say, Gordon-Van Tine's, which irresistibly bring to mind some farmer squinting and licking a stubby pencil to underline "the barn is brown in color"—well-written. Aladdin's advertising was aggressive and imaginative (figure 3.9). Besides the famous "Dollar-a-Knot Guaranty," Aladdin also declared its "Houses Sold by the Golden Rule"—and its business flourished. "This is the fifteenth year of Aladdin success," the company's 1919 catalog proclaimed, "practically every year the history of the business shows a doubling and trebling in the number of houses sold" (p. 3). Branch offices were established: Hattiesburg, Mississippi; Wilmington, North Carolina; Portland, Oregon; and a Canadian branch in Toronto, Ontario. By 1919 Aladdin's catalogs were proudly maintaining that the houses reproduced were not drawings but actual houses standing in Bay City "with just two or three exceptions. *This cannot be said of any similar catalog*" (original italics).

Their house designs were created by "The Aladdin Board of Seven," a group including a master designer, master builders, and factory experts, but no architects. They are duly illustrated in early catalogs, earnestly conferring:

Before this Board of Seven comes every Aladdin house for the acid test of perfection. No detail escapes the keen and searching analysis of these experts. The designer must prove his plans to the complete satisfaction of, First, the Master Designer, for accuracy; Second, the Master Builders, for practicability, strength, and structural harmony; Third, Factory Experts, for elimination of waste, standardization of lengths, and economy of costs. Unless the cost of these high-priced men's time could be spread over a hundred or more houses of each design, the cost would be prohibitive. But when they spend two or more hours' valuable time . . . the cost is not all charged to the *one house*, but to *several hundred* houses of the *same design* sold during the year. No other organization but the Aladdin . . . can afford a group . . . such

as this Board of Seven, because no other organization produces and sells the vast number of houses and buildings."[18]

And sell they did: in 1926, Aladdin's best year, 3600 houses were sold.

Aladdin was old-fashioned in one respect: no financing. They required twenty-five percent with order and the balance on delivery. This policy kept the company in business through the Depression, whereas its principal rival, Sears, Roebuck, which built a far bigger business by offering installment financing, went to the wall in 1937 (as far as prefabricated homes were concerned), when customers lost their jobs and could not meet Sears's mortgage payments, and the company had to repossess its own houses.

Sears entered the architecture-by-mail business a couple of years after Aladdin, around 1907 or 1908 (figure 3.10). Legend maintains that Richard Sears's motive was to prop up slumping sales of house furnishings (if you sell a whole house, you sell a whole lot of furniture to go into it); but it may just have been the ultimate step in a career of selling by mail that began in 1885 when the nineteen-year-old Sears, clerking for the Minneapolis and St. Louis Railway at the North Redwood, Minnesota, station, sold twelve-dollar watches, obtained from a crate abandoned on the platform, by mail for fourteen dollars. Until the twenties, Sears did not rival Aladdin in volume of house sales; according to W. J. Sovereign, Sears approached Aladdin in the teens about selling houses under the Sears name, but Aladdin's founders refused on the grounds that such arrangements too often ended with Sears owning the supplying company.[19] Then Sears got competitive, and by 1928 its *Honor Built Modern Homes* catalog listed almost a hundred house models (Aladdin offered about sixty) and a sales volume running into thousands. Following Henry Ford's example of developing his own factories rather than subcontracting, Sears had established factories in New Jersey and Illinois to cut lumber and a third one in Ohio to make windows and doors.

3.9 Demonstrating Aladdin's imaginative sales approach is this advertisement from *Aladdin Homes* catalog 25, third edition, 1914. The text explains how Aladdin bungalows are insulated for northern climates: ''On the outside of the studding we furnish sheathing, and on the outside of the sheathing, bevel siding. Four inches in from this outside wall we furnish plaster board for lining the inside walls, ceilings, and partitions. Between the plaster board, sheating and siding on the outside is a four-inch dead air space which in itself is one of the best non-conductors of heat and cold.''

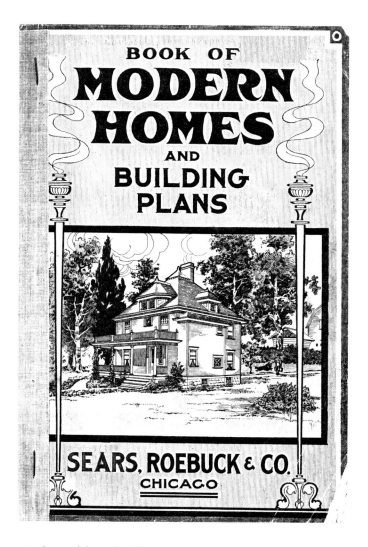

BOOK OF
MODERN HOMES
AND BUILDING PLANS

SEARS, ROEBUCK & CO.
CHICAGO

3.10 Cover of the earliest Sears, Roebuck catalog (1908) features a foursquare farmhouse, still strongly Picturesque in concept. The lamps are in a vaguely Art Nouveau style still much favored on a popular level.

Montgomery Ward, Sears's great retailing rival, was also active in mail-order housing by this time and in comparable volume[20] (figure 3.11). Both firms pushed appliances and furniture, as Aladdin did not; they were, of course, in the business of selling everything, not just houses. Their original customers were farmers. It was people on the remote farmsteads of late nineteenth-century America, the kind of places so vividly evoked in the first chapter of *The Wizard of Oz*—"the house was grey and the fields were grey and Uncle Henry was grey"— who benefited most from contact with the great world of Chicago via mail-order catalogs and who were most likely to buy from them. That these were the very people hit with a double whammy, first by the sudden fall in land prices in 1920 and then by the Depression, contributed not a little to Sears's and Ward's demise as mail-order architecture suppliers in the 1930s.

It also explains the curiously *retardataire* styling of so many of their early offerings (figure 3.12); these are farmhouses, after all, with a bathroom available "for a small additional charge." By the 1920s this had changed, and the big firms were supplying very competent Academic designs (figure 3.13)—so competent, indeed, that most Sears and Ward houses soon passed for the work of local contractors and architects. It is a measure of how rapidly times are changing that Sears now has an archivist toiling in Sears Tower, identifying Sears houses, collecting old mail-order house catalogs, and compiling a guide to Sears houses by roof type.

These were the big firms supplying prefabricated houses, but there were all sorts of smaller ones. One was Harris Brothers of Chicago, who in the mid-teens was already advertising such diverse styles as Craftsman bungalows, Dutch Colonial cottages, Georgians, and foursquares, aimed at the burgeoning suburban market. Another was the Huntington (West Virginia) Lumber and Supply Company, which became Minter Homes in 1919 (and, like Aladdin, required a down payment with order and the rest on delivery and so survived the Depression and remains in business). Minter specialized in supplying cheap homes for company towns—which

Read **Wardway** Ready-Cut Specifications

All dimension lumber throughout is of proper size for the purpose for which it is intended. The best engineering practice has been employed, and our long building experience insures that every piece of lumber in all the houses in this book is amply large to carry all loads placed upon it, and to withstand all strains and stresses.

Girders and Girder Posts are No. 1 Yellow Pine, cut-to-fit.

Girders, Box Sills, Wall Plates, Joists, Studding, Rafters, Blockings, Cripples, Lookouts and all Dimension Lumber are No. 1 Yellow Pine surfaced and edged, cut-to-fit. Every piece is marked and bundled for easy handling.

Scaffolding and Braces are furnished for two sides of the building; also roll of tar paper for covering lumber.

Bridging. A row of double 1 by 3-inch cross bridging is furnished on all joist spans 12 feet and up. Cut-to-fit.

Stair Horses for all stairs and porch steps are cut-to-fit.

Sub-Flooring is furnished for first floor of all houses of 1 by 6-inch No. 2 Yellow Pine tongued and grooved, surfaced two sides, cut-to-fit.

Finish Flooring for first floors 1x3 (2⅜-inch face), for second floors, 1 by 4-inch (3¼-inch face) clear flat grain Yellow Pine. This flooring is clear—no knots or defects of any kind.

Lath for all inside walls and ceilings, No. 1 soft leaf Yellow Pine, guaranteed to make a first-class job. 85 per cent of these lath are 4 feet long, 15 per cent are 32 inches long. No lath furnished for cellar or attic.

Cellar, Grade and Attic Stairs. Treads, risers and strings cut to convenient length for fitting. See page 10 for main stairs.

Grounds, ¾ by ¾ inch Yellow Pine, furnished around all inside doors, and double course for all baseboards, as a guide for plaster.

Backing Strips, 1 by 6 and 1 by 3-inch Yellow Pine, to make solid angles for plaster. Bundled and marked.

Roof Boards, 1 by 4-inch No. 2 Yellow Pine, surfaced two sides, cut-to-fit, bundled and spaced on 6-inch centers. All angles for hips and valleys cut-to-fit.

Wall Sheathing, 1 by 8-inch No. 2 Yellow Pine shiplap, surfaced two sides, or 1 by 6-inch No. 2 Yellow Pine dressed and matched CUT-TO-FIT. Each section tied up in bundles, marked. Angles cut for gable sheathing.

Roof and Wall Shingles, perfect, Edge Grain, 5 to 2 (100 per cent clear—100 per cent vertical grain) Red Cedar, the highest grade and most weather resisting shingle known. All roof shingles laid 5 inches to the weather.

Attic Flooring, No. 2 Yellow Pine, dressed and matched for all houses with attic stairway. CUT-TO-FIT and marked.

Cornice Plancier, ⅝ by 3¼-inch clear Yellow Pine matched and beaded. Where rafter ends are exposed under the cornice we furnish 1 by 4-inch clear ceiling, CUT-TO-FIT, bundled and marked.

Outside Finish, clear grade for exposure to the weather. Includes corner boards, fascia, outside base, frieze, porch beams, belt, porch steps and risers, lattice frame, etc., as shown.

Siding, clear Louisiana Red Cypress or California Redwood, spaced 4½ inches to the weather, absolutely free from knots or defects. Furnished for all houses except where illustration shows shingles or stucco.

Stucco Exterior, for the outside walls of stucco homes we furnish 1 by 8 No. 2 Yellow Pine shiplap, waterproof building paper and self-furring expanded metal lath. The metal lath is of heavy grade with corrugations 4 inches apart. Shiplap cut-to-fit. This is the warmest and most durable construction and is specified by the best architects and contractors.

Building Paper, red rosin sheathing paper to be used between double floors, under siding, and around all door and window frames.

Outside Mouldings such as crown, bed, belt, water table and cove moulding are clear White Pine or Fir, of proper size and design to correspond with each building.

Porch Columns and Rail (as shown) clear Washington Fir. Top and bottom rail with square balusters, cut to convenient lengths.

Porch Flooring: 1 by 4-inch clear edge grain Washington Fir. Full length pieces, bundled and marked.

Porch Ceilings: ⅝ by 3¼ clear Yellow Pine or Fir, matched and beaded. Long pieces bundled and marked.

Outside Frames for all windows, sash and doors, CUT-TO-FIT, bundled and marked. Window jambs plowed and grooved and bored for pulleys. Pulleys furnished. Door jambs rabbeted for doors. All made of clear White Pine.

Windows and Sash are made of clear White Pine, glass set in and puttied. Double strength glass in windows larger than 24 by 28 inches. All two-light windows are check rail and made to hang on weights.

Doors: Front doors are manufactured with clear Douglas Fir panels and White Pine stiles and rails, are first quality high panel design. Interior doors are two-panel design with handsome slash grain fir panels as shown on pages 10 and 11. Rear and grade doors are glazed. All doors mortised for locks.

Hardwood Thresholds furnished for all outside doors.

Interior Finish clear, slash grain Douglas Fir, craftsman pattern in casings, base and mouldings. Ends squared. Bundled and marked. Chair rail furnished for bathroom. All

A. Posts, girders and bolsters.
B. Joists.
C. Box Sill.
D. Sub-flooring.
E. Bottom Plate.
F. Studding.
G. Double Top Plates.
H. Window Framing.
I. Shiplap Wall Sheathing.
J. Ceiling Joists.
K. Roof Sheathing.
L. Rafters.
M. 2nd Floor Joists.

All Prices on Wardway Homes are Based upon the above Specifications

3.11 This page from a 1927 Montgomery Ward catalog reminds us that balloon framing remained the basis of all ready-cut houses, as had been recognized from the beginning: "To lay out and frame a building so that all its parts will come together, requires the skill of a master mechanic, and a host of men and a deal of hard work to lift the great sticks of lumber into position. To erect a balloon-building requires about as much mechanical skill as it does to build a board fence. . . . If it had not been for the knowledge of balloon-frames, Chicago and San Francisco could never have arisen, as they did, from little villages to great cities in a year. . . . Balloon-frames stand as firm as any of the old frames of New England, with posts and beams sixteen inches square." (Gervase Wheeler, *Homes for the People*, 1867, p. 412)

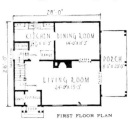

3.12 In its 1908 catalog, Sears offered a mail-order version of vernacular types with echoes from as far back as Downing and trim derived possibly from the Eastlake Picturesque Gothic popular as a high style in the 1870s.

3.13 By the later 1920s Sears and other companies were offering mail-order houses in much more correct Academic styles. This Beverly model from Montgomery Ward's 1927 catalog can be fairly compared with architect-designed houses of the same time.

The "Beverly"—*A Stately Colonial Home*

PICTURESQUE, and true to a type of Colonial architecture which has been popular in America for many decades. This home has the staunchness, character and simplicity of the homes of our early forefathers—with all modern conveniences added.

The harmonious blending of lines and color, an interior arrangement which carries us back to a time when homes fairly radiated hospitality—these are features of the "Beverly" which you will warmly appreciate.

The Exterior: Walls of stucco, which can be made particularly attractive by clinging vines. Well placed Colonial windows with especially designed crescent shutters; the quaint entrance with its tall, narrow columns; a brick floor and steps, and an old fashioned paneled door. Then a large, open porch, extending 20 feet along the right end of the home, completes an exterior Colonial effect strikingly individual and appealing.

6 Rooms and Bath
$1940

Price Includes

Complete set of Plans. All Lumber, Lath, Shingles, Flooring, Inside and Outside Finish and Mouldings, Doors, Windows, Frames, Built-in Kitchen Case, Linen Closet and Towel Case, Nails, Hardware, Tinwork, Building Paper, Paint, Varnish. Everything to build your home with the exception of Heating, Lighting, and Plumbing equipment, and Masonry materials.
Unless otherwise requested, we furnish White Paint for Trim. Walls are Stucco.

Options

Oak doors and Woodwork for Dining Room, Living Room, Vestibule and Stair, $179.95 additional.
Radio Slate Surface Asphalt Shingles with tight roof Sheathing, $23.90 additional.
Galvanized Wire Screens for all Windows and outside doors, $53.80 additional. Storm Sash and Doors, $89.10 additional.
Shades for all windows and outside doors, $19.92 additional.
See complete descriptions of all options on Page 13.

See complete specifications on Pages 8 and 9, also Heating, Plumbing and Wiring information on Pages 91 to 96.

Vestibule: A pleasing vestibule with a convenient closet for wraps is provided.

Living Room: The spacious living room is cheery and well lighted by two large windows and the glazed French doors which lead out onto the open porch. The Colonial fireplace and the attractive specially designed Colonial stairway add greatly to the charm of this homey living room.

Dining Room: A pleasant, well lighted room which is connected with the living room by a wide cased opening. There is ample wall space for placing all dining room furniture.

Kitchen: The kitchen, with its efficient arrangement of built-in cases, stove, sink and ice box, will appeal strongly to the housewife because it is a time saving layout.

Bedrooms and Bathroom: Three large bedrooms and a bathroom on the second floor. All bedrooms have cross ventilation and large closets. A built-in linen case is located in the hall. Study the unusual convenience of the second floor arrangement.

FIRST FLOOR PLAN

SECOND FLOOR PLAN

Size of Home, 28 feet wide by 26 feet long

[25]

does not mean substandard, just small and economical. These were not, as people in those times were fond of repeating (though their descendants have often forgotten) European workers sardined away in barracks or monotonous row houses, but American workers who needed, wanted, and got independent houses on their own plots of ground. Minter's big feature, "The Tuckaway Bath—A Sanitary Sink Plus a Luxurious Bath," actually a bathtub on rollers which slid under the kitchen sink boards, is in itself both a piece of social history (in its derivation from the Saturday night bath ritual in the farmhouse kitchen) and a national cultural expression (*workers* taking baths in their own rooms?). Minter also supplied (like many companies with this kind of speciality) churches, schools, and garages as required. A similar company was Fenner, of Portland, Oregon. According to their series of brochures, they could provide "Small Homes, Five-Room Homes, Six-Room Homes, Large Homes, as well as Barns, Built-in-Fixtures and Special Designs reproduced from the architect's original perspective drawings . . . very modern, high-class designs." But their staple was small homes for company towns. The biggest supplier of such small homes was Liberty Ready-Cut Homes of Bay City, Michigan. Liberty started life as Lewis Manufacturing Company, Millworkers, in 1911. W. J. Sovereign contracted with them for millwork when Aladdin began; but when Lewis saw how good Aladdin's business was, it broke away and became a rival company in 1915, specializing in the low-cost market (figure 3.14).

Pacific Systems of Los Angeles; Rogers & Manson, Home Builders of Chicago; Ernest Hodgson and Fred Hodgson, who supplied "Practical Bungalows" all up and down the Pacific Coast; Southern Mill and Manufacturing Company of Tulsa; Bennett Lumber Company of Tonawanda, New York; Houston Ready-Cut House Company of Texas—the list of companies might continue indefinitely. All provided about the same service— and it was a service fundamentally innovative enough to constitute a new chapter in the history of architecture (figure 3.15).

3.14 Order form for a prefabricated, shipped-by-rail house, from the Liberty Homes Company 1915 catalog. So simple a form, faintly printed on poor quality paper, could get someone a home!

3.15 Signboard and demonstration home for the A. C. Tuxbury Lumber Company of Charleston, South Carolina, as seen at Tampa's 1920 South Florida Fair. The "Quickbilt Bungalow" was a mean little house, perhaps, the sort parodied in Laurel and Hardy movies. But it *was* a real house; it *did* provide a home for a family quickly and cheaply; and it was thanks to these little firms as well as the big ones that the American dream of free citizens all enjoying the liberty of life in their own private spaces came closest to realization. (Photo courtesy Tampa/Hillsborough County Public Library System, from James M. Ricci, "The Bungalow," *Tampa Bay History*, 1979)

The Practice of Mail-Order Architecture

What was it like to buy and build a Comfortable House?

I'll never forget the excitement of waiting for the catalog to arrive. We pored over it many, many times. There were dozens of styles, but most were too expensive. We decided on a one-story bungalow. We didn't have much choice because it seemed they offered mostly two-story houses at that time. I didn't know anyone else who had ordered a house this way, but my husband felt it was the only way that we could buy one.

The speaker is Mrs. Murriel Wells, recalling how she and her husband Opal ordered their first, and only, house in Morgantown, West Virginia, in the fall of 1928 out of a Sears catalog.[21] The Wellses had been living for some years, ever since they were married, in his parents' house. The low price of a prefabricated house gave them hope of realizing their dream of having "A Home of Our Own."

They could have ordered a house from many different catalogs. All had alluring copy (like this for Liberty Homes' Lafayette):

Our architects deserve much credit we feel in preparing this ideal home. Six splendid rooms and bath. Three bedrooms. Closet space. Note the double and triple windows. A bright sunshiny and cheerful home that you all will love. Although the Lafayette is a home of considerable floor space and of much real comfort, the price is amazingly low. This home is a real favorite for those needing accommodation for a large family. Many homes of similar style cost hundreds of dollars more to build than the Lafayette. You have probably worked hard, and have made many sacrifices for a home. Here is genuine and big value for the money you have so thoughtfully saved toward the comfort of your family. Save 30% on labor and 40% on materials. Build one for yourself and one for investment (ca. 1918 catalog, p. 15).

Had they bought a house from Liberty, though, they would have had to put up the total price in cash, no later than on delivery. Instead they opted for Sears's Argyle model: two bedrooms, living room, kitchen, and bath, which cost $2400 delivered, on which they could make payments of $38 a month—$19 interest and $19 on the principal. During the Depression, Sears allowed them to pay only the interest.

All companies expected buyers to have a lot with foundations dug on it. "Of course, all excavation and masonry work must be done on the ground," Aladdin explained:

No money would be saved by including stone or brick or concrete, for every section of the country produces this material and prices vary but little. We furnish you with the foundation plan and will give you figures on the amount of material required for whatever kind of foundation material you decide to use—concrete, stone or brick. Fireplaces or chimneys may be built inside or outside and placed wherever desired or may be omitted. The opening for the chimney is not cut, so that the chimney may be omitted or its location changed from wherever it may be shown in our photographs (1919 catalog, p. 9).

The Wellses had their lot—two, in fact, which cost them $1800—but they had not yet dug any foundations. "Murphy's Law" being just as operative then as now, Sears's house crates duly arrived at Morgantown's railroad station in February 1929, instead of April as intended. The ground was too frozen to dig. The crates had to be stored in a garage. The garage had an earth floor. Some of the lumber got damp and warped. Eventually Opal and a friend got foundations dug, installed cement-block foundation walls, and got the warped lumber replaced. Building operations could commence. The Wellses hired a couple of carpenters who, presumably, would have no difficulty understanding instructions for putting the precut parts together.

There were a lot of those parts. In an Aladdin house, for example:

You get . . . material . . . not only perfectly cut to fit, but cut with a view to saving all waste, which means a direct saving to you. But the saving does not stop there. We mortise all doors to receive the lock sets, all interior finish sanded, and flooring steel scraped.

Bear in mind that when you buy an Aladdin house that the foundation sill, floor joists, the sub flooring, the regular tongued and grooved flooring, the studding, the wall sheathing, the siding, the window and door frames, the outside finish, the rafters, the roof sheathing, the steps, the stairs, all porch framing, are *readi-cut*, ready to nail into place. Is it any wonder that we can save you such a big percentage of your labor cost? (1919 catalog, p. 9).

In addition to the lumber frame itself came, in separate shipments, doors with beveled French glass, windows, hardware, and, Mrs. Wells remembered, "enough nails to build *two* houses!" Plumbing, hot-water heating system, a complete bathroom, kitchen sink. Fireplaces with mantels. Mortice locks, knobs and hinges. Tin flashing, hip shingles, galvanized roof-ridge roll. Paint for two coats on the outside body and trim (any colors; most companies had interior decoration advising departments), putty, oils, stains, varnishes. Lath, plaster, and grounds for lining the entire house. Built-in kitchen cabinets, buffets, ironing boards, medicine cabinets, and closets. Also, if desired, precut additions like back porches (even two stories), back kitchens, sleeping porches.

It sounds confusing just to read, but the instructions insisted that "you can't go wrong." Assembly was promised to be quick and easy. Boards and rafters were numbered and coded to plans, to show exactly where each went. Opal and Murriel studied their Sears instruction packet over and over:

The roof boards for your Modern Home are to be laid tight. The shingles are to be laid ½ inch apart and 4 inches to the weather. . . . Remember these instructions and plans are the result of several years of practical experience. Follow them carefully and no trouble will result. If you do not follow them, errors will occur.

Others were poring over Liberty Homes instructions:

You will receive complete working plans and instructions showing clearly how your Liberty home is to be constructed. These plans are so clear even to those inexperienced in building that it is practically impossible for anyone to make a mistake.

Or:

You will enjoy building the Cresent yourself. The construction is very simple. We furnish of course all necessary blueprints and instructions. You simply can't go wrong. Any of the homes shown in this catalog can be built in just a few days' time.

You wanna bet? After the carpenters had been hammering away for a few days, Opal dropped by after work (he was a house painter) and discovered they had managed to assemble the house backward. The living room and kitchen faced the wall of a neighbor's house instead of the Wellses' vacant lot, as planned. "My husband got rid of the carpenter responsible at once," Murriel recalled, and the house had to be taken down and reassembled. Opal got his Uncle Otis to step in. Otis had no experience, but after this fiasco, there was no place to go but up. Murriel remembers Opal saying that any fool ought to be able to understand those blueprints (and one can imagine the tone it was said in). Murriel, pregnant with her first daughter, undertook to "straw boss" the operation, although, as she recalls, in those days pregnant women were supposed to keep out of sight as much as possible. Opal too started checking on the site every day. In spite of this, the living-room windows got put into the dining room and vice versa; nobody noticed until far too late. They were not going to disassemble the house again, so the windows remain reversed to this day. Once construction was finished, Opal did the painting (it was his trade) but hired a professional plumber and electrician to make water, gas, and electric connections. Altogether the house cost $4500 (exclusive of lot) by the time they moved in. They had no money left over to buy the new furniture Sears urged upon them (nothing new about that story either!).

Opal Wells died in 1978, but Murriel still lives in her Sears Argyle. The lot next door is still empty and lets light into the reassembled living room just as it did in 1929. Few repairs have ever been required. That is typical of prefabricated houses; their materials were first class, just as advertised; the labor-saving constructional techniques were sound, just as advertised. This Comfortable House has withstood a lot of living. Or, as I suppose they would have said in those days, catch in throat, "It takes a heap o' livin' to make a House a Home"—and these houses were designed with a heap o' living in mind.

Mail-Order Towns

Besides houses, mail-order architectural companies had always supplied a wide range of other buildings—barns and sheds, summer cottages. It was natural for them to expand to a point where they could supply whole towns on demand. And they supplied far more than has been suspected. A few famous examples are generally known—Sears's million-dollar order from Standard Oil of Indiana to build the two towns of Standard City and Standard Addition near Carlinville, Illinois, for example, with two hundred houses, sidewalks, the whole town plan. But who has remembered that almost two hundred corporations had placed orders for batches of houses—some for as many as five hundred—with the Aladdin Company, as its 1920 *Low Cost Homes Designed Especially for Industrial Purposes* advertised (figure 3.16)? Some of these obviously represent company towns, and, indeed, in an elaborate 1918 brochure, Aladdin depicted many wholly new towns it had built. *Plan for Industrial Housing* declared:

Industrial housing has been studied to death by these self-styled professors [of urban planning]. The application of straight business judgment . . . will solve the 'problem,' . . . not a professor of electroletic something-or-other. There should be nothing mysterious, theoretical or psychologically complex in the planning and completion of a modern, sanitary, and attractive community of workmen's homes (p. 3).

What such communities might have looked like we gather from the front and back covers of Aladdin's 1920 *Low Cost Homes Designed Especially for Industrial Purposes* (figure 3.17). Here is an almost eighteenth-century idealization of industrial progress, showing Art-Nouveauish plumes of smoke from factory chimneys rising skyward as assurances of secure employment for the workers who inhabit the rows of new homes in front (managers' and owners' houses are not to be seen, of course; in contrast to eighteenth- and nineteenth-century practice, they now live out of sight of the factory). What sets this scene apart from eighteenth- and nineteenth-century European industrial towns, and from the conventional "dark Satanic mills" stereotype still common today, is the variety and individuality of these houses. Each has a lawn at front and sides and a backyard, and several different forms are recognizable—what we will be calling in the next chapter foursquare, bungalow, and homestead temple-house forms. Of course, this is the cover of a company catalog, presumably intended to demonstrate the variety of Aladdin's wares in the best possible light and after enough time had elapsed for some amenities to appear. What these new towns looked like immediately upon construction was illustrated by the company, with commendable candor, in Aladdin's *Plan for Industrial Housing* (figure 3.18).

Aladdin offered model communities with names, just like their model houses: McKinley City, Production City, Sovereign City, and so on. The company laid out streets and supplied stock designs for stores, churches, and schools. Today it is hard to locate and identify many of these towns. For example, McCloud, California, is obviously a lumber company town, whose rows of houses, on dozens of streets, were obviously built from several stock plans and were probably prefabricated. But though there is a chamber of commerce that supplies a data sheet on noteworthy events in the town's history, nobody remembers or cares to remember which firm built its houses. I have made similar futile inquiries about former company towns that are recognizable in parts of

3.16 List of corporations using Aladdin's *Low Cost Homes Designed Especially for Industrial Purposes*.

Corporations Having Purchased and Erected Aladdin Readi-cut Homes

(*Quantities up to 500*)

Abertham Construc. Co.
Acme Cement & Stone Co.
Aetna Chemical Co.
Aetna Explosives Co.
Alan Wood, Iron & S. Co.
Albany Car Wheel Co.
American Cement Pl. Co.
American Net & Tw. Co.
American Sewer Pipe Co.
American Z. & Chem. Co.
Appalachian Power Co.
Atlantic Elevator Co.
Atlantic Mills, Inc.
Atlas Powder Co.
Austin Motor Co.
A. D. Julliard & Co.
Bantam Ball Bearing Co.
Barnes King, Dev. Co.
Bay City Homebldrs. Co.
Bessemer Coke Co.
Bickford Machine Co.
Blair-Cambria-Coal Co.
Blue Mountain Min. Co.
Bridgeport Homes Co.
Bristol Brass Co.
British Government.
Buchanan River Coal Co.
Calcium Products Co.
Calumet and Hecla
  Mining Co.
Cantrall Coal Co.
Carleigh Mills Co.
Casparis Stone Co.
Central Land Co.
Cinclare Central Fcty.
Climax Coal Co.
Coalburgh-Kanawha
  Mining Co.
Coale Co., Wm. L.
Cochran Coal Co.
Coghlin & Gray.
Consolidation Coal Co.
Corry Develop Co., The
Craig-Gould Coal Co.
Cudahy Refining Co.
Cuyahoga Shale Brick Co.
C. A. Hughes & Co.

Dominion Coal Co.
Dow Chemical Co.
Dupont Powder Co.
Eagle Lock Co.
Eastern Steel Co.
E. Dillon's Sons, Inc.
Edison Port. Cement Co.
E. J. Lavino & Co.
Ellsworth Colliers Co.
Federal Ft. & Cold St. Co.
Federal Refractories Co.
First Nat'l Bank of San
  Jacinto.
Ford Co., J. B.
Ford Collieries Co.
Forest Hill Elevator Co.
Fourseam Block Col. Co.
Frick & Son.
Galloway Co., Wm.
Gas Engine & Power Co.
Gay Coal & Coke Co.
General Refractories Co.
Good Hold Farm Co.
Golden Fairview Brick
  Clay Co.
Goodwin-Gallagher Sand
  & Gravel Corp.
Goshen Coal Co.
Graff Brothers.
Gratiot Coal & Lbr. Co.
Grazier Mining Co.
Greenbrier Coal & Ck. Co.
G G G Metal Stamp. Co.
Hatfield Coal Co.
Haverhill Cement St. Co.
Hazelton Oil Co.
H. E. Bell & W. G. Zoller.
Helmar Coal & Min. Co.
Hercules Powder Co.
Hope Coke Co.
Huron Mining Co., The
H. L. Barber & Co.
International Powder Co.
Interstate Water Co.
Investment Realty Co.
Irondequit Coal & Sup-
  ply Co.

John A. Logan Co.
Juniata Ganister Co.
Kellys Creek Colliery Co.
Kent Mfg. Co., The
La Belle Coke Co.
Lehigh Coal & Nav. Co.
Lehigh & Wilkes Barre
  Coal Co.
Linen Thread Co.
Littlefield Realty Co.
Logan Nat. Gas. & F. Co.
Louisville Coal &
  Coke Co.
Lowe-Moor Iron Co.
Lukens Iron & Steel Co.
Manhasset Mfg. Co.
Manufacturers Gas Co.
Mark Mfg. Co.
Mass. Con. Min. Co., The
Mead Toliver Coal Co.
Massillon-Belmont Coal
  Co.
Meyers-Crump Stone Co.
Michigan Tanning &
  Extract Co.
Mineral State Coal Co.
Monarch Coal Co.
Moshannon Collieries Co.
Mt. Vernon Ladies' As-
  sociation of the Union.
M. A. Hanna Mining Co.
National Acme Mfg Co.
National Vaccine & Anti
  Toxin Institute.
Oil Well Supply Co.
Oneida Community Co.
Pearl Ridge Realty Co.
Pennsylvania Coal &
  Coke Corp.
Pennsylvania R. R. Co.
Pere Marquette R. R. Co.
Phoenix Refining Co.
Piney Fork Coal Co.
Pittsburgh Coal Co.
Pittsburg Plate Glass Co.
Postal Hotel Co.

Potter Coal & Coke Co.
Potter Gas Co.
Rattlesnake Jack Mine
Ridgeview Coal Co.
Rich Creek Coal Co.
Robinson Const. Co.
Sandusky Por. Cement Co.
Scranton Anth. Coal Co.
Shadbolt & Boyd Iron Co.
Sheboygan Valley Land
  & Lime Co.
Solvay Process Co.
Stamford Mfg. Co.
Standard Oil Co.
Standard Silk Co.
State of Michigan.
Sterling Salt Co.
Trumbull-Vanderpool
  Elec. Mfg. Co.
The Falls Rivet Co.
The Tide Water Pipe
  Co., Ltd.
The Union Stone Co.
Thompson Connellsville
  Coke Co.
Tonapah Placers Co.
Tropical Plantation Co.
Union Powder Corp.
United Natural Gas Corp.
United States Metals &
  Refining Co.
U. S. Aluminum Co.
U. S. Government.
Valley Camp Coal Co.
Valley Mould & Iron Co.
Warren Axe & Tool Co.
W. A. Stone Fuel Co.
Western N. Y. Water Co.
Willis Coal & Mining Co.
Wisconsin Zinc Co.
West Virginia Pitts-
  burgh Coal Co.
West Virginia Washed
  Coal Co.
Wyoming Sand & St. Co.
Youghiogheny-Pitts-
  burgh Coal Co.

Do Aladdin customers come back to us for more houses? Here's the evidence.
One of the above customers placed the following quantity orders for Aladdin Houses at intervals of from two weeks to eight weeks apart covering a period of a single year.

Sixty Aladdin Houses.
Forty Aladdin Houses.
Fifty Aladdin Houses.
Thirty-one Aladdin Houses.

Sixty-one Aladdin Houses.
Sixty-seven Aladdin Houses.
Twenty-six Aladdin Houses.
Six Aladdin Houses.

Two Aladdin Houses.
Twelve Aladdin Houses.

Can stronger evidence be given than that a great modern business house shall time after time buy and erect Aladdin Houses in large numbers? Doesn't it prove effectively that Aladdin Prices, Aladdin Quality and Aladdin Service are supreme?

3.17 Aladdin's 1920 catalog of *Low Cost Homes Designed Especially for Industrial Purposes,* front and back covers.

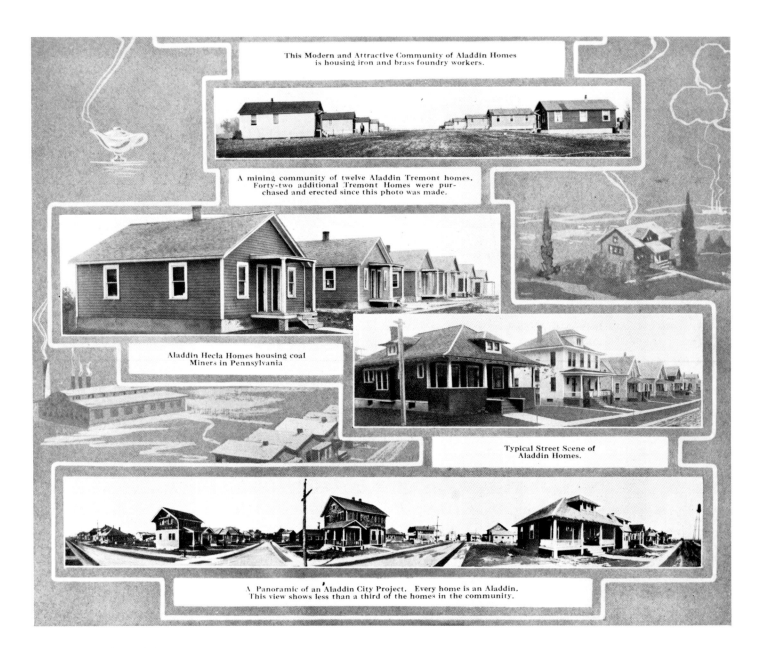

3.18 Illustration from Aladdin's *Plan for Industrial Housing* of new company towns. (Library of Congress)

Sheldon Springs, Vermont (built for the Missiquoi Lumber Company); Pennsgrove, New Jersey; Canton, Mississippi; Washington, Georgia; and many other places. Dozens, perhaps hundreds, of such towns must have disappeared, since they were temporary responses to furious industrial expansion during World War I. Gone certainly is Aladdin City outside Miami, planned in conjunction with a group of Michigan and Illinois businessmen to take advantage of the Florida boom, but caught by its bust instead, to the tune of a $100,000 loss for the company. Vanished also is the village ordered by the Austin Motor Company of Birmingham, England, during World War I—or more exactly the two villages, since the first was sunk in the North Atlantic by a submarine, and a second had to be shipped over. Gone too are the barracks supplied during World War I to several Army posts (Fort Snelling, most notably). But a great many of these structures must remain. According to the 1920 catalog, the company had an

executive staff . . . prepared to meet any situation arising out of housing necessities anywhere. The field staff of the Company includes experienced city planners [Aladdin could even supply sewers and waterworks if necessary], architects, engineers, construction superintendents and foremen. Our field staff has operated in Texas and most of the central western states, in Florida, Virginia, North Carolina, Delaware, Pennsylvania, New York, New Jersey, Quebec, Canada, and in England (p.5).

All this work cannot have disappeared, any more than those Aladdin and Sears and Montgomery Ward suburban houses, which until only a few years ago also seemed gone without a trace. No doubt the explanation for both is the same—quite early it got to be taken for granted that a mail-order house must be something shoddy, so that within a few years a house of any pretension whatever, even a company house, would "pass": "Oh, my house wasn't mail-order; it was built to an architect's plans." Never would *my* home be one of those shoddy mail-order jobs! Such a notion—quite false, it's worth repeating—got no small assist from the architectural profession.

The Great War of Architects with Mail-Order Builders

At first sight, post-Victorian high architecture seems related to mail-order building like the two blades of a scissors: perfectly complementary. This is especially true of a peak period for both, the 1920s. What was officially estimated as a need for a million new small homes could not possibly be met by individually designed houses. Would-be owners could not afford architects' services; nor, for that matter, could they afford the increasingly high cost of skilled labor (brought on by a boom-induced shortage of skilled craftsmen) that custom-built houses involved. In any case, the profit margin on small houses was too small for them to be worth the while of most architects. Only mass-produced mail-order houses could provide the housing needed. And they did provide it. Why then the antagonism between architects and non-architect builders so prevalent through the whole 1890–1930 period?

In part, of course, it was simple cussedness. The more architects thought of themselves as Artists, in a class with Painters and Poets, the more easily their egos bruised, the quicker they were to resent and refute lesser mortals' claims to comparable status. Yet it was by no means all the architects' fault. They were, after all, human, and their resentment was not unprovoked.

Suppose you are a middle-aged architect whose practice rests solidly on years of study at architecture schools, if not in Paris or London, then at Harvard or Yale, or Syracuse, Columbia, Illinois, Wisconsin. You have collected a fine personal library of reference books at great expense. You know all the major styles well and fully share the contemporary opinion that they should be handled "purely," with as little unnecessary mixing as possible. You have been trained to play skillful variations on stylistic themes, and you are a master at it—

something very, very different from jumbling bits and tags from here, there, and all over. Your ingenuity and sophistication in handling these variations are your reasons for being. You then read the kind of tags that appear at the bottom of almost every page of Radford's catalogs:

We have studied economy in construction, and our knowledge of all of the materials which go into a house qualifies us to give you the most for your money. Can any architect do more, even at ten times the cost?

Or you read this, from Aladdin:

The architect, in designing a house, seldom considers the subject of cutting material to waste. He lays out the dimensions of the house, places windows, doors, etc., without any thought of how the material will fit. . . .

When the architect overlooks something or makes a mistake, you pay the bill; when the contractor overlooks something or makes a mistake, you pay for that, too; and when the carpenter uses poor judgment, overlooks something or makes a mistake, *you are the one to stand the cost of his mistake.* It's always your money—not the other's (1919 catalog, p. 16).

Hardly an accurate or fair description of the architect's profession!

Suppose, again, you are a lumber dealer or some other sort of supplier, or a skilled carpenter or plasterer, and mail-order catalogs keep hammering away on the theme of your superfluity. "No broker charges. No wholesale charges. No retail profits. No expensive hand cutting," reads a typical ad (from Liberty). "Don't admit the Hod," admonishes another typical ad (from *Keith's Magazine* for March 1918), use panels instead of plastering. Aladdin writes more expansively, with the same implications—carpenters' skills, acquired by generations of apprenticeship, are superfluous:

The contractor orders so many thousand feet of siding, of flooring, of 2 x 4, of 2 x 6, etc., without any thought as to the utilization of mill-run lengths. You, of course, know that sawmills cut logs in certain lengths, 10 feet, 12 feet, 14 feet and 16 feet, and it comes through the

planing mill in those same lengths. It also comes to the contractor in the same lengths. When the carpenter cuts the siding to fit between two windows, the windows may be 10 feet 1 inch apart: He has to take 14 pieces of siding each 12 feet long and cut each one of them 10 feet 1 inch, wasting 1 foot 11 inches, or about 18% of good lumber absolutely wasted. The principle is the same throughout the entire house (1919 catalog, p. 16).

Or in sum:

Modern power-driven machines can do BETTER work at a lower cost than hand labor. Then every bit of work that CAN be done by machine SHOULD be so done. The steel worker with a little hack-saw trying to cut and fit the steel girders of the modern skyscraper should be no more out of place than the modern carpenter cutting sills, joists, and rafters. The skyscraper framework is cut to fit by machines in the steel mills, marked and numbered ready for erection. The lumber in the Aladdin house is cut to fit by machines in the Aladdin mills, marked and numbered ready for erection. The steel system is twenty-six years old—the Aladdin system fifteen years old (1919 catalog, p. 17).

Of course you would be apprehensive. Where is all this going to end? With the disappearance of all professional craftsmen, that's where! Of course you would begin to talk; and the mail-order builders would have to counter: "Please don't confuse Liberty Homes with cheap, flimsy, portable affairs. Of course, the prices on Liberty Homes are low—very low. But our goal and ambition has been to perfect a system . . . whereby everyone can own a . . . home" (ca. 1918 catalog, p. 11). When the mail-order builders advertise, "It will cost you more to go to your local dealer. If he says, 'Don't buy out of town,' ask him where *he* gets *his* materials," suppliers like the American Steel and Wire Company, urging the superiority of their mesh-backed stucco, have to explain "The Function of the Architect, the Material Dealer, and the Builder in Constructing a Home":

A beautiful home need not be expensive. Skill and good taste need be used, and attention given to such details by the home-builder will amply repay in happiness derived from a snug nest.

Architects have brought the master-craftship of ages down to the present time, so that what kings did not enjoy in many years past, is now to be had within reasonable means.

The advice of an architect is always advisable when contemplating the building of a home. However the builder may think with regard to certain plans, yet it must not be forgotten that the architect represents the most ancient, scientific and practical of the liberal arts. It is a lifetime study, and what has taken him a lifetime to acquire, with the science and teaching of ages back of him, is most useful for the home builder to know. . . .

In every vicinity, therefore, is ample artistic and practical advice obtainable and we present the following descriptions of homes as mere suggestions to be used as helps in designing a home that will be sure to bring contentment and happiness (1921 pamphlet, p. 3).

But this all sounds a bit pompous, pretentious, hollow and was not an effective response to what many were beginning to consider a *crisis*. The public should be told *directly* just what these mail-order people produce. Their stuff is *vulgar:* "stucco warts, bumps, and swellings which infest the land," "small homes of vicious architecture . . . slapped together by carpetects," "pretentious caricatures";[22] they even produce "'Colonial Bungalows'—a weird hermaphrodite, a creation of jarring elements and hitherto unimagined discords . . . Shades of the Pilgrim Fathers, a *Colonial Bungalow*. Mark you that, my countrymen!"[23] A certain professor of architecture at Stanford leaped into the fray with a treatise on *Art Principles in House, Furniture, and Village Building,* copiously illustrated with his own photographs. He proposed to show the path to enlightenment about bungalow building. My oh my, what wasn't wrong with them! "Monstrosities in their ugliness . . . freaky details . . . inconsistent use of materials," "overemphatic sloping chimney," "exaggerated porch," "boastful use of brick," "the brackets and vertical lines in the gable are disturbing." His conclusion: "Lack of intelligence is the trouble—the crime of crimes and the breeder of all vulgarity."[24] Now we know.

Name calling was not enough, however. More positive action was needed, and in 1919–20 it was taken by two organizations of architects, the Home Owners Service Institute and the Architects' Small House Service Bureau. ASHSB was founded by a group of Minnesota architects in 1919[25] to meet the competition—no, that's not how it was put—to respond, rather, to the profession's altruistic concern that "it is the right of every American child to grow up in a real American home." A real American home, one gathers, could only be one designed by an architect (which, if true, would mean that most American children must go forever homeless—a paradox that plagued Wright's Usonian home projects later):

People who may be selling lots have no particular interest in the quality of the houses that may be put upon them. The contractor is interested in neither the land nor in the owner's advantage. The financier has demonstrated his unwillingness to consider either architectural or land values. The architect alone is interested in unifying all the elements that make up the building of a house and in maintaining the relationships between the various factors that make the home successful and valuable to the owner.[26]

ASHSB would protect "the general public—those who cannot avoid seeing it or else must live in close proximity to it." "It" was the "small house" produced by "cut-rate draftsmen-designers and stock plan publishers," whose work represented "a violent architectural epidemic" that showed signs of "spreading rapidly to large homes and buildings, making very definite inroads on the legitimate professional practice of architecture" and that, simply by weight of numbers, was "inevitably going to give the dominant architectural tone to entire neighborhoods and indeed to the country at large."[27] In 1920 the Minnesota organization was endorsed at the AIA's annual convention and became the Northwest Division of the Architects' Small House Service Bureau of the United States. Ultimately, there were twelve other divisions, each mandated to design and publish stock plans for small (that is, with six or fewer principal rooms) houses and thereby, hopefully, rescue the whole country from those "bumps" and "warts" and "caricatures" currently disfiguring it.

The second champion of architecture over near-architecture and non-architecture was the Home Owners Service Institute, whose leading spirit was Howard Atterbury Smith, AIA, ASCE, compiler of *The Books of a Thousand Homes.* "The aim of HOSI . . . is to create the desire for and to educate the prospective home owner to build better homes, where happiness and contentment will reign."[28] It promoted these goals principally by a "Small House Page" feature in the New York Sunday *Tribune* ("that famous newspaper . . . founded by Horace Greeley," subscribers to the HOSI service were reminded), which illustrated plans and elevations and provided advice under such headlines as "Architectural Supervision Reduces Costs of Home Building." HOSI also featured an "Own Your Own Home" service library.

How could such ideas, with such organizations behind them, fail? For modest sums, the smallest small-house builder could get professional architectural services—houses designed by name architects, with working drawings and construction specifications—for a few dollars per principal room; advice on landscape planning, furnishing, decorating, and financing; and plans of the organizations and discussions of their ideas of good and bad architecture. With popular magazines like *McCall's, House Beautiful, Popular Mechancis,* and the *National Builder* (not to mention their own publications) behind them, plus the enthusiastic support of suppliers of building materials (like the American Steel and Wire Company, quoted above), they should have been howling successes. In fact they were not. HOSI did only moderately well, ASHSB never captured more than a tiny fraction of the small-house market. Why? It is a question relevant to many aspects of architectural history, a variant of one of the big questions about Modernism—why, with command of all the media and all the architectural schools, did the Modern movement never

manage to produce a house that anyone other than cultural elitists would buy, certainly not the middle or lower-middle classes? In both cases the reasons are fundamentally similar.

ASHSB, especially, seemed unable to grasp the economic realities of small-house design and/or sale. All too often its "small house" plans were just scaled-down versions of expensive homes for the well-to-do. And as for presentation, the ASHSB was all too fond of formalistic technical presentations instead of the kind of elevations and plans and cutaways provided by Aladdin or Sears—always an eye cocked, it seemed, for other architects' approval rather than purchasers'. But there was another and deeper reason. Somehow these architects could never bring themselves to pander to Public Taste. That would betray their mission to Educate the Masses in Good Design. William Gray Purcell, a product of the old Prairie school then active with the North Pacific Division of ASHSB in Portland, complained to the national bureau director:

The variation in judgement among Architects as to what is a good house and what is not . . . well . . . I just listen, that is all. They turned down a home the other day for which seven different persons had put up a deposit with three different realtors, inside of two weeks. In my opinion an excellent American House . . . and I honestly believe *they* turned it down *because people did like it.*[29]

Only rarely did ASHSB admit, as in a 1926 flier, that spec and precut houses had merit: "It is undeniable that small house architecture has improved since the war. . . . In many large and small cities will be found types of houses . . . not well done, having been built without plans, but with certain inherent qualities of superiority."

Even more rarely did they try to adopt or imitate successful technical ideas from their rivals. Critical standards were not only pedantic but often self-defeating, all too often boiling down to the less ornament, the better. The buzzing noise these practitioners of Colonial and Tudor styles thereupon heard was a saw going through the limb on which they sat. It sounded another time, when the president of the American Institute of Architects approached Sears, Roebuck with an offer of professional assistance in their mail-order architecture department. After some short discussion the offer was declined. "It was difficult for them [Sears] to see the point of view of the Institute," the AIA organ *Octagon* reported.[30]

Saws buzzed again whenever AIA's relationship to the ASHSB operation came up at annual meetings and "professional dignity" was defended. Should Artists like Us cooperate with a new house-plan service initiated in the *Ladies Home Journal* late in 1919? For only one dollar the *Journal* would send so complete a set of working drawings, details, and elevations that any carpenter, contractor, or amateur could "make as many blue prints as are necessary." Absolutely not! So cheap an offer "belittled the value of the article sold and therefore . . . architectural service."[31] Finally in 1935 the AIA withdrew its endorsement of the Architects' Small House Service Bureau altogether. The diehards' victory was hollow; the architectural profession was in dire straits and Sears was going out of the small-house business as unprofitable. The small-house boom was over.

And worse than hollow—it was pyrrhic. The conservative elitists who had so defended their dignity to the bitter end had in fact destroyed their own position. For having taken a stand on the premise that good architecture is a matter of sensitive aesthetic reactions, produced by judicious manipulation of solids and voids, that it is not a language shared with clients but something only architects really know about, there was no reason to maintain any historical style at all. Or to put it another way, by denying merit to popular/commercial building, these conservatives destroyed any possibility of effective resistance to the Modernist invasion then about to cross the Atlantic.

4

Diverse Forms of Comfortable Building

Style and Type: Definitions and Distinctions

Architecture of all sorts, at all times and places, necessarily involves the creation of visual metaphors of the society that produced it—images that both promote and express the values and validity of those social institutions for which and through whose agency architecture must come into being. Of such visual metaphors, the Comfortable House of the years 1890–1930 is an admirable example. It exemplifies especially well how such images are composed of combinations of style and type.

"Style" and "type" in architecture are easily confused, but the distinction between them is important. Most broadly, "style" is a matter of visual effects; "type" is a matter of physical use and social function.

The visual effects that constitute "style" are of three kinds: ornament, proportion, shapes. Identificatory ornament may consist of shapes (abstract or representational) added to a building, be inherent in the texture of its materials, or consist of patterned forms.

Identificatory shapes may result from either functional or nonfunctional considerations. Reproduction of some recognizable shape may well have constituted the earliest kind of architecture, and such shapes persisted for a long time. Egyptian pyramids were a coalescence of mimetically reproduced shapes; the Sainte-Chapelle was a jewel box; the Sun-Temple at Konarak was a reproduction of the Sun God's wheeled wagon. As late as the nineteenth century, North America had some *architecture parlante* shapes imported from Revolutionary France, and later on, some odd identificatory shapes of the old sort. Plenty of popular/commercial examples of this practice survive to this day.

But in high and ordinary architecture, an identificatory shape means something like a chimney, which may be a stylistic feature as well as a device for conveying smoke; a hooded fireplace may equally well be both a functional heating device and an identifying feature of the Craftsman style. Some such shapes are even found

in Modern architecture; despite the claims of early Modernists that theirs was an architecture with no "style" but was only the natural and honest way to build, in fact strip windows, pilotis, angular ferro-concrete blocks, and glassed-in staircases soon became identifying stylistic clichés.

Identificatory proportions may result from repetition through folk habit or from a consciously repeated module. As Henry Glassie felicitously noted:

The skins of houses are shallow things that people are willing to change, but people are most conservative about the spaces they must utilize, and in which they must exist. Build the walls of anything, deck them out with anything, but do not change the arrangement of the rooms or their proportions. In these volumes— bounded by surfaces from which a person's senses rebound to him—his psyche develops; disrupt them, and you disrupt him.[1]

A style may be recognized through a combination of ornament, shape, and proportions; or it may be a single feature only, like a "Jacobean" gable. Sometimes styles may be recognized by no more than a hint or two, or even by subliminal references (thus many eclectic styles maintained a ghostly existence throughout Modernism). But whatever combination of effects determines a style, the identification is primarily by eye. Eyes are trained to recognize styles by seeing numerous examples. An architectural historian recognizes styles in much the same way as ailments are diagnosed by physicians—by analogy with what has been seen before. Visual memory is critical and indispensable.

The names by which styles are commonly known tend to be retrospective, as the names borne by styles in their own times lose usefulness and have to be replaced by new ones more meaningful to later times. Thus (to pick an obvious example) what we call Gothic was originally called modern art (*opus modernum*) or, outside France, the French style (*opus francigenum*). Fifteenth-century Italian humanists called the style Gothic, meaning "barbaric," an allusion to Goths who supposedly despoiled the later Roman Empire. Eighteenth-century Enlightenmentalists expanded Gothic's meaning to include not only "barbarous" but "horrid." But by the end of that century "horrid" had come to have romantic overtones, which became the predominant notion of Gothic style in the nineteenth century. Or, another example, what we call the picturesque nineteenth-century Italianate style was in its own time more usually called Renaissance (the term survives in the nomenclature of nineteenth-century furniture). What we call Second Empire was at that time more usually called Modern French. And so forth.

Types, by contrast, nearly always go under those names by which the original builders knew them: mansion, garage, church, factory (mill), theater, lodge hall, office building. Identification of types requires, theoretically, some kind of objective verification; unlike styles, types are not identifiable simply by looking at their forms. We know a mansion for a mansion because important and wealthy people go in and out of it, a garage for a garage because cars stand inside, and so forth. In theory, such structures might be meetinghouses or castles or laundromats. In practice, however, building types and subtypes tend to be readily identifiable by sight, because function and visual habit combine to associate certain features with certain types and thereby constitute a basic vocabulary of architectural design.

To begin with an axiom: buildings of the same type may be widely divergent in style. All the prefabricated garages in figure 4.1 have the same use and social function, hence all belong to the same type—or more precisely, to the same general typological category of "shelter" and subtype "shelter for machine/vehicle: automobile garage." All have the same immediate prototype: the carriage house, out of which they evolved in response to suburban needs around 1900. By contrast, none of the buildings is similar in style (except that the style in each case is vestigial and not self-conscious). That is because in each case the visual effect is recognizably different. The Peerless has brackets and wide eaves, visual details recalling the Craftsman style. The Winton's most distinctive visual feature is crossed boards, like the old picturesque Stick style. The Maxwell is distinguished by being swathed entirely in shingle; when

4.1 Four styles of garage offered in Aladdin's 1919 catalog.

shingles are the most striking feature of high-style buildings, they have been called Shingle style. The Packard's
"broken roof lines . . . give it an individuality immediately apparent." Houses and mansions with such features, and without apparent use of associative reference,
we have called Picturesque Eclectic Survival, and such a
garage would fit in well with them.

As for grander types like homesteads or mansions or
churches, throughout the nineteenth century it was
common to find "stylistic jackets" applied to them, originally with some discrimination as to meaning, latterly
with little or none. Even in the early twentieth century
we can find examples like the drawings by Lawrence
Buck of Chicago reproduced in H. H. von Holst's *American Homes* of 1911, made to "show the possibilities of
variation in the exterior style of the house after the plan
has been decided upon" (figure 4.2). All represent the
same *type,* that is, mansion, in the typological rather
than descriptive sense. (I make a distinction between
mansion and homestead on the basis of primary social
function; the social function of mansion is primarily to
proclaim or inadvertently express social status and only
secondarily to raise a family, whereas the social function
of homestead is primarily to serve the institution of the
family and only incidentally if at all to proclaim class
status.) All have the same plan. But each represents a
different *style,* created by superimposed details (and
identified, with the vagueness characteristic of the Academic era in architecture, as "Colonial," "English Country," "Italian feeling," and so on).

A second axiom: any and all buildings above utilitarian level have style (whether high style, popular/com-
mercial, vernacular, or vestigial). Style, and the sense for
ornament that is an integral part of it, seems to fulfill an
instinctive human need. Repressed, that need comes out
in vulgarized forms.

Which leads to two claims. First, to study style is not
just antiquarianism or aesthetics or unscientific romanticism; it is a civilizing, humane activity. And second,
style, properly understood, has a genuine social function. Because early Modernists thought of style in terms

4.2 "Studies of Different Exterior
Treatments of the Same Plan,"
by Lawrence Buck, Architect, of
Chicago. (From H. H. von Holst,
American Homes, Chicago, 1911)

Colonial Type of House with Hip-Roof. This May Be Executed in
Wood, Plaster, or Brick

A Plaster or Brick Design. The Hip-Roof Combined with the Arches
Gives It an Italian Feeling

A Colonial Design with Gable Ends—Brick Material

An English Type of House. Plaster or Brick Would Be Suitable
Materials for This Design

Design Has the Feeling of an English Country House of Brick or
Plaster, with Small Windows

First Floor Plan

of "stylistic jackets" that could be donned or doffed by caprice, they saw it as some sort of useless and pompous excrescence that had to be abolished if architecture were to be restored to health. But they were misled by a transient and temporary situation in late-Victorian architectural practice. *As properly used and understood throughout most of history, styles were not capricious but rather a way to make architectural types work more effectively.* Some styles are more effective on some types than others. Also, some styles change their associational values and meanings according to the types of buildings on which they are used, hence their effectiveness in creating visual metaphors.

All the historic styles of North American architecture appear in the period 1890–1930, but not always in relation to the types with which they were associated earlier. In fact, four quite distinct relationships of historic styles to building types can be identified:

1. Consciously correct Academic revivals of historic styles and types. These present no problems of identification. A good example is the New England saltbox; as reproduced by post-Victorian designers, it invariably has ornamental detail and decorative materials appropriate to its historic shape/type. Or, to cite a particular case, the Low house in Bristol, Rhode Island, grows out of precedents in Colonial homestead types, but it is plainly not a revival or a reproduction but a work of high architectural art in its own right.

2. Survivals of older types reproduced by mail-order builders or contractors usually have stylistic tags appropriate to the historic style associated with that type. The problem is that there is no way, or at least no way apparent to me, that such work can confidently be distinguished (without physically dismantling the building and looking for stamps on the materials) from vestigial survivals of historic styles and types perpetuated unselfconsciously by folk builders or even from *retardataire* buildings resulting from uncritical copying of familiar forms.

3. Ornamental details drawn from recognizable historic styles added to more or less traditional forms of one-, one-and-a-half, and two-story houses. Here there usually is no great problem. Details drawn from English

Colonial architectural sources define an "English Colonial house," and so on; that is, the house's "style" becomes whatever stylistic details are tacked onto it. In amateur (read "mail order") hands, to be sure, astonishing combinations of details that defy such forthright identification sometimes appeared; if art historians were permitted accountants' luxury of a "garbage" category, that is where it would be concentrated. Fortunately there are relatively few extant examples of really indiscriminate mixings (whether because they were never built or were too outrageous for later generations to endure is a nice but irrelevant point).

4. Houses with forms developed in the 1890–1930 period (or finding ultimate form then) that were distinctive enough to constitute new styles in themselves. To such forms, too, ornamental details from recognizable historic styles were added; and that is why they are most often what the post-Victorian house owner has in mind when asking, "What style is my house?"

I think these new stylistic forms are distinctive enough to be called products of the 1890–1930 period. Most do not have generally accepted names. I propose here to refer to them as the bungalow, the foursquare, and the homestead temple-house. Within these broad forms a fairly easy distinction can be perceived between big (1½-2½ stories) and small (1 story or 1 + attic) versions. The bigger ones often have been known, in diverse places, by specific names of their own (the "American foursquare" refers to the big version of foursquare; the "suburban cottage" to the big version of bungalow, for example) and sometimes carry applied ornament specific enough for such further refinements of nomenclature as "Colonial foursquare" or "Italianate four-square." The small versions might be referred to as "worker's" foursquares or homestead temple-houses—one does occasionally find the prefix "workingman's" attached to them, but that seems a bit pedantic. Attempts to further refine nomenclature of small versions by stylistic tags as well would go beyond the pedantic to the absurd. But of all that, more later. In this study I propose first to consider the origins and development of the stylistic house

forms characteristic of the 1890–1930 years—bungalow, foursquare, and homestead temple-house—and then to consider the historic styles applied to them—their origins, their appeal, and their application to the Comfortable House.

Diverse Forms of Comfortable Building

The Bungalow

The bungalow was hardly known in 1900, but by 1910 thousands of houses were being built under the generic name "bungalow." They were hailed as quintessentially American creations, the wave of the future. Already in 1920 they were going out of fashion; the term "bungalow" had become pejorative, implying something small-townish—Woodrow Wilson accused Warren Harding of having "a bungalow mind." By the 1930s bungalows had been almost entirely superseded by "Williamsburg Colonial" as a small house form, and their revival in certain kinds of split-level houses after World War II was only vestigial. Only recently has serious interest in them revived and has attention been paid to the origins and definition of the bungalow type, which turn out to be the subject of as much contention now as when bungalows so suddenly appeared on the American suburban scene.

Historians as distinguished as Vincent Scully, Reyner Banham, and Harold Kirker have attributed invention of the bungalow form to architects Charles and Henry Greene and claim for them the first bungalow built, in 1903.[2] On the other hand, Barbara Rubin flatly rejects that attribution, noting that its basis "seems to reside solely in the notion that architectural introductions and innovations invariably filter down, never up."[3] Robert Winter's *Bungalow* (1980) supports Rubin's contention: "Contrary to popular impressions, Charles and Henry Greene . . . were only slightly involved in the paternity" of the bungalow.[4] For students of popular/commercial arts, things are looking up indeed: only ten years ago such controversy over the lowly mass-produced bungalow would have been unimaginable.

The debate pivots on the way "bungalow" is defined. Define it as a kind of house whose preeminent characteristic is the interpenetration of interior and exterior space, as Arthur C. David did in a 1906 article on the Greenes, and its invention as a respectable building form is logically attributed to them:

Its whole purpose is to minimize the distinction which exists between being inside and outside of four walls. The rooms of such a building should consequently be spacious . . . finished in wood simply designed and stained so as to keep . . . natural texture and hue. The exterior should . . . sink its architectural individuality and tend to disappear in its natural background. Its color, consequently . . . should be low in key and correspond . . . to natural wood. Its most prominent architectural member will inevitably be its roof. The type . . . is most completely and happily fulfilled in the houses of Messrs. Greene and Greene.[5]

With that, everyone could agree. David is not claiming that Greene and Greene invented the bungalow type, only that they made of it a work of architectural art which had "an aesthetic character . . . wholly picturesque . . . highly successful, largely because they so frankly met economic, domestic, and practical conditions."[6]

What has caused most of the definitional difficulty was the persistent tendency of writers in post-Victorian years to indulge in vague associative symbolism that depended, ultimately, upon subjective impressions. As it was put so well in *Keith's Magazine* in 1916, bungalows represented "the dominance of an idea over the form in which it is embodied." Thus "bungalow" is often used as a kind of synonym for "home" and symbol of "naturalism" or "Americanism"—all muddy associations at best. Because the word includes sounds as irresistible to real-estate copywriters as the "o" of "cozy" and "homey" and the "u" of "cuddly" and "comfortable," the temptation to apply it to any and every sort of small dwelling was overwhelming; even the prospectus writers for the Architects' Small House Service Bureau, who should have known better, succumbed. Equation of "naturalism" with "bungalow" had a respectable

provenance; the British had from the first thought of bungalows as places of retreat, whether from the natives of their empire or from the artificialities of home society.[7] But this idea too could easily be misused, as was spectacularly demonstrated by Henry Saylor's 1913 *Bungalows,* which, by defining bungalows as anything embodying "naturalness," managed to identify and describe ten bungalow subtypes that included a large and elaborate summer hotel made of logs in the Adirondacks, a Prairie school bungalow whose only point of resemblance to any other bungalow buildings seems to have been possession of a verandah, and a two-story bungalow with eleven rooms which even he admitted "perhaps should not be included in our classification or in these pages at all, for the reason that it is in reality not a bungalow at all."[8]

A further predictable result of identifying "naturalness" with bungalow forms was that the Craftsman style (that is, emphasis on natural expression of materials and construction) and the stylistic form bungalow were confused from the start (and remain so). So, for example, Glenn L. Saxton, a mail-order house supplier in the 1910s, could describe his house 865-B, a two-story vestigial Georgian in form, with a double porch in front and a full attic and full basement, as a "bungalow home" because it had wide eaves with prominent brackets in vaguely Craftsman style. That bungalows frequently displayed the heavy, tapering verandah posts of wood, clinker brick, or cobblestone typical of Craftsman styling and Craftsman-like heavy fieldstone foundations does not mean that these are characteristics of the stylistic form "bungalow"; rather, they are characteristics of the Craftsman ornamental style applied to the bungalow style form.

Bungalows *per se* could be (and were) found with ornament from any and every style—Colonial, Classical, Shingle, Spanish. And precisely because they were not (at least in many people's minds) associated with any style in particular, they came to be thought of as "American." "As a reward for a life of thrift, a woman gained ownership to the spot of land reputed to be the center of the United States," begins a blurb for the Plaza bungalow model in Alladin's 1919 catalog. "It was well worth her time to search far and wide for a beautiful home design for this enviable location. The center of the United States—heart of liberty—was deserving of the best. It is unnecessary to say that the home for this location must be rock-ribbed American in architecture." The result of her search? Naturally, Aladdin's Plaza:

It is a thoroughbred bungalow and bungalow architecture is American. The very essence of American architecture makes up its attractive lines. The West is portrayed in the beautiful California pergola porch, the East in the interior of the home. The sunny South finds credit in the spacious porch, while the North has loaned the shingled side walls representing northern homes in the early days of American history.

To identify and describe bungalows for our purposes, we need to get away from these vague associations and talk about origins and formal characteristics.

The bungalow seems to have had two origins. Narrowly, the bungalow as a house form originated in British Bengal, from which came even the name, derived from *bangala,* signifying typical native dwellings. Quite similar forms could be found in other parts of Britain's tropical empire—Ceylon, parts of Africa.[9] But more broadly the bungalow as a kind of impermanent dwelling is rooted in the earliest decades of North American history and its entire frontier tradition.

As a house form, the bungalow seems to have been transplanted from the British Raj to Britain, Canada, and the United States almost simultaneously, around 1880. In Britain it acquired extensive gardens, a kitchen added to a verandah, bathrooms and bedrooms carved out of a central living space, and associations of "retreat from care." In Canada it appeared as a dwelling in coastal British Columbia, where there was a climate like England's appropriate to bungalow dwelling and large numbers of retired Englishmen to dwell in them. Bungalows as a house form also soon appeared in the Pacific Northwest and California.

The bungalow as an impermanent dwelling seems to have appeared first in resort areas of New York's moun-

tains and along the New England coast.[10] In California, thanks to a benign climate, impermanent dwelling and regular house form fused early. Although as late as 1912 an advertisement in Cheney's *Artistic Bungalows* made a distinction between "bungalows" and "residences"—residences, from the context, including a cellar and attic—already by 1900 the word "bungalow" had come to mean, at least in the Los Angeles area, "small, low suburban house" in addition to "vacation cottage"; and this low suburban house soon began to exhibit enough diversity for Clay Lancaster to cite it as evidence that conditions in California made architects, carpenters, and spec builders more creative there than elsewhere![11] California soon had a "bungalow industry" advertising this diversity:

This industry has also reached a point where bungalows can be built to suit all pocketbooks. For that matter, we are in a position to supply a bungalow for either the workingman or the millionaire. For many years a host of architects and designers have confined almost their entire efforts to the perfection of this class of dwelling.

Unless one accepted Saylor's enormously elastic definition of "bungalow," there were not too many millionaires satisfying their lust for homeownership with bungalow forms. But California did make its varied bungalows so synonymous with "sun and fun" that between 1900 and 1920 "California bungalow" was the most common way of referring to the form.

How exactly is "bungalow" to be defined today? That depends on whether the bungalow is considered an early twentieth-century house form proper with specific origins or one later manifestation of a vernacular tradition of impermanent dwelling, indigenous to American frontiers from earliest times. Between 1900 and 1915 so many variants appeared that any system of identification is bound to be arbitrary. I suggest the simple definition of "bungalow" as a house form proper is a house having at least three of the four basic features of the "original," that is Bengali, bungalow form.

In an 1880s drawing of a *bangala,* four essential features may be perceived (figure 4.3).

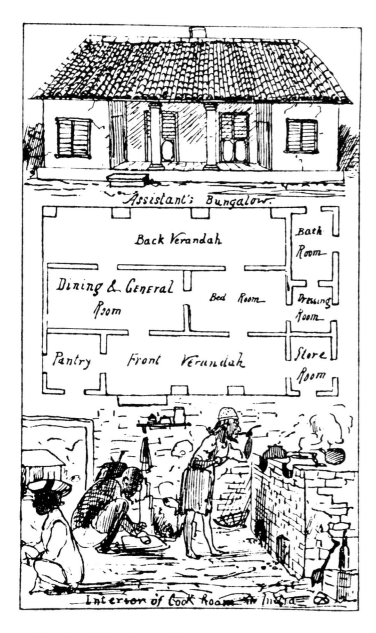

4.3 Drawing of a bungalow used by an assistant on an indigo plantation in Bengal, ca. 1880. (From Michael Edwardes, *British India*, London, 1967)

1. There is no basement.

2. There is a roof sweeping over a verandah. ("The direct attribute of a bungalow that catches the eye of the casual observer and makes him cry out 'Bungalow' as he approaches, is of course the broad expanse of roof," says a writer in 1910.[12] Furthermore, it is a "low sloping roof with eaves at the ends almost touching the ground" that makes a "genuine bungalow."[13]

3. Visually, the bungalow is a one- or one-and-a-half-story house; the second floor, if any, is disguised by some device such as a roofline breaking through. For, as one writer noted in 1916, "Those who insist upon a bungalow with an upper story must call it by another name. For the minute you put on a [palpable, obvious] second floor, away flies your bungalow roof. You may have a house, but you haven't a bungalow."[14]

4. There is interpenetration of inner and outer space. This is most often achieved by the sweeping roof and verandah; even the primitive 1880s *bangala* had both front *and* back verandahs. It can be achieved in other ways, for example by living and dining rooms constituting a flowing space and both carried outward by porches or bay windows. An ingenious way of achieving this freedom and informality without sacrificing privacy and formal structuring was use of a screen wall; screen walls were often the most elaborate element in a bungalow interior. Open, they facilitated flowing space; closed, they preserved the formal integrity of both spaces.

By such a definition, Sears's Corydon model of 1927 is a bungalow (figure 4.4): long sloping roof, no cellar, bedrooms on the first floor, and interpenetration of inner and outer space achieved by the roof/verandah and to a lesser extent by hood-like roofs over bay windows and rear doors. So too are all the upper row of models advertised by Sears in the 1914 issue of *Bungalow Magazine* (figure 4.5). But others in that advertisement are less easily identified.

The second and fourth down on the left side are advertised as bungalows but they look quite different. They represent at best a variant of bungalow, but one which can be found in great numbers through the whole 1890–1930 period, offered by all major companies (see also figures 4.6 and 4.7). Advertisements frequently call it "especially suitable for a working man to afford." This is really, in fact, a sort of "practical bungalow"—at first sight a contradiction in terms, given the origins and association of bungalows with sun, fun, naturalness, and escape. Its qualifications for bungalow status are minimal. There is the sweeping roofline, but nothing like one "gently sloping near to the ground"; there is some interpenetration of space, and the second floor is somewhat disguised by balconies and dormers. But it has a full second floor, containing all the bedrooms; it has a full basement; and the general visual effect is quite self-contained. What we have here is in fact a representative in the "bungalow age" of a form originating in the mid-nineteenth century: the worker's home in the country.

Until the advent of railroad, trolley, and auto, most American workers had to live on the outskirts of cities or towns, where European peasants had had to live before them. But these were not European peasants or proletarians content, even thankful, for some hovel or tenement let from a local landlord: "Intelligent working men in America," wrote Andrew Jackson Downing in 1850, "ought, more than the same class anywhere else, to feel the value and dignity of labor, and the superior beauty of a cottage home which is truthful, and aims to be no more than it honestly is."[15] This cottage home as Downing defined it was small, for use by a family without servants or with at most one or two (such as the farmer's "hired man"). It generally combined the parlor and the living room and therefore lacked even vestigial middle-class formality. But it stood sturdily independent, built by, and visual metaphor of, workingmen of sturdy independence and dignity, capable of owning, and by right entitled to, homes of their own.

By 1887 when the Pallisers published *New Cottage Homes*, the term "cottage" had acquired (in part from its associations with living in the country) the meaning of "summer cottage" in our modern sense, and the Pallisers included some very elaborate examples, almost villas. But "cottage" still kept working-class associations, and they offered one for a narrow city lot (figure 4.8): an "honest workingman's" home, a story and a half high,

4.4 Corydon bungalow, from Sears's 1927 *Honor-Bilt* catalog.

4.5 Panorama of Sears house models, in a 1914 advertisement from *Bungalow Magazine*.

4.6 One of the most popular mass-produced prefabricated house forms was the bungalow cottage. Although often called simply a bungalow, it characteristically had a full second story housing all the bedrooms and a full basement. This example is design 7045B from *Radford's Artistic Bungalows*, 1908.

Size 19'0"x26'6"　　**DESIGN 14018**　　6 Rooms and Bath

Design No. 7045=B

Size: Width, 30 feet; Length, 25 feet

Blue prints consist of basement plan; roof plan; first and second floor plans; front, rear, two side elevations; wall sections and all necessary interior details. Specifications consist of twenty-two pages of typewritten matter.

PRICE

of Blue Prints, together with a complete set of typewritten specifications

ONLY

$12.⁰⁰

We mail Plans and Specifications the same day order is received.

First Floor Plan　　　　Second Floor Plan

DIMENSIONS

Width over all.....21 ft.
Depth over all.....50 ft.
Ceiling height, 1st floor
..............8 ft. 6 in.
Ceiling height, 2nd floor
..............8 ft. 2 in.
Height of basement..7 ft.

Give every family a home of its own with lawn, trees and garden and crime will disappear.

A home like the above will generate an environment of love, kindness and happiness that can only promote good will and charity to all.

Rent money in a few years will pay for your home.

Call and inspect material and secure full particulars.

(56)

4.7 A bungalow cottage from *Walker Bin's Book of Homes*, a catalog published in Penn Yan, New York, in the early 1920s. The aggressively Tuscan columns look almost Post-Modern!

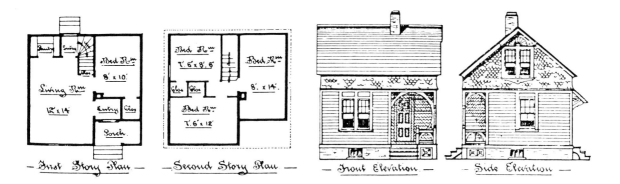

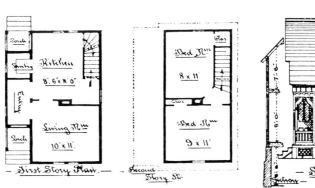

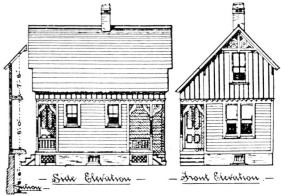

4.8 Ancestors of the bungalow cottage, from Palliser's *New Cottage Homes*, 1887.

with a big dormer (or gable functioning as a dormer) allowing for bedrooms in the upper story, without projections into surrounding space.

Such designs are precedents for the "practical bungalow" or "bungalow cottage" of post-Victorian spec, pre-fab, and catalog builders. This updating of name from the obsolescent (for workers) "cottage" to the fashionable "bungalow" corresponds to an update in place—the form is now characteristic of suburbs rather than rural outskirts of cities. But it remains an image of "intelligent working men in America," with homes of their own instead of planned barracks, and of their upward mobility.

Another bungalow variant imaging upward mobility is the very small form found especially in California cities (figure 4.9). It is extremely versatile, and its plan on occasion was adjusted to fit on platforms in hillsides or to accommodate garages. It was called "bungalow" when

4.9 Characteristic of the small "beginners' bungalow" of California is this house in Berkeley of ca. 1910: all rooms on the first floor, no basement, interpenetration of space suggested by doorway treatment. (IMG:NAL)

built, and still is; yet features of the bungalow form proper, as defined by reference to evolution from the *bangala*, are rudimentary. The same is true even of more developed forms like Aladdin's very popular Pomona model (figure 4.10), whose blurb nevertheless alleges it to be the quintessential California bungalow, designed to "typify the bungalow-craft for which the sunset country is renowned." This kind of small bungalow might well be called the "beginners' bungalow," for two reasons. First, the term suggests that its first turn-of-the-century builders and/or owners thought of it not so much as permanent as a start on the way to something larger and better—a bungalow proper, perhaps, or some other suburban form; second, it implies that evolution from the *bangala* was not the only point of bungalow origin, that it also can be related to the "impermanent architecture" of the "beginners" on the continent's earliest frontiers.[16]

Other suburban forms developed in the 1890–1930 years, the foursquare and the homestead temple-house, derive from the reigning Classical Revival styles of America's first "national rebuilding" of the years 1820–50.[17] But the bungalow's characteristic elements as well as its basic social function can be recognized on that first American frontier, where "all, no matter what their circumstances, were beginners,"[18] and, indeed, on all those subsequent westward-moving frontiers which only vanished in the years when the Comfortable House was taking form:

House construction and barn raising were inescapable first steps in a process of homesteading that was central to the American experience for over three hundred years. It required the planter/settler/pioneer/sodbuster to select from his or her carpenter's repertoire of building types and construction methods those best suited to immediate circumstances.[19]

Geographically that process may have ended around 1890, but psychologically it continued in the expanding 1890–1930 suburbs. The beginners' bungalow exemplifies those origins and associations (which may or may not have been entirely subliminal).

4.10 Pomona bungalow, from Aladdin's 1919 catalog.

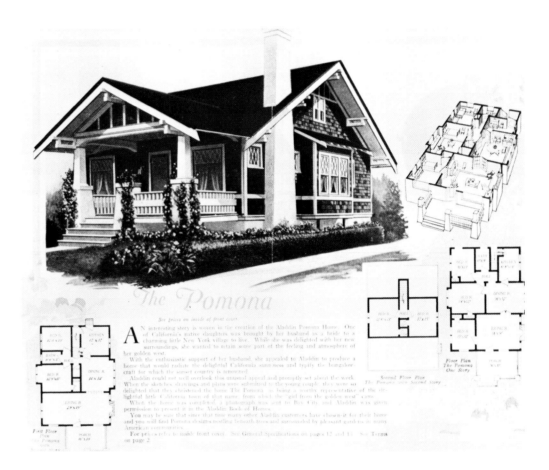

The Foursquare

Two stories high, set on a raised basement with the first floor approached by steps, a verandah running the full width of the first story, capped by a low pyramidal roof that usually contains at least a front dormer, and an interior plan of four nearly equal sized rooms per floor plus side stairwell—that is the form of house known variously as the box, the classic box, the double cube, the plain house, and here as the foursquare. In contrast to the interpenetration of space characteristic of bungalows, the foursquare's basic ethos is a classical self-containment. Despite commonly having only three instead of four columns across the front, asymmetrical placement of porches, irregular fenestration, and side bay windows breaking up boxy outlines, the fundamental visual effect is balanced and symmetrical. Everybody knows this form; every North American town built before 1930 has dozens, thousands of them, and the countryside is full of them as well (figures 4.11, 4.12, 4.13).

The foursquare was one of three essentially new house types evolved in and for those new post-Victorian suburbs. Its Americanness was often stressed at the time: "Thoroughly American in architecture, it is a house anyone will be proud to identify as 'My Home,'" was Aladdin's description of its Willamette model. "Massive" was another popular adjective for the foursquare: "The ever-popular square type which gives an air of massiveness," says one advertisement, while another praises "the square, significant of massiveness and strength." The American foursquare thus appealed to that same need for stability and solidity which on another level was satisfied by associations with English or colonial American roots.

Every mail-order company offered variants of foursquares between 1900 and 1925. The examples in figures 4.14, 4.15, and 4.16 show how the foursquare's massiveness could be powerfully emphasized by predominant horizontal lines—by long straight eaves running

4.11 The front walls of this foursquare farmhouse near Mill Run, Pennsylvania, have been asphalt shingled, but the side walls retain their original horizontal clapboarding. So standard it could have come from several ready-cut companies, it is typically located near a railroad—the one that in 1920 carried crates for one of Aladdin's summer cottages, ordered by the Kaufmann family of Pittsburgh. Later the Kaufmanns replaced their Aladdin cottage with a bigger house designed for them by Frank Lloyd Wright. They called it "Fallingwater." (IMG:NAL)

4.12 Location of a chimney was often specified as "free." The chimney on the near side of this foursquare farmhouse in the vicinity of Clear Spring, Maryland, is an obvious, and visually not very happy, addition. Rough concrete-block walls have been painted over in Williamsburg green and the roof has been reshingled. Otherwise this quite expensive (in its day) foursquare looks about as it did when completed ca. 1910–15. It probably came from a Sears catalog, as concrete block construction was a Sears speciality. (IMG:NAL)

4.13 A rotting frame foursquare in Washington, Oklahoma, could serve as an illustration to *The Grapes of Wrath*; it could well have been abandoned in the 1930s (thirty-odd years before this picture was taken) by some family like the Joads, gone forever to California. This house was probably built from a Radford design; the truncated pyramid roof was a favorite Radford feature in foursquare models ca. 1903–10.

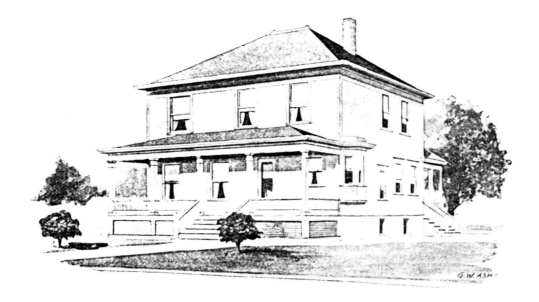

4.14 A Radford foursquare, design 566 from *American Homes* of 1903. The elevation is signed "G. W. Ashby, Architect."

4.15 Massiveness was a quality much admired in foursquares. It was achieved through shape and reinforced by a variety of devices—heavy rooflines and eaves, concrete block. This taste undoubtedly accounts for the emphasis on overhanging roofs in Ward's Norwood model from the 1927 catalog, where it makes even the half-verandah massive. Ward, Sears, Aladdin, and the others offered many foursquare models that differed only in minor details of eave and wall treatment and in what auto dealers call "accessories." The aim, apparently, was to create an impression of unlimited flexibility.

A SQUARE HOUSE OF COLONIAL DESIGN
Design No. 6-G-6

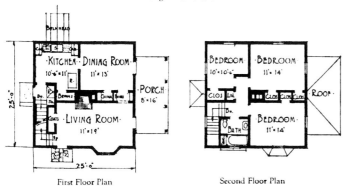

First Floor Plan   Second Floor Plan

4.16 The Architects' Small House Service Bureau disguised the four-square as a "Colonial" in its 1929 New England Division catalog. The resulting hybrid is enough in itself to explain why the ASHSB never flourished. Even the lowliest mail-order house suppliers knew that the people who bought foursquares wanted to come out of their front doors onto their porch and that they very rarely owned a spacious separate lot that would permit a patio opening from the living or dining room on to a garden.

the full length of the walls and by verandah roofs running across the facade and often extending past the edges of the house. Often the second-floor line was picked out as well, by eaves or simply by decorative strips. Frequently the foursquare was extended horizontally, to become a heavy oblong. Additional mass was gained by doubling, trebling, or quadrupling the porch columns or by turning them into squarish pillars. Another favorite massing device was the use of concrete block.

Foursquares seemed to burst suddenly upon the American suburbscape. There seemed to be none in 1890 and hundreds by 1900. Where did they come from? A vogue of this magnitude can hardly be attributable to any one source. Symbolically, foursquares were an inevitable product of the idealistic 1890–1930 years, and in form they resulted logically from the impulse toward more restrained ornamentation evident everywhere from the 1880s on.

The ancestor of the foursquare was the eighteenth-century Georgian mansion (see figure 2.1); put another way, the foursquare was a Georgian mansion reborn in middle-class form. By the 1850s the vogue for picturesqueness had already begun to tack brackets and arcaded porches on the older forms (figure 4.17); by the 1860s towers and gables and wraparound verandahs were swathing them (figure 4.18). The old square or cubical shape became only a core for houses in High-Victorian Picturesque styles like General Grant and Queen Anne (see figure 2.2). In the 1880s the process began to reverse, as part of a growing reaction against the Picturesque villa's aimless and chaotic pretentiousness. Slowly the square form began to resurface, and the American foursquare of post-Victorian suburbs emerged from its Picturesque chrysalis (figures 4.19, 4.20, 4.21).

4.17 This Italianate house in Evansville, Wisconsin, ca. 1855, is a gussied-up version of basic Georgian. (IMG:NAL)

4.18 During the Picturesque mania of the 1850–80 years, even simple houses were disguised by a plethora of ornamental additions, as here exemplified by a Gervase Wheeler design for "Addition to an Old House" in his *Homes for the People,* 1867.

4.19 By about 1890 the basic square with pyramidal roof emerged from its swaths of gables and bays and turrets. This design (number 1130), when published in *Radford's Modern Homes* of 1909, was decidedly *retardataire.* Signed "William Schroeder, Architect."

PL. LXXXV.—ADDITION TO AN OLD HOUSE—ELEVATION.

4.20 By the early 1900s, taste for Picturesque was being superseded in knowledgeable circles by Academic correctness, and the process is traceable in mass-prefabricated designs a decade or so later. These houses of ca. 1905 in Calgary, Alberta, represent a stage in the opposite process from Wheeler's "Addition"; these are foursquares emerging from their Picturesque chrysalis, still retaining vestiges of their larval state: corner turrets with hexagonal witch-cap roofs, flagpoles, widow's walk on the roof peak. Here, plainly, was a spec builder out to please both incoming and outgoing architectural taste!

4.21 In the process of remodeling this ca. 1908 concrete-block foursquare farmhouse into a mini-office building housing a bank and two realtors in Potomac, Maryland, the foursquare evolution is reversed: massiveness is disguised and picturesqueness revived. (IMG:NAL)

The Small (Workingman's) Foursquare

Counterpart to the foursquare proper is a one-story version of the same form. Because it was much favored for company towns, it was in its time sometimes referred to as a "workingman's home." But all small mass-prefabricated house forms were often so tagged; furthermore, small foursquares were by no means inhabited only by proletarians. It is in essence a smaller version of the big two-story foursquare; but it has some distinctive features and precedents of its own.

What distinguishes this form is primarily its squarish plan capped by a pyramidal roof, and, secondarily, a tendency to cut verandah or porch space out of the basic square of the house. A third common, though not definitive, characteristic is a basement raised high enough for the house proper to be approached by a steep (and usually broad) flight of wooden steps.

Like the foursquare proper, the small foursquare had origins in Classical Revival vernacular variants, specifically the Classical cottage of the 1835–1855 period (figure 4.22). By the 1860s the small foursquare appeared as a mass-producible form, advertised by Woodward; by the 1880s the form was fairly common, as evidenced by design 124 in Palliser's 1887 *New Cottage Homes* (figure 4.23). In the 1890–1930 years the form came into its own as a complete mail-order house whose producers showed extraordinary ingenuity in devising variations. The range is suggested by comparing Sears's Modern Home 106 of 1908 (figure 4.24) with Ward's Gary of 1927 (figure 4.25). Sears's 106 had a pyramidal roof pitched high enough to accommodate a bedroom and, on the main floor, besides the kitchen and another bedroom, a sitting room and parlor—curiously backward for a big-city operative in 1908. The square ground plan of Ward's Gary was divided into four near-squares, for the kitchen, two bedrooms, and a living room.

Even in the smallest houses porches were often cut out of a corner of the main plan, so strong was the "square" instinct (figure 4.26). In such houses, rooms were squeezed into the attic pyramid, called grandilo-

4.22 "Classical cottage" of ca. 1835, an ancestor of the small foursquare of later times. This is the manse of St. Andrews Presbyterian Church at Niagara-on-the-Lake, Ontario. (IMG:NAL)

quently on the plans, the "second floor," as if in compensation. The instinct for massiveness also survived (figure 4.27).

Unlike foursquares proper, which can hardly be mistaken for anything else, the small foursquare is easily conflated with other forms. Sometimes, provided with porches and bay windows to effect interpenetration of space and with bedrooms on the ground floor, it could be (and often was) called a bungalow. But the commonest mix was of small foursquare and the temple-house (figure 4.28).

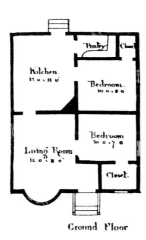

Ground Floor

Front Elevation.

4.23 An ancestor of the small foursquare in Palliser's *New Cottage Homes*, 1887.

4.24 Model 106 from Sears's 1908 catalog is a big version of the small foursquare, with rooms in an attic story. Part of the space was taken up by the ceremonial "parlor" even this late. It cost $1,137.

4.25 Ward's Gary in the 1927 catalog (presumably the name is suggestive of industrial towns) is the basic small foursquare. It cost $598.

4.26 A characteristically West Coast version of the small foursquare is represented by this house built ca. 1920 in Victoria, British Columbia. It has dormers on each side and porch space cut out of the main square, and the whole is set on an elevated basement. (IMG:NAL)

4.27 Many mail-order houses got Permastoned in later times, like this small foursquare in Aberdeen, Maryland; simulation of stone helped give an impression of massiveness, always supposed to be a quality of foursquares. (IMG:NAL)

4.28 A mixture of small foursquare and temple-houses in Elkton, Maryland. (IMG:NAL)

The Homestead Temple-House

One of the goals of a reincarnated Rome in America, so Thomas Jefferson is reputed to have believed, was to provide every American with a family temple-house; Frank Lloyd Wright is credited with propounding a similar idea. For them the goal was utopian, however, because it involved setting that temple-house on its own Arcadian acre or so of land. It was the near-architects and mail-order builders of the 1890–1930 decades who made that goal something of a practical reality, with their mass-produced homestead temple-house set in its own plot—limited, yet distinctly separate. True, what they provided was not exactly the "templed hills" celebrated in *My Country 'Tis of Thee,* but it was a unique body of architecture nevertheless. Regional painters like Charles Burchfield appreciated its especially American qualities as early as the 1930s (figure 4.29).

The homestead temple-house is easily recognizable as a temple-house if you mentally replace the one-story verandah or porch common on the basic type with a Classical temple front (figures 4.30, 4.31). In fact, there are plenty of examples with good approximations of Classical porticos and colonnades (figures 4.32, 4.33). Indeed the homestead temple-house must have owed some of its popularity to either conscious or unconscious associations with the vernacular Georgian/Colonial/Classical house developed between 1830 and 1870.

To tell where vernacular survival stops and mail-order or prefab building begins is not easy without documentation, and is perhaps impossible, for at least two reasons. First, in the countryside, homestead temple-houses often had side wings that produced the effect of two temple-houses set at right angles to each other. That practice had a long history in both vernacular building, where the Classical temple-house proper often had such a configuration—the Caples and Sinclair Lewis houses are representative (figures 4.34, 4.35), and pattern books since at least the 1880s. Second, homestead temple-houses also preserved the vernacular Classical Revival temple-house plan with the door set to the side of the facade and opening directly to a straight staircase.

The reasons for such an arrangement differed vastly: in the later case, it was to provide separate access to upper floors that might be rented out; in the earlier, to provide space for the formal front parlor still requisite in houses of any pretension—and Classical Revival houses were always presumed to be mansions, as we shall see.

Unlike the bungalow or the foursquare, the homestead temple-house is not obviously suburban. Seeing homestead temple-houses in their current context, one hardly thinks of them as suburban at all, but rather as veritable images of teeming northeastern cities—an impression strengthened by their being so often two- (or more) family dwellings used as rental properties. When built, however, these houses stood on the outskirts of town and only time has made them seem "inner city." Further, one-family and multifamily homestead temple-houses were customarily found alongside each other on the same streets (figure 4.36).

4.29 For painter Charles Burchfield, the homestead temple-house form evoked uniquely American qualities, represented in paintings like *Six O'Clock,* of a working-class street in Buffalo, New York, ca. 1935. (Everson Museum, Syracuse)

4.30 Chicago House Wrecking Company's design 145: project the eaves outward a few feet, connect them with an architrave, double the height of the porch columns, add a fourth in the middle, and you would have something like the porticoed temple-house of the early Republic.

4.31 Design 373 in *MacLagan's Suburban Homes*, published at the beginning of the century, illustrates many homestead temple-houses still to be seen in northern New Jersey's older cities. Though spec built, they have the spacious proportions of Academic styles.

4.32 Big homestead temple-house form, from *Walker Bin's Book of Homes,* design 14004. Although this catalog is from the 1920s, this kind of house (easily subdivisible, in fact labeled "Two Apartment") was more commonly built in preceding decades.

4.33 A row of four homestead temple-houses on the 200 block of Delaware Street in Albany, New York. For Classical purists, the vestigial Palladian window and tristyle portico strike jarring notes; but the visual intent is obvious. (IMG:NAL)

4.34 Charles and Lucinda Caples homestead, Columbia City, Oregon, 1870: vernacular temple-house survival. (Courtesy D.A.R., Columbia City)

4.35 Sinclair Lewis homestead, Sauk Center, Minnesota, ca. 1880: possibly a Classical Revival; possibly built by locals from a catalog. Classical temple-houses were often enlarged with wings; in vernacular versions, and catalog derivatives, the wing often got as high as the house itself, thus in effect creating two temple-houses at right angles. (IMG:NAL)

4.36 The 300 block of Quincy Avenue, McCloud, California. This street in the McCloud Lumber Company town was built up between 1907 and 1911. The models of cars in this 1980 photograph, and the truck, clearly indicate that it is still a working-class street. At the far end of the street is a medium-size homestead temple-house. A one-family dwelling, it would have been more desirable than the multifamily homestead temple-houses, as indicated by its own picket-fenced yard. (IMG:NAL)

Their appeal and the simplicity of their construction encouraged many variants of the basic homestead temple-house. A one-and-a-half-story version was quite popular (figures 4.37, 4.38). It was a proper suburban form with fronts, sides, and back; gabled porches; and often pseudo- or vestigial Palladian windows in the gable. Then there was a one-story version called variously "bungalows," "shotguns," and "workers' housing" (figures 4.39, 4.40). None of these are very accurate appelations. "Bungalow" the form simply is not. It does have some resemblance to the vernacular shotgun form of the South, but then any long rectangular shape would. "Housing" has proletarian connotations that are the opposite of what the form was intended to imply— independence and thus possibilities of upward mobility. "Small temple-house" not only corresponds to the actual form but also relates it, correctly, to the reigning style of the early Republic. To such historical styles we now turn.

4.37 A medium-size homestead temple-house: the Yale model, from Aladdin's 1919 catalog.

4.38 A street of medium-size homestead temple-houses in Oswego, New York. Diverse porch treatments have diverse causes: variations permitted by catalogs, individual taste, necessary replacements over the years, adaptations as sun porches. (IMG:NAL)

FLOOR PLAN

Size of Home, 24 feet wide by 38 feet long

4.39 The small workers' temple-house, what would probably have been called in its own time, locally, a shotgun: Sears's 1927 Kenmore model. It was intended for a narrow lot but was self-contained. Concrete-block posts maintain the portico effect.

4.40 The porch is a little more elegantly roofed in this small temple-house advertised in Bennett's Better-Built Ready-Cut catalog of the early 1920s.

5

Colonial Revival Styles: Spanish, French, Dutch, German

The Diverse Styles of Post-Victorian Architectural Ornament

At first sight, post-Victorian architectural styling seems a welter of vestigial, half-understood, misused, mixed-up fragments from styles and stances prevalent earlier in the century (figures 5.1, 5.2, 5.3). Is there any coherent way to comprehend them? It is no solution to call them all *retardataire* High-Victorian Picturesque or to invent names for each variant, like Sullivanesque, châteauesque, Western Gothic, Victorian Vernacular Revival, and the like—a meaningless style with a label is no less meaningless than one without. The question to ask is, what principle, if any, underlies this styling? And the answer is ornament. Post-Victorian styles fall into three fundamentally different groupings or categories, depending on how ornament is perceived or handled.

In the 1880s and 1890s there was a crisis in thinking about design comparable in many ways to what has been happening to thinking about architecture in the 1980s. It centered around the role of ornament, and, specifically, on what to do about the excess of meaningless ornament that by the mid-1880s was making all architectural design farcical.

In essence, three solutions were proposed—Academic, Progressive, and Modern.

The Moderns thought ornament had become so useless and meaningless that it should simply be abolished. Their attitude was that all buildings should be designed "scientifically," and ornament had no scientifically demonstrable use. The Modernist point of view is fundamentally peripheral to a study of the Comfortable House, for two reasons. First, Modernists were much less interested in Comfortable Houses than in Scientific ones (the house as an ideological statement of the triumph of technology; the house as machine for living in, etc.), and, second, until the mid-30s, all the outstanding pace-setting practitioners of Modern style were

5.1 Illustrating the diversity of ornament employed by catalog builders is this Venus model from Aladdin's 1919 catalog. It has a Shingle style upper story, clapboarded first story, Classical columns, and Craftsman brackets and hood all mixed together.

5.2 This house on Claremont Avenue in Verona, New Jersey, is plainly Aladdin's Venus; the porch, fenestration, and eaves brackets are identical. But at some point over the sixty years since it was built, the hooded roof over the upper gable windows has disappeared. Only one fluted column remains; and sometime in the fifties, asbestos siding replaced the original wall treatment over the whole house. The front steps, too, have been rebuilt in brick with metal railing. (IMG:NAL)

5.3 Two other houses on Claremont Avenue in Verona started life as Aladdin's Venus. The one on the right preserves Aladdin's shingled upper story, but the porch has been glassed in; the one on the left has its porch rebuilt, shingles and brackets removed, and shutters added—by someone with a taste for English Colonial, presumably. (IMG:NAL)

in Europe. Thus, between 1890 and 1930 only a handful of Modern houses were built in North America. Most of them were designed by minor members of the European Modern movement who had come to this country a decade or so before the great Bauhaus Blitz and were eking out a living on commissions from early representatives of "radical chic"—the Lovell house in Los Angeles of 1929 or Martha Raye's house in Hollywood are good examples. But totally Modern houses were rare, and they have remained so. Despite control of all the public relations apparatus in the art world, Modernists never were able to produce a house that the average middle-class or even upper-middle-class American would buy, let alone one for the working class.

In contrast to Modernists, both Academics and Progressives agreed that ornament was important and should be retained, with disciplined restraint. Although they differed on how it should be restrained, and on what exact principles it should be disciplined, they are much closer to each other than either is to the Modern position.

Academics proposed disciplined revivals of such earlier styles as Georgian, Gothic, and Tudor but granted wide latitude. They could design Classical buildings that were all but exact replicas of ancient buildings or ones that had hardly any recognizably Greek or Roman ornament on them, but had Classical symmetry and proportional relationships. Progressives put their emphasis on elements of texture, materials, and structures to be found in older styles and were willing to depart much further from their models than their Academic counterparts. They might retain Gothic Revival stained glass or Tudor paneling, for instance, but treat such elements very freely; they could take elements from Colonial homestead models and reassemble them in new combinations. Here is the common ground between an elitist architect like Wright and a populist designer like Stickley

and what unites both to vernacular bungalow builders in California or Michigan. But then Academics and Progressives in turn had so many basic attitudes in common that plenty of architects (including major figures) worked easily in both modes as occasion suggested; hence the justification for considering both as different kinds of Academics, as Moderns did when they jeered at Wright as "the greatest architect of the nineteenth century"—that is, not a Modernist at all.

Considering these cross-connections and, further, that during the post-Victorian period all earlier styles were represented in some way, I will take up each style chronologically, beginning with the Colonial styles.

The Colonial Styles: General Observations

"Colonial" was an elastic word, to say the least, in the post-Victorian years. Typically, "Colonial" could refer to a multitude of styles all generally and vaguely associated with "ancestral security" and "roots": a 1926 issue of *Architectural Forum*, for instance, comments that "the Colonial style" is "the lawful and splendid heritage of a large part of our country. . . . It can feel at home in any part of the United States, for it is the style that is best suited to the average American temperament"[1]—whatever that might mean. The vagueness and generality are useful, perhaps, in helping explain how Spanish and Dutch Colonial, English Georgian, and Cape Cod could all cohabit under the same shaky roof; but to understand what Colonial styles really have in common, it is essential to consider their original common social function.

All Colonial styles had as their basic function the transmission—by reproduction of familiar environments, symbols, and associative shapes—of the institutions of the class-structured states of the Old World to the New, and, in due course, from older to newly settled regions within the New World. The class-structured state was maintained by defined rights, privileges, and duties pertaining to hereditary social classes; those distinctions were maintained through clothes, speech, manners, and architecture, among other means. It follows that each colonizing power could in theory have brought to the New World styles corresponding to and identifying, as well as promoting, its three classes: an aristocratic high style, a peasant folk vernacular, and middle-class styles exemplified in urban dwellings.

So in theory there could be an almost infinite number of Colonial styles. English Colonial would include diverse aristocratic high styles like Georgian as well as diverse folk vernaculars like Cape Cod; Spanish, French, Swedish, Dutch could each have high, vernacular, and middle-class substyles. In practice the number is limited, because few immigrant groups brought over a complete social structure from their homelands and reproduced all its constituent architectural metaphors here. Nevertheless Colonial styles are complex. We take them up here in order of their appearance in the New World (roughly), not necessarily in order of their first Academic appearance or of their popularity in the 1890–1930 period.

Spanish Colonial Revival Styles

The Original Spanish Colonial Styles

Imperial Spain, formed by the union of Castile and Aragon under Ferdinand and Isabella in the late fifteenth century, was Europe's premier power throughout the sixteenth century. Imperial Spain was the first mature nation-state, as contrasted to the smaller sort of principalities, dukedoms, and city-states of fifteenth-century Italy and Flanders. It was also the first mature example of a dynastic class-structured state, the principal visual metaphors of which were the Escorial Palace, near its new capital of Madrid, and the rebuilding of Rome with money from Spain's New World conquests.

Impetus for those conquests, and the model for the colonization procedures, was the final reconquest of the Iberian peninsula from Moslems who had overrun

nearly all of it in the eighth century. Granada, last of the Moorish kingdoms, surrendered to Ferdinand and Isabella in 1492. There the Catholic kings lie buried, in Granada Cathedral's Royal Chapel, and there Isabella commissioned Christopher Columbus to find new worlds to conquer, new infidels to convert. They found new worlds in those parts of North and South America most like Spain in climate and topography—a pattern in all North American colonization.

And they conquered New Spain on the pattern of the reconquest of Spain itself: "natives" (Indians) were to be converted so as to become the "peasant" base of a class structure capped by lords and soldier-adventurers from Spain. Many of the "exploiters" sincerely believed that they were acting in the Indians' best interests. To them, people like Indians who lived "natural" lives must be miserable and brutish; incorporation within the calm confines of a class-structured state would in the end guarantee greater happiness than possible outside it (a kind of thinking applied to their own peasants too, of course!).

Once grasp this controlling model and the distinctive characteristics of Spanish Colonial architecture in the New World become self-evident. Its churches and shrines were splendid because they served as palace surrogates, as images of the dominant class. Of course the finest ones were in Mexico, but even in California some of the Mission churches were extraordinarily grand in relation to the time, place, and available resources (figure 5.4).

Its homesteads were insignificant. Many were just Amerind dwellings or adaptations of Amerind techniques to a debased vernacular Spanish tradition, with stuccoed adobe walls and tiled roofs (figure 5.5). Substantial homesteads or mansions were very few; most of those in what is now the United States came in the last years of Spanish rule (the Vallejo house in Petaluma is an example).

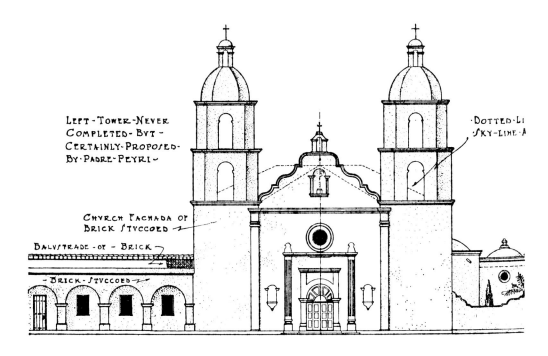

LEFT-TOWER-NEVER
COMPLETED-BVT-
CERTAINLY-PROPOFED-
BY-PADRE-PEYRI-

·DOTTED·LI
·ʃKY-LINE·A

CHVRCH·FACHADA·OF
BRICK ʃTVCCOED

BALVʃTRADE·OF-BRICK

-BRICK-ʃTVCCOED-

5.4 Restoration drawing of mission church of San Luis Rey de Francia, California. (HABS)

5.5 Adobe in the vicinity of Los Angeles, ca. 1840, demolished ca. 1900. (Special Collections, UCLA Library)

The Appeal of Spanish Colonial Styles

Such remains alone would have rendered Spanish Colonial among the least appealing of all possible models for post-Victorian imitation, one might have thought. Certainly to Americans of Downing's generation, reviving their style would have been inconceivable. Romantics though they were, they were still aware in a dim way that architecture was *about* something, that it involved a visual metaphor of values, and they would have considered the associative values of Spanish Colonial reprehensible. Spain was the enemy in two of America's nineteenth-century wars—the 1840s war with Mexico (though independent, the Mexicans were still thought of as Spaniards), and the 1890s war with Spain itself. In both cases, justification for the war was the corruption and degeneracy of Spanish forms of government. In none of the territories won in the Mexican–American war did the idea of copying native Spanish styles of building enter the conquerors' heads. Both in Texas and in California, the immigrant Anglos reproduced the vernacular building—and in due course, the high styles—of those parts of North America from which they had come. (Occasionally, for want of timber, they had to use adobe, as in the Larkin house in Monterey; but using adobe did not make the house Spanish Colonial, only a New England type built of sun-dried mud brick, with a necessarily wider overhanging roof for protection).

How peculiar, then, that in the 1890s, while a war was still going on to save poor Cuba and the Philippines from the clutches of a decadent monarchy and a corrupt *junta* that were reducing native populations to futility and beggary, Americans in California were copying Spanish styles; by 1920 Spanish Colonial houses could be found all over the country. How truly extraordinary that, hardly thirty years after the Spanish–American war, American communities like Santa Barbara could put up elaborate courthouses in elaborately Spanish style—atria, cloisters, towers, and all (figure 5.6)—which, according to the city's promotional booklet of 1931, was not only "an expression of the traditions of this area," but also "was built to provide a fitting home for the type of government which the people are striving to develop and perpetuate." A misprint? No, for on the back page we are reminded that "such a courthouse must, in time, attract and hold in the service of the community men and women interested in advancing the science of government." How to explain it?

5.6 Santa Barbara County courthouse, California. Completed 1929 on designs of J. J. Plunket, with Wm. Mooser & Co. of San Francisco supervising. (IMG:NAL)

Part of the explanation is that the Spanish Colonial Revival in California was well launched before the Spanish–American war of 1898; in California, Mexico had long ceased to be thought a dangerous enemy, and things Spanish could therefore become part of a romantically viewed past. But the main reason was that in the course of the nineteenth century the whole notion that architecture appealed by means of literary, historical associations had been superseded by the primacy of visual appeal.

As early as the 1850s the authors of *Village and Farm Cottages* devoted several pages to lambasting Classical Revival styles, on grounds that "we would aid in our humble measure, to banish entirely a style of building which possesses so little of real beauty, variety and power, and thus direct the popular mind toward other modes which combine all these qualities."[2] They apparently did not conceive of Greek Revival, or any other style, being built to convey abstract ideas like liberty or republicanism—and this just a few decades after the Classical Revivals were introduced for precisely that sort of reason! How much further down that road were architectural apologetics in the 1890s! As late as 1926 the city fathers of Pasadena could still refuse Bakewell and Brown's design for a city hall with a Mission campanile, demanding instead that the architects design a dome "in the well-developed and familiar tradition of American capitol buildings, appropriate to the seat of a municipal government"[3]; but they were by then distinctly the exception and Santa Barbara distinctly the rule. By then, the visual appeal of "beauty, variety and power" (in this case dappled contrasts of light and shade on stuccoed walls, the play of convex and concave patterns in tile and ironwork, and so on) had been everything, or nearly everything, for several generations.

Of course there were associative values and inspirations in Spanish Colonial as well. If for purposes of war propaganda "Spanish" could be used pejoratively to connote the shiftlessness, softness, and frivolity bred by corrupt monarchical government, for purposes of promoting real estate in California or Florida "Spanish" could be associated with the easy-going, relaxed, fun-loving life-style of a semi-tropical people, attainable by stern, hardworking Anglos should they settle in some southern state. The mythical contrast of dreamy romantic Latins and stern, workaholic Yankees is generally considered to begin with Helen Hunt Jackson's novel *Ramona* of 1884, whose "glucoside sentimentalizing over the years of Spanish and Mexican control in the Southwest"[4] was assiduously promoted over the next dozen years by books calling California variously "the Golden Land," "the American Italy," and "the Land of the Afternoon."[5] Promoters of Florida were soon singing similar tunes:

No real valuation can be placed on this Florida architecture . . . [outside] the life of which it is a part. Florida is not a serious place. It is a region of winter resorts, some gay and some restful; a place to which people come to escape from everything that reminds them of the North. It is a place of clear skies, of temperatures mild to semi-tropical; a place, in short, where architecture may well assume its least serious and most festive guise,—where, indeed, it *should* assume such a guise, if it is to be at all appropriate to its setting. It must assume a glad, gay, holiday garb.[6]

This surely explains why Spanish Colonial Revival was for over forty years a favored style for big resort hotels: in Florida, at the Ponce de Leon in St. Augustine, a glorious mixture of bits and pieces of tile, stucco, and terracotta all applied to a classical frame and plan of the Beaux-Arts sort usually favored by its architects Carrère and Hastings (1884+); in Honolulu at the Moana (small, vaguely Mediterranean, 1901) and Royal Hawaiian (big, pink Spanish Baroque palace); in New Mexico at the Alvarado Hotel in Albuquerque and the Sanatorium (a deluxe resort hotel, if you like) at Alamogordo, both by Charles F. Whittlesey (1901–5); and most of all in California, at Riverside's Mission Inn (figure 5.7), at

Pasadena's Green Hotel (F. L. Roehrig, 1889, later additions) and Wentworth-Huntington (Myron Hunt, 1911), at Santa Barbara's Potter Hotel (John Austin, 1901), at Los Angeles's Hotel Ingraham (ca. 1906) and Beverly Hills Hotel (Elmer Grey, 1912). New settlers in California and Florida buying a "beginners' bungalow" could enjoy comparable associations.

The pleasing associations of Spanish Colonial with fun, sun, and leisure are still promoted, indirectly, by such events as the Pasadena Rose Parade[7] and the end-of-term student festivities at Fort Lauderdale. But in the teens Spanish Colonial acquired a new and even more compelling appeal: association with Hollywood glamor. By 1915 the American movie industry was concentrated in Los Angeles's suburbs, especially Hollywood. Romance, in every sense of the word, was what the movie industry seemed to be all about—transporting audiences out of the lackluster Podunks and Mudvilles into realms of fairyland. Hollywood stars were exotic, and they often appeared to the world in Spanish Colonial dress—mansioned in complexes of pools and arcades, atria and balconies, that looked for all the world like stage sets. How compellingly Hollywood associated Spanish Colonial with the glamorous life is suggested by the movie theaters themselves: they took appropriately exotic Mediterranean/Spanish names—Alhambra, Alcazar, Granada, Rialto—with architecture to match. By the 1920s it was as normal to have a theater in vaguely

5.7 Mission Inn, Riverside, California. Begun 1905 on designs of Arthur Benton; additions by Myron Hunt and G. S. Wilson. (IMG:NAL)

Spanish style as to find them in Art Deco in the 1930s.
Sometimes the style was what we would call Moorish, a
descendant of the old habit of making pleasure-palaces
exotic and Eastern-looking which goes back to London's
Vauxhall, the Regent's Palace in Brighton, and McKim,
Meade, and White's Madison Square Garden of 1889,
with its tower like La Giralda in Seville. When J. W.
Lindstrom of Minneapolis included plans for a "small
motion picture theater" in his *Duplex and Apartment
Houses* of ca. 1920, it seemed entirely natural to him to
make it Spanish Colonial, with tiles, vaguely Spanish-
looking stucco walls and specifically "Spanish tile cor-
nices," and an ornamental iron canopy (figure 5.8). You
can see just such a theater on the main street of Marfa,
Texas, next to the Presidio County Court House (figure
5.9).

Time and again the first Spanish Colonial building in
towns outside California was, if not the hotel, the theater. Marfa is typical. The town is promoted to tourists
as a "delightful place to visit and live," which it surely
is, and as full of examples of early Spanish Colonial architecture, which it surely isn't. None of Marfa's early
buildings are Spanish. The Presidio County Court
House of 1886 might just as well have been built in the
1870s in Ohio or Pennsylvania. The county jail of 1900 is
a Gothic castle. In fact, not until 1919 did a Spanish Colonial building appear—and that is the old Texas Theater. Until then Marfa, like Texas towns everywhere,
had sternly resisted early Progressives' attempts to find
merit or models in buildings of the Spanish period or in
buildings using Spanish techniques. It was movies that
made the difference. The glamor of Hollywood wrapped
one Marfa building after another—the old El Paisano
Hotel (Trost and Trost, completed 1930), the Brite Building (1931), then houses both great and small—in Spanish Colonial dress. It was through the movies that
Spanish Colonial mansions came to be built in the fogs
of Seattle, the snows of Ottawa, and the freezing winters of Minnesota, where Spaniards never set foot, by
people whose entire political and social tradition was
antithetical to everything Spanish.

No. 724

DESIGN NO. 724

Contents 86,000 cubic feet.

Design No. 724 is that of a small motion picture theatre.

The building is of brick construction with fireproof
roof and walls. The front is constructed of pressed brick
with common brick throughout the sides and rear.

This building could be constructed of frame and stucco
thereby greatly lessening the cost.

A Spanish tile cornice and an ornamental iron canopy
make this an attractive exterior.

The rear of the foundation has been excavated for a fuel
and boiler room.

The main floor has an auditorium with a seating capacity
of about four hundred. There is a spacious lobby and a
ticket office in the front of the building while the extreme
rear is given over to a small stage and an orchestra pit.
The stage might be utilized for amateur performances.

This theatre plan would give satisfaction to anyone de-
siring a small practical building.

One set of blue prints of working drawings and details,
$15.00. One set of specifications, $5.00. Three sets of
plans and specifications, $30.00.

5.8 "A small motion-picture theater," design 724 in Lindstrom's
Duplex and Apartment Houses (Minneapolis, ca. 1920, p. 69).

5.9 Main Street in Marfa, Texas, showing Presidio County Court House commanding the vista, with (left to right) Marfa Bank Building, Brite Building, and El Paisano Hotel, all fine representatives of the Spanish Colonial Revival of the 1930s in Texas. At the extreme end, next to the courthouse, is the 1919 Texas Theater, the first Spanish Colonial Revival specimen in Marfa. (IMG:NAL)

Spanish Colonial Revival Substyles

General Characteristics

The bulk of Spanish Colonial buildings of whatever substyle are generally identifiable by combinations of tiles, low-pitched roofs, stuccoed walls, and round-headed openings. Ornamental effects include patches of molded decoration set into walls, stained or otherwise darkened exposed wood, and thin wrought-iron grillwork.

Tiles covering all, or at least the visible parts, of the roof constitute Spanish Colonial's single most distinctive characteristic. Magazines of the time often called four-squares or bungalows Spanish for no other reason than their having tiled roofs. Other styles besides Spanish Colonial occasionally had tiled roofs, of course; an advertisement in a 1927 *Architectural Forum* by the Heinz Roofing Company of Denver, Colorado, listed tiles in Old English Shingle style; tapered Italian Mission; tapered Spanish Mission; long, hand-fluted Dutch; cut-face French flat. But tiles in general signaled Spanish Colonial. In keeping with that post-Victorian taste for historicism at once learnedly accurate in detail and vague in application, which produced "instant museums" like Vizcaya and San Simeon, the more pretentious Spanish Colonial mansions were roofed with "genuine" tiles imported from Spain. Builders in Coral Gables, Florida, imported vast quantities of "Spanish roof tiles" to lend authenticity, but they got them from Cuba. Orangey-red or reddish-brown were the usual colors, and terra-cotta the usual material; however, painted metal tiles were also available.

Stuccoed walls imitated effects of adobe construction. Stucco proper is a very old building material. Sand and water plus some bonding agent had been used for weatherproofing outside and for ornament within by Egyptians, Aztecs, Romans, and Moslems. By the late nineteenth century stucco chiefly consisted of lime and gypsum plaster. A major development in popularizing Spanish Colonial was the introduction and refinement of "staff," a pseudo-stucco invented in France and first widely used in America at Chicago's Columbian Exposition in 1893 as a means of simulating effects of marble and travertine in a cheap and impermanent material (it was mainly plaster of Paris plus fiber). By 1915, at the Panama–Pacific International Exposition in San Francisco and the Panama–California Exposition in San Diego, staff had been improved by admixtures of cement (making it more permanent) and color (much more visually attractive and versatile); Goodhue used it for much of his elaborate churrigueresque ornament at San Diego. A booklet put out by California Stucco Products around 1919 called staff "California stucco." It became immensely popular among speculative builders for simulating the effects of painted mud-brick walls at low cost. In the East, "California stucco" had competition. Coral Gables required all houses to be given "antiquity in picturesque design" by means of coral rock, tinted stucco

combined with coral rock, or another local stone called Ojus. The American Steel and Wire Company advertised in a 1921 pamphlet on stucco houses that their method of stuccoing onto tough wire mesh made walls as "lasting as stone." Jens Pedersen in his *Beautiful Homes* pushed the use of "Kellastone magnesite stucco on a Flaxlinum Keyboard Base."

These general characteristics identify as Spanish Colonial those rows and rows of low bungalows, built by speculators from plan books or catalogs, that typically line suburban and small-town streets in California and Florida (figures 5.10, 5.11). Spanish Colonial as handled by professional architects for upper- and upper-middle-class clients had, in addition to these general characteristics, others by which four or five distinct variants, or substyles, can be more or less readily identified; and in due course details from them came to be incorporated in speculatively built suburban houses. The result is that whereas substyles are more or less easily recognizable in high or formal architecture by the new features consistently applied, on the popular/commercial level new features coalesce with older ones, so that specific substyles are harder to identify.

5.10 This textbook example of the basic small Spanish Colonial bungalow, in Colusa, California, was probably built around 1923. The ovoid arch is a fairly common variant on round arches. In the Mediterranean substyle, it occasionally comes pointed, an allusion to Spanish North Africa. (IMG:NAL)

5.11 Architects' Small House Service Bureau Design 4B6, from their 1929 catalog. It was "especially intended for a warm climate. . . . terrace/patio allows outdoor living the year 'round." ASHSB reminded us that "the Colonists from Spain transplanted this style of house from the Motherland to America." Well, not exactly.

THE COLONISTS FROM SPAIN TRANSPLANTED THIS STYLE OF HOUSE FROM THE MOTHERLAND TO AMERICA

BASEMENT
CEILING HEIGHT 7'3"

FIRST FLOOR
CEILING HEIGHT 8'6"

Mission

First of the Spanish Colonial substyles was Mission, launched in the 1890s. Its name and some of its identifying features came from a romantic interest in the missions built by Spanish missionary padres from Mexico between the 1780s and the 1820s and strung from southern California to north of San Francisco. (It had nothing originally to do with the "Craftsman mission" furniture produced by Gustav Stickley; Stickley called his populist version of Arts and Crafts "mission" because he felt he had a "mission" to refine and restore American design to good taste.) These mission buildings had mostly been abandoned or "recycled" after the Mexican Revolution of the 1820s secularized them; San Miguel Arcangel, for example, founded in 1797, served between 1824 and 1878 as a saloon, dance hall, sewing-machine agency, warehouse, and store. By the time many missions were reconsecrated in the 1880s (with the new prosperity, population growth, and religious freedom), they were virtual ruins and had to be patched up. They became objects of romantic pilgrimage and, all too often, of romantic restoration as well, for the American population of California.

These missions seemed to give California some special romantic character; they also made it seem long settled—both qualities appealing to its American immigrants. Their "myth" was actively propagated by railroad companies and other speculators, so that when a French traveler, Jules Huret, visited California in 1905, he was amused and amazed by the veneration Americans displayed toward "these walls without history and without architecture, near-secular; the same respect which we experience before our cathedrals of the Middle Ages or the ruins of the Parthenon."[8]

Precisely who developed the Mission style, and where, remains unresolved. There is no lack of candidates. Lester B. Moore of Los Angeles was nominated in the *Craftsman* magazine for 1903. A. Page Brown and Arthur Benton did major early Mission buildings (California Building at the 1893 Chicago fair; Mission Inn, Riverside). Willis Polk has also been suggested. The truth is that no single individual was actually responsible; Mission Revival was an idea whose time had come. The way was prepared for it by the success of the novel *Ramona* about life in Mission times; a number of Mission-like buildings are datable to the 1890s both in northern and southern California; and its development was facilitated in the 1890s and early 1900s by a stream of articles about "Mission building," first in local magazines like *Outwest, The Architecture & Engineer,* and *Sunset,* then in nationals like *Craftsman* and *The Western Architect.* Ultimately Mission houses could be found all over the land—astonishing testimony to the lingering power of romanticism in the first decade or two of the twentieth century (figures 5.12, 5.13).

As Mission developed, it became more complex (especially in more pretentious mansions and hotels) and ultimately melded into Mediterranean. Distinguishing characteristics of Mission were, along with generally "Spanish" features, elements copied, adapted, or supposed to be derived from the mission churches, such as facades resembling mission-church facades, with prominently scalloped outlines and clearly recognizable parapets, sometimes with towers on one or both ends; arcades forming an entranceway or side porch; bell towers (usually on public buildings like railroad stations and city halls, but occasionally on mansions) with tiled roofs covering a series of diminishing squares capped with round or elliptical cupolas; extremely simplified classical details like pilasters and tapering columns; and ceilings treated to resemble open timberwork interior roofs of missions, which in practice meant beams (or boards imitating beams) stained and exposed.

In the century's first decade, Mission details like these were often added indiscriminately to otherwise Tudor or Craftsman or Colonial designs (see, for example, figure 5.14). By the 1920s, however, there was a much more consistent awareness of style; the result was the Mediterranean substyle of Spanish Colonial.

Mediterranean
The Academic impulse toward authenticity became, paradoxically enough, a prime motivation for greater complexity of sources in domestic design, because the Mission model being followed was so plainly inadequate. How could you use churches as the primary models for houses or hotels or public buildings? In many cases bell towers were inappropriate and arcades not

5.12 The Mission style at home: a mansion in Pasadena, ca. 1915. (Special Collections, UCLA Library)

5.13 The Mission style abroad: with full-blown Mission church facade, verandah simulating round-arched atrium, scalloped chimneys, and side gables, this might be supposed a prime specimen of Mission on its native sod somewhere in central or southern California. But this one was built on the Windsor side of the Detroit River, a block or so from the present Ambassador Bridge, ca. 1923. (IMG:NAL)

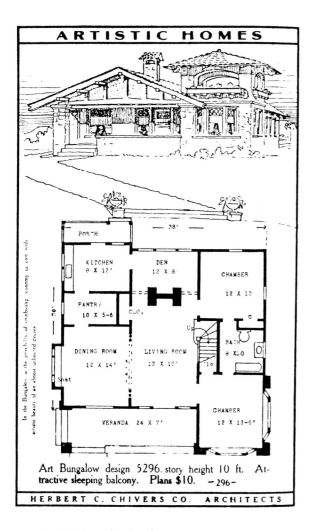

5.14 An "Art Bungalow" with a Mission tower; design 5296 offered by the Herbert C. Chivers Company of St. Louis in its 1910 *Artistic Homes* catalog.

very practical. Churches provided no models for interior plans. Neither did California's missions offer much in the way of ornament, at a time when most people still felt a house without ornament definitely lacked something. So interior plans and ornament in the Mission style were, in general, borrowed: interiors of mansions and public buildings from Georgian or Tudor Revival interiors; interiors of small houses from Gustav Stickley's simple boxlike rooms; ornament from the churrigueresque churches of Mexico.

Once the principle of borrowing from models other than California mission churches was accepted, it was a short step to borrowing any elements that looked more or less Spanish regardless of their origins. This meant using features from the domestic buildings of adobe brick built in California from the late eighteenth through the early nineteenth centuries; Mexican churches (a favorite source, being so close; architectural magazines frequently carried reports and pictures from trips to view romantic Mexico) and then the domestic buildings of Spain itself; Spanish churches; Italian architecture; and finally details from Islamic North Africa. Hence "Mediterranean"—a term that seemed all the more appropriate since California's coastal climate is one of only five areas on earth classified as Mediterranean (the others being southwest Africa, southwest Australia, and coastal Chile). High-style architects, as usual, led the way; but details and concepts from famous mansions like The Breakers at Newport (R. M. Hunt, mid-1890s), the Gillespie house in Montecito (Bertram Goodhue, 1903), or Goodhue's extravaganzas for the Panama–California International Exposition (1915) soon began filtering down into ordinary speculative building. Prosperity in the twenties made some ostentation possible, if not mandatory, even in ordinary speculative building, so that all sorts of ornamental work began appearing. Furthermore, Spanish Colonial became cheaper to build than Craftsman or Picturesque styles, because of the rising cost of timber in California. Consequently, the Mediterranean substyle of Spanish Colonial became a favorite for houses throughout the 1920s (figure 5.15).

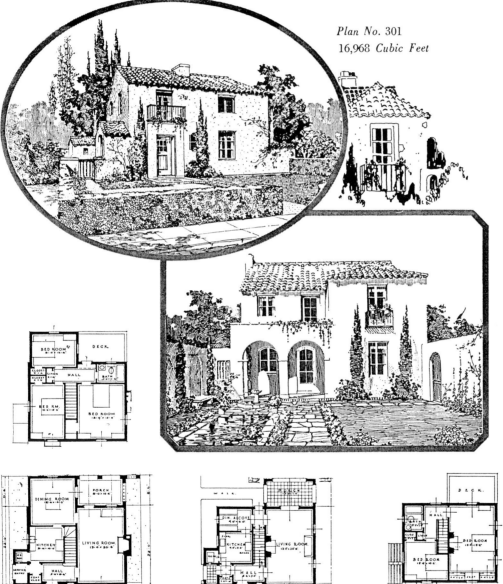

Plan No. 301
16,968 Cubic Feet

5.15 Designs by Louis Justement for four- and six-room Spanish Colonial houses in the early 1920s, from *The Books of a Thousand Homes*, 1923.

FLOOR PLANS OF HOUSE AT RIGHT
(Reversed from perspective)

FLOOR PLANS OF UPPER HOUSE (301)

The most obvious characteristics of Mediterranean are efforts to simulate effects of the atria of Mediterranean domestic architecture by making verandahs into arcaded loggias and/or by extending one or two walls to make an entrance (usually with round-headed arch) into the backyard or garage; much more emphatic color; and a sophisticated play upon arches both outside and in. The typical white or earth-hue walls are trimmed in scarlet, orange, azure blue, and other "Mediterranean" colors, with random paving stones in driveways or walks colored to match. The reddish-orange effects of tiles are dramatized by textural effects resulting from their being laid unevenly and shaped semicylindrically. And in addition to Mission round-headed shapes, flattened and scalloped Muslim types are used. Interior arches repeat outside ones and are often set off by metal grillwork.

Fireplaces set into walls are common, and they often have ceramic tiles of Spanish or Moorish design in addition to or instead of niches. These features also characterize the "Venetian" of Florida—a term meant especially to publicize Miami and Coral Gables, where Merrick and other developers simulated the canals and lagoons of Venice and provided bridges, islands, and other exotica.

By 1920, then, even small Spanish Colonial houses could be quite sophisticated. This sophistication was part of a general trend toward Academic correctness that had set in by the turn of the century. Every style was used more self-consciously than before; and the idea of houses with each room in a different period style, like Hunt's Breakers, was generally condemned by 1930 as absurdly bad taste. And yet this greater awareness of correctness did not mean inflexibility. Not only high-style Spanish Colonial (like the work of George Washington Smith and James Osborne Craig in Santa Barbara or Wallace Neff of Pasadena), but also ordinary middle-class homes showed enormous variety and inventiveness.

Pueblo

Mission substyle dominated the first half of the Spanish Colonial Revival; Mediterranean the second, roughly. Two other movements within Spanish Colonial span the entire 1890–1930 period. One is Pueblo; the other, Proto-Modern.

In one sense Pueblo is not part of the Spanish Colonial Revival because its forms derived not so much from Spanish building as from pueblos (villages) built by Amerinds of the region that became New Mexico; the old pueblo outside Taos is perhaps the most famous of them. These forms were adopted by the Spaniards, more by necessity than choice, because the only labor force available was Indian. The best known of Pueblo models was the Governors' Palace in Santa Fe, originally built about 1609–10; the most drawn upon were the New Mexico mission churches, which differed considerably from their counterparts in California and, of course, the Amerind villages of the region, distinctively built of adobe brick rounded at the edges, with roofs carried on round logs that projected through the bearing walls at uneven lengths (figure 5.16). These latter features became the stylistic mark of popular/commercial Pueblo, a style that has survived long after Spanish Colonial has dwindled into the odd Taco Bell stand and sporadic touches of tile and stucco (figures 5.17, 5.18).[9]

Driving west out of Texas, it is striking how Pueblo begins to appear instead of Spanish Colonial proper as soon as you cross the New Mexico border. Since around 1900, efforts were underway to make Pueblo a regional style especially evocative of New Mexico, the way Mission was of California, and it was even called the "Santa Fe Revival" style. The *Craftsman* magazine in 1911 carried an interesting account of a struggle over the style for the buildings of the new University of New Mexico; its first buildings were in the style of Indian pueblos inspired by the researches of university president W. G. Tight, but a new president, hired from California, wanted the style changed to Mission because he saw it as more "civilized" (19:4, 404–6). Native New Mexicans tell you that Texas several times tried to annex the much

5.16 The distinctive plastered, adobe-brick walls with rounded edges and the irregularly projecting beam ends of the Pueblo style are seen in this detail from the Pueblo in Taos, New Mexico (IMG:NAL)

5.17 Pueblo style house in Las Cruces, New Mexico, ca. 1950–60. Note the matching garage.

5.18 Something unusual—a Pueblo style house very far from home: Revelstoke in the mountains of inner British Columbia. (IMG:NAL)

poorer territory of New Mexico but were resisted because New Mexico was a free and Texas a slave state. Hence New Mexicans have always felt a need to distinguish themselves from their more powerful, rich, and aggressive neighbor, which may be why the Pueblo style marks the border. And of course that may well be why Pueblo continues to flourish: architecture whose social function is still vital never really goes out of date.

Proto-Modern

What I am calling Proto-Modern is a substyle that uses Spanish Colonial in ways that presage Modern architecture. A small number of examples date from before 1900 and some were built well into the 1940s. This substyle is, of course, predominantly represented by architect-designed and usually high-style buildings.

To discuss in any detail how architects like Bernard Maybeck of San Francisco, Irving Gill of Pasadena, or to a lesser degree Julia Morgan, used Spanish Colonial as a vehicle for personal expression is outside our scope. But in terms of Spanish Colonial as cultural expression, this much needs to be said: nothing demonstrates more clearly how much the post-Victorian art world, high and low, was a cultural unity. The Mission style, for instance, so despised in the years of Modern ascendancy, was in its own time often compared to the Secessionist movement in Europe; writers saw in it elements comparable to early Modernism there. David Gebhard has shown how "it was a give-and-take relationship, with Secessionists often receiving more than they gave. . . . The conscious or unconscious task which these men set for themselves was to strip off the specific historic details, and then to think in terms of elemental shapes and forms—the cube, the rectangle, and the arch,"[10] for which process Spanish Colonial was an ideal vehicle. Architectural reformers like Gustav Stickley saw nothing incongruous about supplying interior designs for this "revivalist" style and often illustrating them in his *Craftsman* magazine. And of course Sullivan's ideas on ornament were not without influence in both Mission and Mediterranean. Elements of Mission can be detected in some of the Greenes' work (for example, the Cornelia Culbertson house of 1911 in Pasadena). Practitioners of the more complex Andalusian sub-substyle found it a useful base for relating buildings to their environment, as interpenetrating masses and voids. In the 1930s, Spanish Colonial can be detected in the work of the new breed of Modernists—Schindler, Neutra, Gregory Ain. And of course it was easy for Spanish Colonial to mix with Art Deco in the 1930s and 1940s; theaters were the most obvious places, with their associations with both luxury and Modernism (the Art Deco historic district of Miami is perhaps the best place to see this in operation).

French Colonial Revival Styles

The Original French Colonial Styles

Through much of European history, France was the most powerful nation in Western civilization. In North America, French colonies at one time controlled the mouths of both the Mississippi and the St. Lawrence rivers and threatened all of New England from the great fortress of Louisbourg and the settlement of Acadia (in present-day Nova Scotia). But in a series of land-and-sea contests culminating in the French and Indian or Seven Years War (1756-63), France was essentially driven out of North America. The Acadian settlers were deported in ships, and Louisiana was ceded to Spain. Only Quebec remained, but as a province within the British empire.

None of these colonies was well populated. None had resources enough to erect any palaces or churches comparable to those in Mexico. New France never had more than feeble reflections of such grand palaces and churches of its homeland as Versailles, Notre-Dame-de-Grâce, Saint-Sulpice, or the castle-palaces of the Valois kings on the Loire. Nor did New France have many good examples of middle-class houses except for a few contiguous mansions in Quebec and Montreal, dating from the second half of the eighteenth century. New France's chief legacy to the North American landscape was its Québecois homesteads in the St. Lawrence valley. Their form evolved over three centuries. In the seventeenth century, the building was a simple oblong with a high roof (two-thirds the building's total height), irregular fenestration, and a flexible ground plan (figure 5.19). In the eighteenth century, it had a less precipitously steep roof with bell-cast eaves, dormers of considerable size, and fieldstone walls whitewashed instead of clapboarded for protection from frost (figure 5.20). By the early nineteenth century (figure 5.21), the form was symmetrically fenestrated, stone walls were often left exposed, and a front porch or verandah was standard (less for practical reasons than for prestige: in the seventeenth century, royalty and nobility began calling the second story of their palaces the *première étage* and the first the *rez-de-chaussée*, and distinguished the "first" (main) story by balconies). Also for prestige, homestead chimneys by the early nineteenth century normally appeared on the sides of houses as a sign of upward mobility, thus imitating the practice in town houses, where side chimneys served as firebreak walls in contiguous dwellings.

A variant of the Québecois homestead appears in the Mississippi valley (the Bolduc house in Sainte Genevieve is archetypal), and in Louisiana appears the Cajun house (corrupted form of Acadian, from refugees evicted from Acadia who eventually settled in Louisiana; the Acadian Village in Lafayette offers good examples). A few examples of this original French Colonial homestead type can be found in other parts of the United States also—for example, the Demarest House in Hackensack, New Jersey. But it is interesting to discover that this type was never reproduced as a style for the Comfortable House in 1890–1930. An explanation is to be found in the kind of appeal French Colonial had in that period.

5.19 The Marcotte homestead near Cap Santé represents the seventeenth-century Québecois form, although it was not completed until the 1790s. (IMG:NAL)

5.20 The eighteenth-century Québecois form is represented by this house on the old main street of Cap Santé, ca. 1750. (IMG:NAL)

5.21 Classic form of Québecois homestead is seen here in a homestead at Saint Césaire in the Chambly region, built ca. 1820. (IMG:NAL)

The Appeal of French Colonial

France had been America's indispensable ally in the Revolutionary War; further, leaders of the French Revolution repeatedly declared their indebtedness to American democratic inspiration. But these pleasing political associations did not attach to French peasant homesteads on the St. Lawrence or the Mississippi. The French contribution to American architecture was direct—initially through the work of French architects of revolutionary democratic bent designing post-Revolutionary American buildings (L'Enfant, Godefroy, Hallet, Mangin) and later through direct copyings of châteaux, especially of French minor nobility, because of their picturesqueness and image of polished culture. In other words, the appeal of French culture in the 1890–1930 years was entirely traditional; for a thousand years past, France had been arbiter of taste for Europe and the Western world generally, and its high styles still set the pace.

Given the democratic tenor of the 1890–1930 years, however, "French" did not have identical overtones for everybody. For perhaps a majority of Americans, it implied "cultivated and exquisite" in close to a pejorative sense and "culture" in a *nouveau riche* context. And it was indeed the *nouveaux riches* who cultivated "French taste" most. As early as 1860 LeGrand Lockwood celebrated his rise from poor Connecticut family origins to immense stock-market riches by erecting a French castle in Norwalk, designed by New York's most fashionable architect, Detlef Lienau (figure 5.22). This was a direct ancestor of the colossal Biltmore in Asheville, North Carolina, grandest of the Biltmore mansions, classic of the Loire-castle genre. The model for both was the type of château built in the Loire Valley by French kings and noblemen of the early sixteenth century, which explains the mixture of Gothic and Renaissance features that both display. The appeal of this type, and the social function of this style, is plain. Such houses proclaimed a new American aristocracy, created by mercantile and industrial activity but commanding privileges and luxuries not dreamt of by the old aristocracy of blood and land. Not

5.22 LeGrand Lockwood's mansion in Norwalk, Connecticut, built in 1860 to the designs of Detlef Lienau. (IMG:NAL)

content with mere proclamation of their aristocratic status by a palatial mansion, such people often sought to marry into the old European aristocracy, a kind of double insurance against social insecurity. The archetypal instance was the marriage of Consuela Vanderbilt and the Duke of Marlborough; the most memorable, that of Lord Randolph Churchill and Jenny Jerome, from which union Winston Churchill issued.

All of which for middle- and working-class Americans simply meant snobbery, and worse. Comic strips and popular novels, those invaluable mirrors of popular taste, equated ''French'' with ''affected,'' ''sissy,'' ''immoral,'' ''flighty,'' ''unreliable'': the absurd *punctilio* of *Alphonse and Gaston,* for example; or the stereotyped ''M'soo'' who teaches French in boarding schools or dancing at young ladies' academies—always with little pointed beard, comically punctilious etiquette, but, we may well suspect, surreptitiously given to can-can dancing, ''French safes,'' ''French kissing,'' and other such woeful departures from a hundred percent American values. It follows that French homesteads were rarely if ever models for mass-produced popular house types; what you find on this level, when you find anything, are traces of high-style castles retained for their prestige and out of a lingering taste for picturesqueness.

French Colonial Revival Styles

The château or, as it was more often called, Norman French high style, was never widespread.[11] The relatively few examples of it are famed beyond their due because they include Vanderbilt mansions and were designed by the likes of Hunt. For obvious reasons this was a popular style for apartment houses; from Buffalo to Los Angeles small castle-like apartments punctuate residential avenues. In Canada the château-style hotels built by the Canadian Pacific Railroad from Victoria to Quebec became ideological symbols of the country's unity and aspirations—but that goes well beyond our scope here.

When French-styled suburban houses did appear, it was generally in upper-middle-class settings. Shaker Heights has a good many of them (figure 5.23). What identifies them as Norman are their round turret towers (*tourelles*) set in at angles and corners and their steep-pitched roofs, quite high in proportion to the wall, with dormers breaking into them mansard style. (Such roofs were more often taken from the kind of medieval roofs out of which the mansard developed in the seventeenth century than from true mansards, which have two sets of rafters. The lower rafter slopes at a steeper pitch than the upper, and dormers are set into the lower—something rather too complicated for contractors and ordinary builders. See figure 5.24.) Roofs covered in slate or slate simulations were often considered French, especially if eaves were bell-cast (figure 5.25). Both bell-cast eaves and two-thirds proportion of roof to wall are characteristically Québecois, but their inspiration probably came directly from France, since in early twentieth-century America Quebec was thought of, when thought of at all, as a kind of quaint fossil. More likely still, the principal inspiration came from books like Blomfield's on the French Renaissance[12] and Banister Fletcher's *History of Architecture on the Comparative Method*,[13] which contained such French details as tall chimneys with ornamental brickwork patterns and wide bases; casement windows and windows brought down to ground level (French windows); quoins, leaded mullions, and other obvious conflations with medieval revival styles.

Beginning in the 1950s, the French Colonial homestead proper was revived in popular/commercial forms both in Louisiana and in Quebec, though for very different reasons. In Louisiana the motivation was sentimental for the most part, a kind of regional identification. In Quebec it was part and indeed symbol of the "Québec Libre" movement. Chronologically, these popular/commercial French Colonial houses are far beyond the 1890–1930 limits of this book, but they do demonstrate the value of associations (figure 5.26).

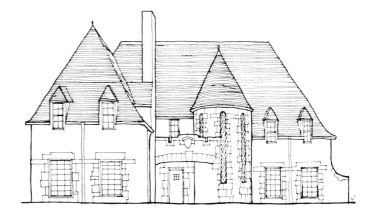

5.23 Norman style house designed for Shaker Heights suburb of Cleveland, Ohio. (Drawing by Patricia Forgac)

5.24 Diagram of the true mansard roof form from *Larousse Encyclopaedia*, 1880 edition.

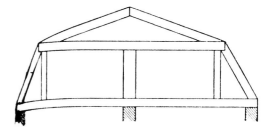

5.25 House designed for Shaker Heights, in French Georgian style. Think away the ground story and you have almost a classic Québecois homestead. (Drawing by Patricia Forgac)

5.26 Development house in suburbs of Nicolet, Quebec. (IMG:NAL)

Dutch Colonial Revival Styles

The Original Dutch Colonial Styles

Besides the major colonizing efforts of Spain, France, and England in the New World, small colonies were planted by Sweden and the Netherlands as well in the seventeenth century; and early in the eighteenth century a large though not state-organized immigration of Germans began. All brought distinctive styles to the New World.

Neither New Sweden, on both sides of the upper Delaware Valley between New Castle/Wilmington and Philadelphia, nor New Netherlands, on both sides of the Hudson from New York/northern New Jersey up to Albany, lasted more than a few decades before being overwhelmed by English arms and settlers. In consequence, the distinctive high styles both had developed in Europe were not solidly transplanted. A mercantile urban house type typical of northern Europe—built of brick, with crow-step street gable and attic storage space—did, however, appear in most Dutch-founded cities, like New Amstel (New Castle), New Amsterdam (New York), and Albany (figure 5.27).

In the countryside of northern New Jersey, western Long Island, and along the Hudson appeared farmhouses with distinctive gambrel roofs flaring over verandahs that came to be called in the later nineteenth century Dutch Colonial. At one time it was imagined that there was some consistent Dutch Colonial usage. Hugh Morrison's *Early American Architecture* quite confidently distinguished English, Dutch (with which Flemish was conflated), and Swedish gambrels:

The "Dutch gambrel" as it is often called, has a distinctive shape. As shown in figure 95 [figure 5.28], the typical New England gambrel of the eighteenth century has a generous and full contour, the upper and lower slopes of almost equal length, and the lower slope quite steep—about 60°. The Dutch gambrel, however, has the break higher up, giving a short upper slope of about 22°, and a long sweeping lower slope of about 45° pitch.

5.27 Stepped-gable urban house built on William Street in New Amsterdam, 1648. (*Valentine's Manual*)

Combined with the curved overhand, the Dutch gambrel is shaped like a wide-flaring bell, and it is certainly the most beautiful of the many varieties of gambrel roof.[14]

Today that confidence cannot fully be shared. But as far as the Comfortable House is concerned, the matter is academic. Only on upper levels was a distinction maintained. For the ordinary suburban builder, gambrel roofs of any kind meant "Colonial." Whether you called them New England, Dutch, Swedish, or Flemish Colonial (or for that matter, French mansard!) was only a matter of sales appeal in a given region.

5.28 Diagram of differing gambrel forms, from Hugh Morrison's *Early American Architecture,* 1952. Top to bottom: New England, Dutch, and Swedish.

5.29 Design for row houses, in Palliser's *New Cottage Homes,* 1887.

Exactly why the distinctive crow-step gable of the Dutch urban mercantile house was not copied more in post-Victorian houses is not clear, at least to me. I suppose it seemed too urban at a time when the predominant taste was for rural (suburban) associations; yet it could easily have been made rural had anyone been interested. Washington Irving's "snuggery" at Tarrytown on the Hudson (Sunnyside, 1832) had crow-step gables of a sort; John Quidor included rural houses with crow-step gables as "Dutch atmosphere" in his illustrations of Irving's stories (for example, in *Rip Van Winkle at Nicholas Vedder's Tavern* of 1839, now in the Boston Museum of Fine Arts); and there are actual standing examples of farmhouses with crow-step gables from the Dutch period (such as the Bronck houses at West Coxsackie). Palliser's *New Cottage Homes* of 1887 even offered several designs for row houses with Dutch urban gables (figure 5.29), and there are nice examples of them in areas with Dutch (that is, German, for in those years little distinction was made) associations, like Lancaster, Pennsylvania (figure 5.30). But the fact remains: this intrinsically romantic and picturesque feature is comparatively rare in the 1890–1930 years.

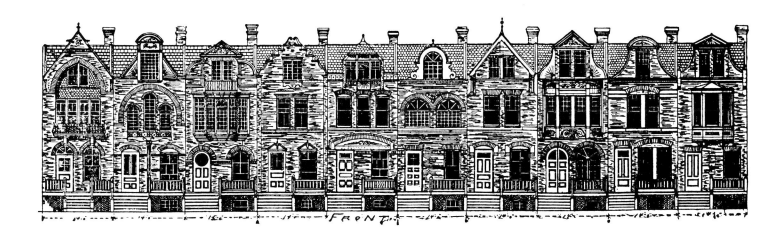

5.30 Row house of ca. 1905 in Lancaster, Pennsylvania. The style is still Picturesque in intent. (IMG:NAL)

The Appeal of Dutch Colonial

Dutch Colonial Revival usage was the opposite of French; only the peasant homestead was copied, and it was copied very widely. What appealed to post-Victorian public taste were the secure, peaceful, quaintly romantic Dutch homesteads of the Hudson Valley. But in the Victorian age they had no such appeal, or any appeal at all. In 1865 Woodward complained in his *Country Homes:*

What can be done with a substantial old farmhouse . . . very numerous about the suburbs of New York City and more particularly in the "neighboring province of New Jersey," where one finds them nestled in the valleys or by the road side. . . . There is, perhaps, nothing more difficult in an architect's experience than to make a fine thing out of a subject so destitute of beauty of form or proportion, and yet preserve the substantial walls and other belongings that have stood for half a century . . . and yet here is a "presto change" that will almost defy the keen eyes of the old settlers to recognize any trace of the ancient landmark that for fifty years has overlooked the beautiful valley of the Tenakill (p. 52; see figure 5.31).

Indeed so. By 1908 tastes had changed. In that year Aymar Embury, II, wrote an article that in effect launched the Dutch Colonial Revival. In *International Studio* he praised the "genuine" old farmhouses for their "picturesqueness" and "old-time intimate air" and attributed these same qualities to houses copied from them. Embury noted (as others have since) that no models for Dutch Colonial gambrels could be found in the Netherlands; his explanation was that immigrant Dutch carpenters invented this gambrel because there were too few long rafters for building straight gables! Embury also noted that mixed materials were characteristic of Dutch Colonial houses; wood, stone, brick, shingle, and stucco might all appear on the walls of the same house (he would later deplore such usage when he saw what speculative builders made of it).

5.31 Remodeling an Old Dutch house in the 1860s, illustrated in *Woodward's Country Homes*.

The early appeal of Dutch Colonial derived from the visual effects of its Dutch gambrel roof and the porch that could be created by extending it and from some romantic regional associations with roots and the solid virtues of sturdy God-fearing pioneers. As the blurb for Ward's Cambridge model of 1927 put it, "a true adaptation of Dutch Colonial architecture . . . [represents] simplicity at its best . . . built low to the ground, its lines take on a massiveness and grace." "Massiveness" had great appeal in Dutch as well as other Colonial styles, connoting stability in troubled times, solid citizen, and the like—connotations as irresistible to sellers of mass-produced houses in the 1920s as the word "mild" to that decade's cigarette-ad writers.

Dutch Colonial Revival Styles

In less pretentious houses older roof forms persisted long after the Revolution, but not without undergoing significant modifications. Thus the gambrel, which then had a great vogue in the regions about New York City, was made lower and flatter . . . an outstanding characteristic of what has come to be known as the "Dutch Colonial" style. It is scarcely Colonial in the strict sense, and not Dutch in origin at all. Nothing analogous is known in Holland.[15]

No matter. By the time of Fiske Kimball's exposé in 1922, Dutch Colonial houses of every description were thick on the ground throughout all the old territories of New Netherlands and were to be found all over the nation. Such popularity had come almost overnight.

William B. Rhoads traces the beginnings of the Dutch Colonial Revival back to a lecture given in 1877 by J. Cleveland Cady to the New York chapter of the American Institute of Architects on "Some Features of the Dutch Farmhouses of New Jersey."[16] But its real popularity came only in the early twentieth century and only after disentanglement from other Colonial revivals. As late as 1900 the Dutch Colonial house designed by Ernest Flagg for himself on Staten Island contained, in addition to a Dutch gambrel "suggested by two-hundred-year-old buildings'' on that island, a huge classically pedimented dormer. Aymar Embury, II, did a number of less eclectic Dutch Colonials after around 1905, which he believed entitled him to be considered ''somewhat responsible for popularizing the Dutch Colonial type'' (figure 5.32).[17] Yet it took about a dozen years more for the style to catch on at a popular level. As late as 1913 a writer for the *Architectural Record* could still claim—in a review of Embury's *The Dutch Colonial House,* which summarized the style's origins and published recent modern examples of it by Embury, Wilson Eyre, Charles Barton Keen, and Myron Hunt—that Dutch Colonial had ''little if any apparent influence on domestic architecture outside its immediate geographic birthplace.''[18]

MacLagan's Suburban Homes catalog of 1898 contained designs for what would later be called Dutch Colonial (figure 5.33). Here were all the signature elements of a suburban cottage form in Dutch Colonial style that appeared in Embury's design: distinctive gambrel, exterior chimney, spacious verandah. But the form was distinctly suburban as contrasted to Embury's quasi-suburban, quasi-rural approach, inasmuch as it was designed to fit onto a suburban lot yet still maintain four distinct sides. Twenty years later, very similar designs were without question labeled Dutch Colonial or Modified Dutch Colonial (figure 5.34).

The designation depended upon Academic insistence on unified stylistic format penetrating to popular/commercial levels. In the 1890s popular/commercial designers from the most pretentious to the humblest cheerfully mixed up stylistic elements in the old Picturesque way, so that gambrels were often put in High-Georgian stylistic settings, and other such anomalies. By the 1920s the Academic attitude had displaced Picturesqueness on all levels; ready-built catalogs were openly featuring Dutch Colonial designs more or less directly derived from Embury's disciplined and refined prototypes

Mr. Flagg's cottage is an excellent example of how the very smallest country or suburban home that is really livable can be made attractive. The use of the heavy brick piers at the corners, with an unusual pattern of brickwork filling below the windows, and stucco walls above, makes the house particularly well worth studying.

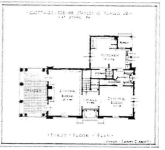 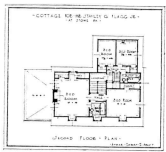

The plan is the common central-hall type, but it is worth noting how closet space has been gained by having only the passageway through the pantry and dining-room from kitchen to the front door

Upstairs there are two distinct parts of the house; the rear wing with its two bedrooms and bath for the housekeeper, and the two main bedrooms and bath between them in front for the owner and guests

THE COTTAGE OF MR. STANLEY G. FLAGG, JR., STOWE, PA.
Aymar Embury, II., architect

5.32 Design by Aymar Embury, II, for the cottage of Mr. Stanley G. Flagg, Jr., Stowe, Pennsylvania. (From Henry Saylor, *Inexpensive Homes of Individuality,* 1912, p. 25)

Design No. 391

Cost about $2000　　　　　　Plans and Specifications $10

5.33 Design 391 from *MacLagan's Suburban Homes*, 1898.

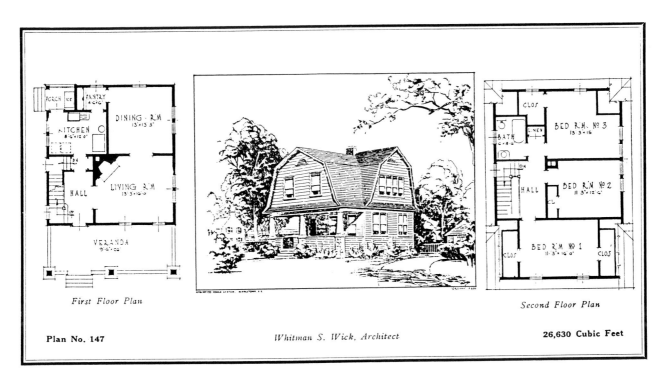

First Floor Plan　　　　　　　　　　　　　　　*Second Floor Plan*

Plan No. 147　　　　　*Whitman S. Wick, Architect*　　　　　**26,630 Cubic Feet**

5.34 "Six-room frame house of modified Dutch Colonial type," by Whitman S. Wick, architect, in *The Books of a Thousand Homes*, I, 1923.

(figure 5.35). On this level, however, practical considerations prompted a distinctive innovation: a variant of the Dutch Colonial gable in which the signature gambrel was encased by a straight, slant-angled gable, providing attic space the full width of the house (figure 5.36). That the resulting configuration approximated the visual effects of the bungalow cottage form no doubt added to its appeal.

Dutch Colonial was always most popular in its geographic birthplace; that is, the old territories of New Netherlands (northern New Jersey, the Hudson and Mohawk valleys of New York). The legend of Dutchness in that region was a kind of counterpart to the Spanishness of California—artificially created, but very powerful. Franklin Delano Roosevelt, whose name was ultimately Dutch, gave powerful impetus to it when, as Governor of New York, he wrote an introduction to Helen W. Reynolds's *Dutch Houses of the Hudson Valley* (1929); later, as President, he proposed and helped carry through a Dutch Colonial design for the post office in

his native Hyde Park. Anything that could conceivably be called Dutch Colonial in that area generally was, in the 1920s and 1930s (figures 5.37, 5.38, 5.39).

Outside the old New Netherlands territories, Dutch Colonial was murkier, and the label more arbitrary. Gambrels that might have signified, or in time came to signify, Dutch Colonial in New Jersey or New York remained simply Colonial in Wisconsin or Minnesota (figures 5.40, 5.41) or even French Colonial in Quebec (figure 5.42).

But, in sum, however variable the designation, Dutch Colonial must be considered one of the most prominent features of the suburban landscape. Like other Academic stylings, Dutch Colonial passed over into popular/commercial when Modernism seized architectural schools, and there it flourishes to this day. Newspapers still advertise house plans with a "Dutch Look: The Gambrel" and advise that "Dutch houses have a neat, orderly look and considerable charm . . . send for a set of complete blueprints with specifications."[19]

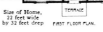

5.35 Cambridge model, from Montgomery Ward's 1927 catalog. This is very similar to the Architects' Small House Service bureau standard Dutch Colonial house.

5.36 In these houses in Verona, New Jersey, ca. 1925, the dormers coalesce into a single quasi-second story, which then extends the full width of the house to produce, in effect, a full second story, yet without sacrificing the Dutch Colonial signature gambrel. (IMG:NAL)

5.37 These houses on East Main Street in Amsterdam, New York, illustrate two points: first, how time changes suburban streets into city arteries—East Main Street is now a five-lane highway and these houses have to be photographed through a maze of wires; second, how the "Dutch Colonial" designation varies with place and time. Originally—the date of ca. 1905 for the right-hand house is confirmed by its neighbor, an "emergent four-square" that retains a vestigial Queen Annish asymmetrical gable—this house would surely have been simply Colonial; now it is known as a Dutch Colonial and has been since the 1920s, especially since it stands in Old Dutch territory on the Mohawk. (IMG:NAL)

5.39 These big homestead temple-houses probably came out of *Mac-Lagan's Suburban Homes* of 1898; with their gambrelled roofs and location in New Brunswick, New Jersey, they would, again, have been designated Dutch Colonial by the 1920s. (IMG:NAL)

5.38 Small homestead temple-houses on Suydam Street in New Brunswick, New Jersey, built ca. 1915. They were probably called Dutch Colonial in the 1920s. (IMG:NAL)

5.40 This house on Bluefin Avenue in Avon, Minnesota, was built ca. 1908 as simply a Colonial cottage, and has remained so designated. (IMG:NAL)

5.41 Workers' housing for a war plant at Beloit, Wisconsin, recorded in *American Architect* for 1918 as Colonial, and still such.

5.42 One of a dozen gambrelled houses built ca. 1910 in Pointe-Gatineau, Quebec, by one of the pulp and paper companies that once flourished on the Ottawa River. Since mail-order housing was no respecter of borders, it could well be that these designs were from some American firm, applied to company housing. They might originally have been called Dutch Colonial; now they are called French mansards. (IMG:NAL)

German Colonial Styles

Although the population with German ancestry or origin probably constitutes the largest single racial block in the United States, manifest German impact on American culture has always been surprisingly small. Two factors are most responsible: first, confusion of German with Dutch (from the German word "deutsch" meaning "German"), and the violent anti-German campaign of 1917–18 and its residue, when almost all traces of Germanic culture vanished even from heavily German areas. Only the odd inscription in stone bears witness to the origins of most of the population in cities like Covington, Kentucky, and Cincinnati, Ohio—Mutter Gottes Kirche, Phillipus Kirche, Evangelische Kirche.

And there is negative evidence as well: in suburban houses of the 1890–1930 period, German Colonial is the one style that almost never appears. I know of only one example, the "Modern German Type" (figure 5.43) in John Henry Newson's *Homes of Character*, before 1917, of course (1910). And even it is obviously a product of that strong Anglophile strain in early twentieth-century German domestic architecture, to which Muthesius's *Das Englische Haus* bears witness. Newson's design recalls early Behrens a bit, and its emphasis on "a touch of brilliant color in the flower box" recalls too those Bauhaus jibes at Bruno Taut for his bourgeois red doors. But mostly what it recalled, to architecturally literate Americans at least, was the English Arts and Crafts style. And one may be sure that after 1918 "English" is how the style would have been designated here and everywhere else (figure 5.44). For in all housing of the 1890–1930 years, English Colonial styles were the overwhelming favorites.

5.43 One of the very few designs to be specifically labeled German Colonial is this "type of cement house having the feeling of modern German work," from John Henry Newson's *Homes of Character*, 1910.

5.44 Like many designs with jerkin-headed gables, open porches, and Arts and Crafts shingled roofs, this design from Jens Pederson's *Beautiful Homes and Plans* of 1919 seems to have stylistic origins, if not in Germany, certainly in Scandinavia. But it is not called German or anything else—just "a cozy home."

6

Colonial Revival Styles:
English

The Original English Colonial Styles

Like other colonizing powers, England transplanted to America the architectural metaphor of a class-structured state—peasant homesteads, set against the ruling class's high-style palaces and other authority symbols, and mercantile townsmen's buildings.

Homestead Styles

In the course of Western civilization, from its beginnings in the ninth and tenth centuries to the time it was transported across the Atlantic, every nation developed distinctive traditions of folk dwellings. England was no exception. When, during the later nineteenth century, interest in the American colonial past quickened, several regional dwelling types were identified: those characteristic of New England, Virginia (The Old South), and Philadelphia (mid-Atlantic region). Facts about these early homesteads were in short supply; romantic notions about them abounded. Research over the last twenty years has continued to upset many early assumptions. But for purposes of ascertaining what influenced the Comfortable House, what ideas about colonial houses its builders held, the following summary will do.

That New England's distinctive "saltbox" farmhouses and town houses (so called from their resemblance to the shape of salt containers) constituted a regional form was recognized early (figure 6.1). Questions about its precise evolution are beyond our scope here[1]; more relevant is the possibility that its distinctive shape resulted less from necessity than from status-signaling, hence that it was really more a mansion type than a homestead, which might explain its usage during the 1890–1930 years.

Also recognized early as a New England type—by President Timothy Dwight of Yale in 1800 , in fact—was a small, simple, one-and-a-half story house called the Cape Cod cottage, evocative of that region's ancient reputation for plain living and high thinking (figure 6.2).[2] Cape Cod cottage walls are most commonly shingled or clapboarded; occasionally they are made simply of

boards. Shingles and clapboards early acquired and long retained pleasing New England associations, and they are endemic to The Comfortable House; bare boards were a little *too* plain, if not too virtuous, for that generation's taste, which still displayed fondness for picturesque variety.

In what was romantically called The Old South, another characteristic homestead type was identified—the hall and parlor, with attic–sleeping quarters above and a broad stepped exterior chimney at one or both ends (figure 6.3).[3] The belief that it was most commonly built of brick or stone led to suburbs (more in the 1930s and 1940s than in the 1890–1930 years) filled with brick adaptations of it. Recent researches indicate that the early Southern house form was a much flimsier affair, closer to those "wretched" and "ugly" structures Jefferson was complaining about in his notes on the early nineteenth-century Virginia landscape.[4]

Yet another early homestead type developed in Philadelphia and the adjacent Delaware Valley. It originated with an early kind of mass-produced house made for quick rebuilding of London after its great fire in the 1660s and was transplanted to Philadelphia to serve the housing boom of Penn's Great Town. It was intended as a continuous row house and thus had blank side walls. It was two stories high and was especially noted for a pent eave (literally suspended by hooks) projecting over sidewalks to protect passing pedestrians. This type was carried into the countryside by Philadelphia builders and is found in farmhouses all around the Philadelphia region and across the river in southern New Jersey. In Salem and adjacent counties, a local subtype developed, distinguished by elaborate brickwork patterns on the blank side walls (figure 6.4).[5] The pent eave especially was adopted by knowledgeable architects as a regional characteristic, but it never entered the mass-prefabricated market.

Out of this Philadelphia (or more properly, mid-Atlantic) form developed the I-house, which geographer Fred Kniffen made famous as the archetypal folk farm-

The Most Talked-of House in America

6.1 Page from *The Books of a Thousand Homes* published in 1923 for the Home Owners Service Institute, showing sketch for a "modernized replica" of the Long Island saltbox once lived in by John Howard Payne, composer of "Home Sweet Home," and the original. The replica, sponsored by the General Federation of Women's Clubs, was built of concrete block stuccoed with white Portland cement. Don Barber and Whitman S. Wick, architects.

THIS house was built in the Spring of 1923 as a modernized replica of the home of John Howard Payne to commemorate the one hundredth anniversary of the writing of his immortal song, "Home Sweet Home." It also represents the official demonstration house in the National Capitol for the "Better Homes in America" movement. The house was built in the shadow of the White House and officially opened by President Harding, after which it was presented to the General Federation of Women's Clubs as a permanent demonstration point for home economics. The funds which paid for its construction were provided by the Home Owners Service Institute through contributions of materials and money from the various nationally known manufacturers who are co-operating members of the Institute. Complete plans are available for this attractive home as described on Page 24, where floor plans are shown. The architect for the house as built in Washington is Donn Barber but the interior arrangement has been changed for general use as shown in the floor plans after redesigning by the Home Owners Service Institute.

ABOVE is shown a photograph of the original John Howard Payne house which still exists on an estate in Long Island. It is interesting to note how well the architect has maintained the original lines, making only changes necessitated by modern homeowning requirements.

Photographs of the completed house shown on Page 41.

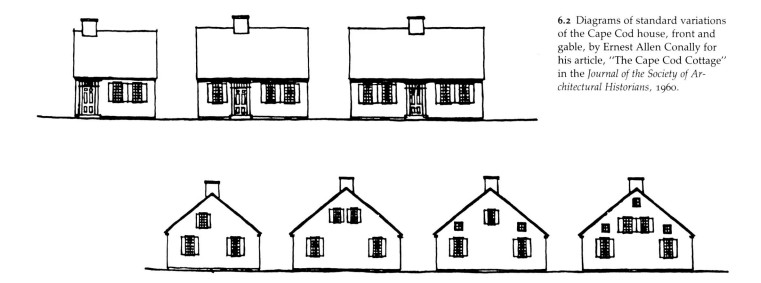

6.2 Diagrams of standard variations of the Cape Cod house, front and gable, by Ernest Allen Conally for his article, "The Cape Cod Cottage" in the *Journal of the Society of Architectural Historians*, 1960.

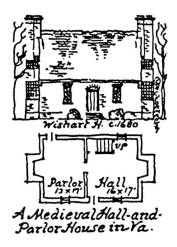

6.3 Elevation and plan of the Wishart hall-and-parlor house of ca. 1680. From Henry Chandlee Forman, *Virginia Architecture in the Seventeenth Century* (Williamsburg, 1957, p. 39).

house of the Midwest (figure 6.5).[6] As one might suspect, the I-house was indeed a stock type in early mass-prefabrication, though more as survival than revival, as was what might be called the Southern Cabin form of hall and parlor (figure 6.6).[7]

Common to all these homestead forms is a quality best called "naturalness." They use materials in straightforward and unselfconscious ways; their plans are revealed by the disposition of windows and doors, which is seldom regular. They are the products of generations and centuries of family living, gradually adjusting to proportions that have come to "look right" in just the way certain pronunciations came to seem right and others wrong, producing a regional accent in speech and cognate vernacular forms in arts.

Deliberately contrasting with this natural quality was the formality of houses intended to indicate their owners' higher status. In English Colonial, houses styled to serve this kind of social function go under the general rubric of Georgian.

6.4 William and Sarah Hancock house at Hancock's Bridge, New Jersey, dated 1734 on the elaborate blue and red brick patterned gable, which also has initials of the husband and wife as landed family founders. This is an HABS photo made ca. 1940 before the existing alterations; it shows the resemblance to Philadelphia town-house forms very well. Many other Salem County patterned-brick houses had Swedish gambrelled gables.

6.5 An abandoned I-form house in its heartland, near Principio, Maryland, illustrates very well the basic characteristics as defined by Fred Kniffen: "gables to the side, at least two rooms in length, one room deep, and two full stories in height." Porches may run the full length of the house or only part of the way. The "tail" is also characteristic. (IMG:NAL)

6.6 Southern Cabin form of the hall-and-parlor Southern house form. (Drawn by Henry Glassie for his *Patterns in the Material Folk Culture of the Eastern United States*, 1968)

Georgian

Since the 1890s "Georgian" has been used to describe everything from great mansions for the land's very richest to small working-class houses sporting a fake shutter or two. Even if we confine it strictly to more pretentious high-style houses, "Georgian" is an almost meaningless word, since its reference is to the reigns of four King Georges in England spanning from approximately 1715 to 1830. Furthermore, folklorists can talk (quite justifiably) about a Georgian vernacular still vigorous into the 1860s—full Georgian, two-thirds Georgian, one-third Georgian houses quite recognizable even when decked out with Italianate brackets or French Second Empire mansards. Even if "Georgian" is limited to the three Georges who ruled in America, there is still a vast stylistic change during the period. Here I use it simply to denote both the high style brought to the American colonies from England between approximately 1680 and 1780 that was used to compose authority symbols for a class-structured state and the equivalent qualities of design and plan.

Balance and symmetry, as visual metaphors of reasoned order, are eminently desirable design elements in symbols of authority, and they are the basis of High-Georgian compositions. Proportions carefully follow a module—the original intent was to create a visual metaphor of that reasoned order which was held to justify a structure of society in which each individual has a hereditary place and is required to "do my duty in that station in life to which it hath pleased Providence to call me," as the old Anglican prayer book put it. In addition, the palace type had applied ornament, while the homestead did not. This ornament was drawn from ancient Greece and Rome via the Italian Renaissance; it alluded to sources of authority that justified the social status of the owner.

In its own time, the style was known as Renaissance, Italian, or Roman, all alluding to its origins in the so-called rebirth of antiquity promoted by Italian humanists two or three centuries before, or as Venetian, alluding to the great influence in England of the *Four Books of Architecture* by the Venetian architect Andrea Palladio. Georgian had three basic social functions: to help create an image of authority, to help create an image of successful landed-family founding, and to proclaim partnership in the British empire.

The first of these is very well demonstrated in the first Georgian to appear in the colonies, the Foster-Hutchinson house on North Square in Boston, built ca. 1688 (figure 6.7). Besides size, it was distinguished from neighboring ordinary houses by a number of typically Georgian features: pronounced symmetry created by a central entrance axis, balancing sets of windows (themselves internally balanced by mullions), and matching pilasters molded into the brickwork; balustrade across the roof creating a horizontal accent; balcony above the main door; and a cupola. Every one of these features signals authority, and every one of them contrasts with the homestead's haphazard naturalness. Symmetry and balance proclaim the reason supposed to be particularly incarnate in the dynastic prince and to justify a hierarchically balanced social order. Horizontal accents proclaim stability and solidity, in contrast to medieval verticality. The balcony is an old royal appurtenance, originating with papal balconies of appearance, later transferred to royal and noble palaces. The cupola is a variant of the dome, most venerable of all images of sacred and royal authority, developed over millennia out of sky and tomb shapes.

All these features combined to proclaim Thomas Foster's rise from small origins to high rank in the colony, as a member of the Governor's Council and a judge, and to make his house a suitable residence for Governor Hutchinson later on. How effective a symbol of authority the house became is indicated by its repeatedly being the target of mobs rioting against royal authority in the Bay Colony.[8]

6.7 Thomas Foster's mansion, later the residence of Governor Thomas Hutchinson, on North Square in Boston, built ca. 1688, demolished around 1832. (Woodcut from J. H. Stark, *Stark's Antique Views of Ye Towne of Boston,* 1907)

John Hancock used similar features for the same purpose in the mansion he built for himself on Beacon Hill in Boston from the proceeds of successful trade and commerce (figure 6.8). The Hancock house, though demolished in 1863, proved to be the single most influential model for Academic (and in due course, popular/commercial) Georgian design in the country. It had corner quoins instead of pilasters as framing accents; it had dormer windows with alternating curved and triangular pediments (in good Italian Renaissance fashion); and it had doorways and a central window framed by much more correct Classical columns, pilasters, and pediments. But these were largely matters of more sophisticated taste and greater erudition about Roman and Renaissance architectural details. What might be called the subliminal pattern of solidly grounded rectangle/oblong, subdivided into a pattern of balanced parts whose interrelation is perfectly clear, is the same as in the Foster-Hutchinson house and constitutes the basis for the appeal of the Georgian style, then and later.

By the middle of the eighteenth century, Georgian was being employed everywhere to proclaim dramatic upward mobility, even by tanners at Appoquinimink Creek (see figure 2.1). Any standard history of American architecture will contain dozens of examples of what you might call these incipiently Revolutionary houses, with their implicit challenges to hereditary authority by those whose social standing was self-made. Georgian details were successively refined in shape, proportion, and articulation, thus enabling the style to create far subtler and hence more effective images of the successful founding of landed families. Compare, in this regard, the kind of integrated and sophisticated statements of family success made by the great eighteenth-century Georgian mansions of Virginia with the naïvely patterned brick walls of homesteads in Salem County (see figure 6.4)!

6.8 John Hancock house on Beacon Hill in Boston, built ca. 1744, demolished 1863. (Woodcut from Robert Sears, *Pictorial Description of the United States*, 1838)

As for partnership in the British empire, one particular feature emphasized that: the Venetian or, as it is more learnedly called today, Palladian window (figure 6.9). In contrast to the normal windows of Georgian style—sash with rectangular mullions in balanced four-over-four or six-over-six pane arrangements (an enormous improvement both practically and symbolically over the medieval casement, whose ventilation was not so nicely controllable and whose irregular diamond panes implied irrational verticality)—Venetian windows were usually decorative (symbolic) in intent. They rarely opened. Usually they were located in the middle of facades, lighting central stair landings and so marking the center of the house. They referred, when used consciously, not to the romantic Venice of nineteenth-century travel but

to that aggressive, empire-building, mercantile, and oligarchic Venice so immensely admired by eighteenth-century British aristocrats and taken as an archetype of their own oligarchy based upon seapower.[9]

The first two of these social functions, and the details that proclaimed them, were preserved in post-Victorian suburban houses. To live in a grand mansion of revived Georgian style was to proclaim wealth and power, or aspirations to them. It was the most popular style for the very rich and the upper-middle class all through the 1890–1930 years, and it filtered down through Shaker Heights status to the humblest mail-order Georgian prefab. Until about 1960, to own a home was also under-

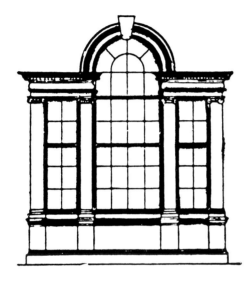

6.9 The Venetian or Palladian window.

stood as symbolic family-founding; it was the big step away from renting and living with Mom and Pop. Today you can still find vestiges of that concept, not so much in initials and dates on houses (though that too persists surprisingly often) but in mailboxes and even lawn signs ("The Joneses live here" or "Mary and Mike Jones").

As for the Palladian or Venetian window, its associations with the first British empire had long been forgotten by those years, but enough association with Englishness survived (assisted, no doubt, by the Queen Anne style) to make it the most popular extra feature in mail-order architecture, *the* decorative feature if customers could afford no other.

Georgian/Homestead Fusions

In a rigidly class-structured society, homestead and palace types might remain strictly segregated for centuries; in old Europe that did in fact happen. But America was never a rigidly class-structured society; it was always distinguished by upward mobility. This upward mobility fueled the Revolution; it was also a principal cause of Georgian and homestead types being mixed up. Colonial Williamsburg is the great example of Georgian mansion/Colonial homestead mix. Since such a mixture typified "Colonial" suburban houses throughout the 1890–1930 period, mention of Colonial Williamsburg is justified here, even though its restoration properly belongs in the 1930s (in the 1920s John D. Rockefeller was restoring Versailles). Colonial Williamsburg in effect climaxed the truly national popularization of Colonialism begun with the Wayside Inn in South Sudbury and in Deerfield. It is therefore not facetious to say that captions in the early official Williamsburg guides read like real-estate advertising copy for prospective suburban-home buyers or like descriptions of ready-cut Colonial cottages from Sears or Aladdin catalogs.

Consider something like this, from the 1964 Williamsburg guide:

Duke of Gloucester Street—East to West. Captain Orr's Dwelling. Partially restored. Erected sometime before 1743, this simple but comfortable dwelling has stood through the centuries with little change. The rear cornice has a two-foot overhang which makes a wider roof and thus adds needed space to the second floor. Another pleasing irregularity of this familiar over-all house design is the placing of one of the end chimneys inside the house, the other outside (p. 44).

The result of such copy was predictable. Thousands, then millions came to Williamsburg, walked along Duke of Gloucester and other streets, guidebook in hand, looking at those "simple but comfortable" dwellings in

Georgian/homestead style—and then went home deter-mined to get one for themselves. Models already ex-isted. Many mail-order firms, and both ASHSB and HOSI, already had them in stock, only under other names (figure 6.10); it was a simple matter to change the 1920s "English Colonial" into the 1930–1960s "Williams-burg Colonial." This Georgian/homestead style, combin-ing the Georgian mansion's formal symmetry with Colonial homestead cottage hominess of proportion, ma-terial and ornament, produced the perfect image of up-ward mobility for the American suburban house, the ultimate Comfortable House. It is with us still.

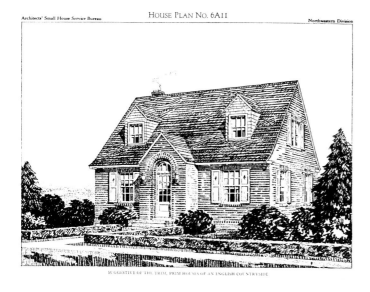

Architects' Small House Service Bureau   HOUSE PLAN NO. 6A11   Northwestern Division

SUGGESTIVE OF THE TRIM, PRIM HOUSES OF AN ENGLISH COUNTRYSIDE

6.10 ASHSB's plan 6A11 of ca. 1925, "suggestive of the trim, prim houses of the English country-side"—then still called English Co-lonial, although its actual inspira-tion is the hall-and-parlor Southern form in brick. Not until the 1930s and later would this form be labeled Williamsburg Colonial.

The Appeal of English Colonial Styles

The general reasons Colonial styles so appealed to Americans have already been set out: they fulfilled one of the oldest social functions of the art of architecture—to provide a cushion against future shock, to provide a sense of roots without which humans cannot long or happily live. It is easy to make fun of the almost hyster-ical nostalgia of someone like Joy Wheeler Dow, whose 1904 *American Renaissance* is an almost inexhaustible mine of amusing quotations:

A home should express that its owner possessed, once upon a time, two good parents, four grandparents, eight great-grandparents, and so on . . . that bienseance and family order have flourished in his line from time im-memorial . . . and that he has inherited heirlooms . . . to link him up properly in historical succession and pro-gression.

And if perchance an American were so luckless as to lack such an ancestral home to occupy? Then he should "pretend" that he had one, and build an "ideal home-stead" in revived Colonial style which would help make "the world appear a more decent place to live in. . . . Let us pretend that God has been good to us, and that we have proved worthy of His trust."[10] Aymar Embury sounds pretty quaint and dated too with his praises for the Georgian style of Charles Platt's Cheney house in South Manchester, Connecticut: "emphatically the most suitable residence imaginable for a modern gentleman descended from the old Puritan stock."[11]

Yet to call such feelings nostalgic does not refute their usefulness or (it is not too much to say) necessity. Surely it is no accident that long before post-Victorian times, in the decade before the Civil War even, artists began painting and selling pictures of serene countrysides with what are plainly English Colonial homes nestled in them, and that after the Civil War firms like Currier and Ives sold prints of such scenes by the thousands (figure 6.11).

a

b

6.11 Two of Currier and Ives's
American Homestead series: *a. Spring,*
apparently intended to be a vaguely
Southern house form, and *b. Winter,*
taken from a painting by George H.
Durrie of New Haven, who special-
ized in nostalgic images of rural
New England. (Library of Congress)

In such images homestead and Georgian styles are indiscriminately taken to mean "home." The painters were interested in Colonial architecture only insofar as it projected a general nostalgic impression of times simpler, earlier, and, above all, more secure, of the time before the terrible rending of the land by civil war, before the idealized high-thinking, plain-living Yankee and the equally idealized courtly Southern gentleman took to killing each other's children. Earlier Colonial Revivalists thought along similar lines. So, if the Connecticut pavilion at the 1876 Philadelphia Centennial looked more like a picturesque pastiche than anything close to an actual Colonial dwelling, it was not because designer Donald G. Mitchell didn't know what old Connecticut houses looked like, but because he was a romantic (author, in fact, of a nostalgic book called *Rural Studies,* published in 1867) who liked vague images of pastness created by patches of shingle and half-timbered walls far more than he liked accurate copies (figure 6.12). A similar spirit

motivated Currier and Ives's depiction of *The Birth-Place of Washington* (figure 6.13): to "improve upon" old Virginia homesteads by making them longer, lower, more ground-hugging, and cozier than they in fact were.

That kind of Colonial appeal motivated Gustav Stickley's model Craftsman house of 1911 (figure 6.14) in Morris Plains, New Jersey. One recurring theme in his writings in the *Craftsman* magazine was the desirability of creating images of roots:

Of course, the most desirable thing one can have in the way of a home is an old house built by one's grandfather or great-grandfather or modified by each successive generation until it comes into one's own possession as an embodied history of the life and nature of one's forefathers possessing a ripeness and sense of permanence that are eloquent of long years of comfort and usefulness. But the next best thing is a home planned so entirely in accordance with one's own individual tastes and habits that every nook and corner of it is so inevitably the right thing that no alteration would be possible and "moving" is never to be thought of.[12]

6.12 The Connecticut pavilion at the 1876 Philadelphia Centennial Exhibition. Contemporary print.

6.13 Currier and Ives's print *The Birth-Place of Washington*. (Library of Congress)

6.14 Gustav Stickley's model Craftsman home as it looks today, outside Morris Plains, New Jersey (IMG:NAL). It was originally built as a community house for his Craftsman Farms school and published as such in *The Craftsman* for November 1911.

It is this common desire to find appropriate form for a visual metaphor of continuity and roots—in a small house built by oneself—rather than ignorance or a copying of one from the other, that explains the otherwise curious resemblance between Washington's birthplace and Stickley's Craftsman house; indeed, this desire was the real source of Colonial appeal from beginning to end.

Colonial Homestead Revival Styles

Colonial appeal being at first and for long a matter of vague nostalgia, revivals of specific homestead types are hardly to be looked for until well into the twentieth century. The first real evidence for Colonial homestead revivals came in a taste for what were presumed to be typical homestead materials—logs and shingles.

The "Log Style"

The "log style" originated in an old myth that the first settlers from England built log cabins. This is now known to be quite false; once above a primitive level, they built houses of pit-sawn boards, as Harold Shurtleff demonstrated in his 1938 *Log Cabin Myth.* Log construction, like stoves and many other useful homestead devices, was probably of German origin. In any case, the "log style" was never of much importance to post-Victorian suburban building. A few mail-order examples of it can be found (figure 6.15); Gustav Stickley's use of peeled and oiled logs in the main living space of his Craftsman farmhouse could be counted an instance of middle-brow use; and the style could also claim some high-brow examples like El Tovar on the edge of the Grand Canyon in Arizona (1904) and Château Montebello in Quebec, originally built in the 1920s as a private seigniory club with construction supervised by a Finnish log-building expert, and still, despite its steel framing throughout, billed as the largest log structure in the world. But "log" was never a serious suburban style; it soon tended to be associated nearly exclusively with summer houses and cottages, like the "country home"

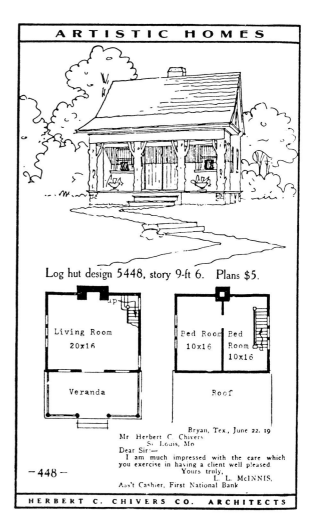

6.15 Log hut design 5448, from Herbert Chivers's *Artistic Homes,* 1912.

illustrated in *Keith's Magazine* for February 1918 whose walls are entirely logs and boulders, whose beds and tables and chairs were all made of small birch branches "in white birch jacket."

The Shingle Style

Shingled walls as an ornamental or stylistic feature existed long before Vincent Scully sought to make "shingle" an autonomous style in his first book, *The Shingle Style*.[13] His interpretation has, however, colored all later writings about "shingle." According to him, the Shingle style was a matrix of Modernism (this was typical line-of-progress thinking, which evaluated *everything*

by its relevance to emergent Modernism; he may not hold the same opinion today). Thus the Low house of 1887 in Bristol, Rhode Island (figure 6.16) constituted a "climax and kind of conclusion" for the Shingle style because McKim, its designer, decisively broke away from any ornamental use of shingles as characteristic of the Queen Anne style in favor of a direct expression of the nature of the material in a proto-Modern way—without paint or stain or undue shaping. It followed that McKim's subsequent abandonment of Shingle in favor of Academic Roman Revival and Renaissance stylings was seen as a tragic turning off the high road of progress.

6.16 W. G. Low house, Bristol, Rhode Island, completed 1887 to the designs of C. F. McKim of McKim, Mead and White. (HABS photo, Library of Congress)

That the fondness for shingled effects came out of a matrix of quite distinctively American taste is unquestionable; shingled walls and gables and turrets were among the most popular sorts of ornamentation from the 1860s on. More arguable is the assumption that Progressives' use of Shingle was somehow more honest, expressed the nature of the material more directly, than before; after all, the natural form of wood is in a tree, and once you hew or saw it, you give it some kind of artificial form. That is to say, shingles on walls are inherently ornamental as well as utilitarian or physically functional; as ornament, they are subject to associations, subliminal and direct. It would be hard to believe that no associations with images of Colonial homesteads like Washington's birthplace ever entered the heads of either McKim or Low, especially given the persistence of such associations on the popular level down to the 1930s. From 1890 on, shingled walls were widely used by mail-order and spec builders of all sorts, and had Professor Scully come along fifty years or so earlier to popularize

the term, "Shingle style" would undoubtedly have studded the pages of every mail-order catalog. But he was tardy, choosing to adorn a later generation; therefore, my use of "Shingle style" here in a mail-order context has to be retroactive.

Any suburban house of the period 1890–1930 visually dominated by an expanse of shingle, patterned or otherwise decoratively used, might in theory be designated Shingle style. Thus we might well speak of a Shingle style foursquare (figures 6.17, 4.15), a Shingle style bungalow (figures 4.5, 4.6), or Shingle style homestead temple-house (figure 4.38, left); and less easily of a Shingle style small foursquare or small temple-house, for in these smaller houses the form itself tends to be a more obvious stylistic designation than any ornament. But it would be redundant to speak of a Shingle style Queen Anne or Cape Cod, for shingles are a constituent part of those styles.

6.17 The Fulkerson house, a Shingle style foursquare built in 1908 in Weiser, Idaho. (From Don Hibbard, *Weiser: A Look at Idaho Architecture*, Boise, 1978)

Saltbox

The New England saltbox was the only Colonial homestead form specifically reproduced as such during the years 1890–1930. As early as 1887 Pallisers *New Cottage Homes* offered one, described as a "type not at all uncommon in the New England states, built sixty to one hundred years ago, many of which are still in a good state of preservation, thanks to the honesty and good material used in their construction." In 1923 it was a New England saltbox, replica of the Long Island home of John Howard Payne, composer of "Home Sweet Home," which the Home Owners Service Institute chose to erect near the White House as a model for good architect-designed housing (see figure 6.1); and throughout the 1920s the Architects' Small House Service Bureau supplied saltbox designs, many of which are still to be seen in upper-middle-class suburbs (figure 6.18).

But curiously enough, on the level of near-architects and non-architects (spec and catalog builders), the saltbox is as good as nonexistent. Neither the shape nor the name appears, for reasons unknown to me. One might argue that ready-cut suppliers could not, unlike architects, afford the luxury of offering models perceived by the broad public as exotic. But why the saltbox should be perceived as exotic throughout the 1890–1930 years, when the Pallisers obviously did not consider it so in 1887, remains a mystery.

Cape Cod

A comparable mystery is why Cape Cod does not appear in ready-cut house suppliers' catalogs as a style either. Not only did the term exist, and had, indeed, for almost a century; not only had the leading Colonial revivalist Royal Barry Wills at one time proposed mass-producing a "Cape Cod cottage" to provide the populace once and for all with a truly well- (that is architect-) designed house; but several popular small house models on the mail-order market resemble it in

6.18 A saltbox on Sunset Avenue in Verona, New Jersey, ca. 1925. (IMG:NAL)

many ways. In Aladdin's 1919 catalog, for instance, something very like a Cape Cod appears, and is, furthermore, called The Plymouth. But Cape Cod *per se,* did not become a popular style until the 1950s.

Southern Cabin

Ready-cut house suppliers also offered a number of models which we today might recognize as perpetuations on a popular/commercial level of the vernacular Southern Cabin form and which may well have owed much of their popularity to unconscious approximations of it (figure 6.19). Their lack of identification as such is not a mystery, however, inasmuch as that term then existed only as an epithet. In fact, intimations of "primitive" and "backwoodsy" then attaching to the form perhaps explain its popularity for summer cottages; since the principle of summer-cottaging involves a reversal of progress, giving up running water and vacuum cleaners and central heat for kitchen pumps, brooms, and fireplaces, why not revert all the way to a primitive house form built for hot weather?

I-form

Since the I-form was the lowest-common-denominator frontier house, and since the frontier was perceived as expanding throughout most of the post-Victorian years, it is no surprise that early mail-order-house catalogs have a number of I-form offerings. Most, like Gordon-Van Tine's plan 64 of ca. 1905 ("It is plain, but appears well . . . distinctly a farmer's home and its arrangement is adapted solely to farm life," without plumbing or central heating) and Aladdin's ca. 1912 Thorndale (figure 6.20), also without those luxuries, look like I-forms externally, but are not true I-forms because the plan shows them two rooms deep instead of only one. By contrast, Sears's 105 of 1908 *is* a true I-form on plan but externally has been gussied up by gables and fretwork (figure 6.21). Equally predictable is the disappearance of I-forms from these catalogs by the 1920s, coincident with the disappearance of the frontier.

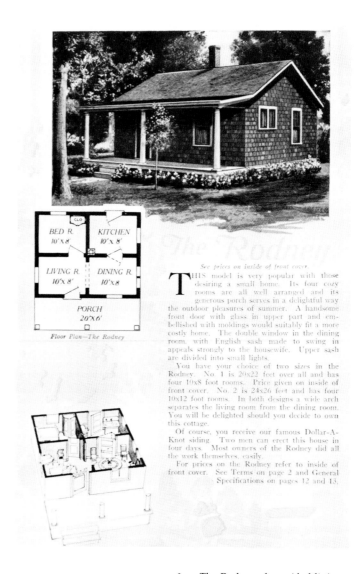

6.19 The Rodney, from Aladdin's 1919 catalog. Shingle style Southern Cabin, with English Colonial porch columns. A popular item out of Aladdin's Hattiesburg, Mississippi, plant. Ward's Charlevoix model was very similar.

THE THORNDALE

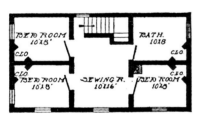

Second Floor Plan, The Thorndale

6.20 The Thorndale, a quasi-I-form house from Aladdin's 1908 through 1914 catalogs. It did not later reappear. The plan calls for a house two rooms deep so as to provide "a ten-room house. Imagine, at this price!" But, the blurb goes on to explain: "If you haven't use for so many rooms, we will furnish the house leaving out the partitions between the two downstairs bedrooms or . . . upstairs partitions between any two rooms"—in other words, make it a regular I-form.

6.21 Sears's Modern Home 105, from the 1908 catalog. An I-form farmhouse is revealed by the plan.

MODERN HOME No. 105

The arrangement of this house is as follows:

FIRST FLOOR.

Parlor - - - 11 feet 6 inches by 11 feet
Bedroom or Library - 9 feet by 11 feet
Kitchen - - 11 feet 6 inches by 12 feet
Pantry - - - - - 4 feet by 6 feet
Front Porch - - - 20 feet by 5 feet
Rear Porch, 4 feet 6 inches by 6 feet 3 inches

SECOND FLOOR.

Bedroom - - - - 10 feet by 11 feet
Bedroom - - - - 10 feet by 11 feet

Two Closets, 5 feet 6 inches by 2 feet 6 inches.

Entire length of building, 27 feet 6 inches by 22 feet wide, not including porches.

This house has an excavated basement under the entire building, 6 feet 6 inches from floor to joists. First story measures 8 feet 8 inches from floor to ceiling. Rooms in the second story measure 8 feet 4 inches from floor to ceiling. We specify solid "A" grade yellow pine inside doors and yellow pine trim throughout. The plans, specifications and bill of materials are absolutely free to you as explained on page 2.

FIRST FLOOR PLAN

SECOND FLOOR PLAN

Complete Hot Air Heating Plant, for	coal, extra..... $ 54.00
Complete Hot Air Heating Plant, for	coal, extra..... 56.00
Hot Water Heating Plant, extra..	152.00
Steam Heating Plant, extra..	132.00

SEND FOR OUR FREE SPECIAL CATALOGUE OF MILL WORK.

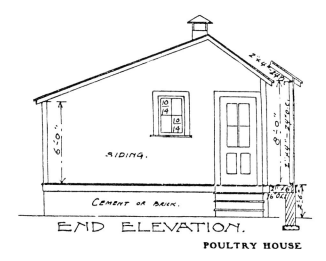

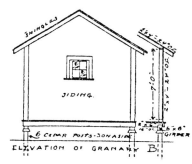

POULTRY HOUSE

6.22 Granary and henhouse available from Gordon-Van Tine Company's 1908 catalog.

Survivals of Traditional Utilitarian Forms

From the eighteenth century to the present, popular/commercial arts have perpetuated older forms, types, and stances dropped by avant-garde arts, wherever and whenever such older traditions retain a social function.[14] Thus it is not surprising to find early prefabricated-building catalogs offering a wide range of traditional forms for sheds and outbuildings, granaries and henhouses (figure 6.22); it is a counterpart to their perpetuation of Cape Cod, Southern Cabin, and I-forms.

Georgian Revival Styles

It is difficult to fix when Georgian survival ends and Georgian revival begins. Certainly the 1827 restoration of Independence Hall was survival; so perhaps was Arthur Gilman's Arlington Street Church in Boston of 1859. After that—was restoration of Mount Vernon in the 1870s revival or survival? Given the contemporary state of high styles, revival it must be considered. A revival of English Colonial was endemic in the stance of the 1876 Centennial; by the Columbian Exposition

of 1893, there was no doubt about it. Revival was dramatized by the number of state pavilions that chose English Colonial reproductions in contrast to the Picturesque styles that had dominated the 1876 state pavilions in Philadelphia (see figure 6.12). Now only a few states (Michigan and Idaho, for example) chose Picturesque; what most clearly represented up-to-date taste and the wave of the future were the Colonial pavilions, like New Jersey's (figure 6.23), Louisiana's (figure 6.24), and Massachusetts's (figure 6.25). The New Jersey pavilion had a "reproduction of Washington's headquarters at Morristown," albeit wrapped with a generous porch that smacked more of Cape May. Louisiana had "a reproduction of an old plantation mansion . . . a typical Southern home"; and Virginia's was modeled upon George Washington's Mount Vernon. But the *pièce de résistance* acknowledged by all was the Massachusetts building: "The Old Bay State has done herself infinite credit in the building she has erected. It is a reproduc-

6.23 New Jersey pavilion at the 1893 Columbian Exposition in Chicago, from James W. and Daniel B. Shepp, *Shepp's World's Fair Photographed* (Chicago and Philadelphia, 1893). Based on Washington's headquarters at Morristown, but given a ceremonial entrance with Palatial Georgian pediment and full (High Victorian) wraparound porch.

6.24 Louisiana pavilion at the 1893 Exposition, from *Shepp's World's Fair Photographed*. Based on Parlange plantation house in New Roads, Louisiana.

6.25 Massachusetts pavilion at
the 1893 Exposition, from *Shepp's
World's Fair Photographed*. Based on
the Hancock house, but given a
cupola and a two-story portico
something like that on the Vassall-
Longfellow house in Cambridge.

tion of the old Hancock Mansion, once to be seen on
Beacon Street, Boston.'' Well, not exactly: there was a
prominent cupola set up in the roof; there were four
identical dormers instead of three (two triangular and
one round pedimented); there was a two-story portico
encasing the central facade features; there was a one-
story columned porch on one side. The pavilion was, in
a word, considerably more palatial. But that befitted its
function and the general idealization of the Founding
Fathers.

Palatial Georgian

The differences between the Hancock house and its "reproduction" at the Chicago fair were deliberate—that's
the important point. Departures from the original were
not the result of ignorance but of intent. In fact the Hancock house had been thoroughly measured and drawn
just before its demolition in 1863; and I agree with Mar-

garet Henderson Floyd's contention that this set of measured drawings was pivotal to the whole Colonial
Revival. No American house had been so recorded before. It made the Hancock house a rallying point for
fashionable Boston architects, an iconic form for the likes
of Arthur Gilman and John Hubbard Sturgis. Especially
significant here is the date, 1863—right in the middle of
the Civil War. Massachusetts had taken upon itself the
role of champion of the Sacred Union proclaimed in
1776, whose preservation was the prime objective of that
conflict. John Hancock's name appeared first among
signers of the storied Declaration. That a revival of
American patriotism and a revival of Colonial architecture should proceed together was almost inevitable.[15]

In the Massachusetts pavilion, the primary Colonial
image shifted from homestead to Georgian mansion. A

chief mover in this development was Boston architect Robert Peabody (whose firm of Peabody and Stearns was responsible for the pavilion). Peabody had represented the Boston Society of Architects at the 1876 Philadelphia Centennial, where emphasis was on seventeenth-century founders and romantic homesteads, and his own early work showed this influence. But by 1893 he contended that the great colonial Americans were not founders like Winthrop or Roger Williams, but signers like Hancock and Washington and Jefferson. The most perfect Colonial Revival models accordingly were the kind of palatial mansions these great men had built and lived in. The best remembered and most effective promoter of this idea was Fiske Kimball, who between 1910 and 1930 authored architectural histories and biographies (on Fairmount Park in Philadelphia, on Thomas Jefferson, on American architecture) and who established American rooms in the Philadelphia Museum of Art, was instrumental in Colonial restorations, and was by profession a practicing Colonial Revival architect. Patriotism, romanticism, and academic correctness were promoted by him in equal measure; and that is what the Georgian Revival was properly all about. You can see that plainly in the Massachusetts pavilion's numerous successors, emulators, and unconscious imitators.

The Massachusetts pavilion, like its model the Hancock house, was demolished (immediately after the 1893 exposition) and is known only from photographs. But its influence lingered on in a taste for Palatial Georgian Revival style, not only in architect-designed homes where you might expect it, but also in spec and mail-order houses where you might not; Sears, Ward, Aladdin, and others early and long had a Palatial Georgian model at the top of their line. In *MacLagan's Suburban Homes* catalog put out in Newark about 1910, Palatial Georgian models seem to rival all others in popularity; many of them show, by their combination of giant portico and gambrel roof, influence from the Massachusetts pavilion in Chicago (figure 6.26), while others show influence

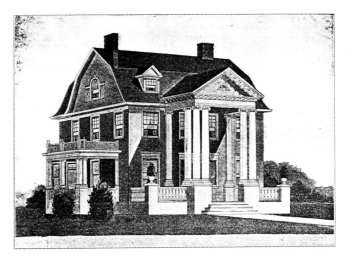

6.26 Adaptation of the Massachusetts pavilion for a Palatial Georgian model in *MacLagan's Suburban Homes*, ca. 1910.

from the New Jersey pavilion. Top-of-the-line in Glenn L. Saxton's 1914 *Plan Book of American Dwellings* was "A Beautiful Georgian Colonial. . . . There is no style of architecture in the world that is as commanding." It owed much to the Massachusetts pavilion and cost $8000. For the less ambitious, he offered what could most properly be called a Palatial Georgian suburban cottage, featuring a two-story portico built into a much more modest body, and more humbly priced at $2900. This he called simply "A Comfortable Home." Sears's top-of-the-line Palatial Georgian was called the "exclusive Magnolia" and was advertised in the 1918 edition of Sears's *Modern Homes* as "a Colonial type of residence" which "from the days of George Washington to the present time has housed the greatest figures in American history, science, and literature," a group that for only $5,140 Sears's customers could join. The caption is on shakier ground when it declares that "many will recognize its close resemblance to the famous residence in Cambridge, Mass., where poet Longfellow composed his immortal works." Not even "poet Longfellow" would immediately have noticed the resemblance, but its ultimate peroration that "leading architectural authorities declare this type will continue to win favor for hundreds of years" has so far been borne out.

Technically, most of these designs had the kind of "appended portico" characteristic of Classical Revival architecture in the years 1820–1850, especially in the South—classical porticos tacked on to the fronts of Georgian mansions (Andrew Jackson's Hermitage is the classic example). It would be unprofitable, however, to make such fine distinctions in popular/commercial designs of the 1890–1930 years, especially since the most favored portico was not a full classical one but something high and narrow, as is actually found on the Hancock house. The use of various devices to signal English Colonial intentions is the important consideration (figures 6.27, 6.28, 6.29).

6.27 Palatial Georgian house in Botkins, Ohio. It is actually a four-square with appended portico like that on the Massachusetts pavilion. (IMG:NAL)

6.28 Homestead temple-house forms on Alpin Street in Albany, New York, ca. 1910, with two-story portico effects, Venetian/Palladian windows in the gables, and Shingle style walls. (IMG:NAL)

6.29 Vestigial Palatial Georgian house in Toledo, Washington, ca. 1946–50. (IMG:NAL)

Modified High Georgian

Not everybody could afford Palatial Georgian's two-story front porticos; for many, they seemed ostentatious. Frequently then these porticos were modified into various types of entrance porches, and other Palatial Georgian decorative elements were simplified as well (figure 6.30). Thus was created a kind of standardized Georgian, except on the architect-designed level, where throughout the 1890–1930 years Academic taste tried, with some success, to maintain regional accents. These were most pronounced in New England, where actual research into American Georgian architecture had begun earliest and gone deepest (the *White Pine Series of Architectural Monographs* was overwhelmingly concerned with New England, for instance). But Colonial Revival architects in other regions had increasingly rich resources to draw upon as well: a "Pennsylvania High Georgian" style could be created with some confidence on the basis of books by William Davenport Goforth or Harold Donaldson Eberlein, for instance; a "Maryland High Georgian" from J. Martin Hammond's *Colonial Mansions of Maryland and Delaware* of 1914; a New Jersey counterpart from Weymer Jay Mills's *Historic Houses of New Jersey* of 1902; and so on.

This Georgian regionalism is of course a counterpart to the preference for Dutch Colonial in northern New Jersey, Long Island, and Albany; or for Spanish Colonial in the Southwest and California. It brings to mind that

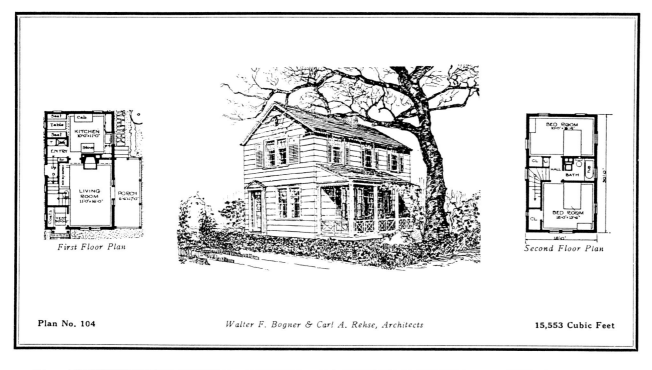

First Floor Plan

Second Floor Plan

Plan No. 104   *Walter F. Bogner & Carl A. Rehse, Architects*   **15,553 Cubic Feet**

6.30 Typical Modified Georgian "simple little home of four rooms," offered as plan 104 in HOSI's *The Books of a Thousand Homes.* Walter Bogner and Carl A. Rehse, architects.

much older America of communities more tightly knit than now, of an American army that went into battle in regional units (20th Michigan; 7th Alabama), when pride in one's local region was taken for granted—that regionalism which avant-gardists both European and native attacked with such scorn from the 1940s onward as an obstacle to social (read "scientific, planned") progress but never quite destroyed. Regionalism was never so marked at the other end of the social and economic scale. What mail-order builders spread across the country was a lowest-common-denominator sort of Modified High Georgian, becoming from model to model more simplified, more sparsely decorated and, in general, a bit more picturesquely irregular.

Georgian Homestead

The humblest form of English Colonial Revival is the Georgian Homestead style—a pastiche of various elements culled from Palatial and Modified Georgian styles as developed in the post-Victorian era (figure 6.31). The Georgian Homestead style really did not come into its own until after 1930, indeed, not until popular/commercial buildings of the late 1940s and 1950s. Not, that is, until after Academic confidence had shrivelled under Modernist scorn and the devising of an imagery of roots and stability was left to popular/commercial builders because the Modernists never seemed to understand that suburban architecture has to be *about* something— specifically, about the concerns of those who live in it.

This part of the struggle to maintain an American identity, like most other aspects of it, had long been abandoned by intellectuals and did not again become their concern until Venturi's Post-Modernism of the late 1960s and 1970s. Whether Post-Modernism will be able to effectively concern itself with the traditional social functions of architecture remains, at this writing, to be seen; as yet, the bulk of middle- and lower-midde class houses continues to be the province of speculative builders and their style to be the legacy of the Comfortable House.

6.31 What the ASHSB called a "Colonial bungalow," house plan 4B15, designed about 1925, was destined for a long life: millions of houses like it, though not necessarily deriving from this or any one single prototype, were built in expanding suburbs from the late 1940s onward.

7

Classical Revival (National Democratic) Styles

The Original Classical Revival (National Democratic) Styles

The American Revolution had two distinct aspects. On the one hand, it was a nationalistic movement, born of a sense that the thirteen colonies were big enough and adult enough to constitute an independent nation, free of direction from or allegiance to any other. In that sense it was no more than the latest in a series of struggles for freedom from domination by foreigners, in a line with the Swiss struggle against Austria, the Dutch against Spain, the Swedes against Denmark. On the other hand, it was an ideological struggle, growing out of eighteenth-century Enlightenment theories about the natural goodness of Man being suppressed by despotic institutions and the marvels possible when those institutions were supplanted by democratic republican government. Enlightenment enthusiasts were fond of citing ancient Rome, especially that version of ancient Roman history represented by Edward Gibbon's *Decline and Fall of the Roman Empire.* According to this view—naive, more than a little misinformed, based upon propaganda taken too literally—republican Romans were paragons of virtue. The period from Augustus to Hadrian was the most glorious epoch of peace and prosperity ever known to mankind, when "first citizens" ruled on behalf of their people. Then somehow, unaccountably, this model republic and noble race fell under the tyranny of corrupt rulers, vicious laws, and enfeebling superstitions (Christianity), just as earlier, equally unaccountably, the pristine democratic city-states of Greece had been corrupted by the intrigues and bribery of despots from degenerate Asia. First in the Renaissance, later in the Enlightenment, however, ancient republican virtues had been rediscovered and their revival promoted by enlightened philosophers. Now finally in the glorious American Revolution mankind had a unique chance to revive and restore them.

The proper architectural forms for a reincarnation of the virtuous republics of antiquity could only be their own architecture. That is to say, Americans progressing to ever-greater perfection via democratic institutions supposed to be based upon the republics of Greece and Rome should properly be housed in temples (an idea that actually goes back to a 1540s guidebook to Rome written by Andrea Palladio and still, incredibly, being taken as reliable and used as late as the 1820s), should conduct their business in architectural forms derived from Greece and Rome, should in fact model their whole environment on a Classical Revival style. That style, like the new state itself, was to be purged of all corruptions: no mixings of details drawn from different periods; no adulterating them with derivations from Italian Renaissance generalized Classicism. "Pure" Classicism was what the hour called for. Unfortunately, since so little was actually known about the Greek and Roman worlds, in practice the "pure" revival of Classicism meant two things: reliance upon a few specific models from antiquity, readily recognizable to anyone even slightly acquainted with architecture; and insistence upon only one style per building, preferably of studied correctness (if one knew, of course, what the "correct" Classical forms might be for a shopping arcade, a temple-dwelling in frigid Vermont, a Presbyterian church in Alabama, a privy, or a Unitarian school).

The two most common "model symbols" for Classical Revival (or better, National Democratic) buildings were both considered to have come from the reign of Augustus: the Maison Carrée at Nîmes in Provence, a rectangular structure set on a high platform approached by steps with a Corinthian portico in front; and the Pantheon in Rome, a dome-and-portico combination. That the Maison Carrée had actually been dedicated to Augustus as a god (in 2 AD) was a fact yet unbelieved or unknown by the early Republic's leaders, who still took at face value the propaganda put out by Augustus and his courtiers, which made him out to be one among equals, a kind of predecessor of George Washington. Still unknown too was the fact that the Pantheon had not been built by Augustus at all, despite the inscription across its portico frieze, but assembled by Hadrian a hundred years later to honor the empire's gods, including himself. No matter; it's not what happened in history but what people *think* happened in history that shapes destiny. And so the Maison Carrée, supposedly the ideal temple described in *De Architettura* by Augustus's architect Vitruvius, and the Pantheon's portico-plus-dome combination became models for countless buildings in the early Republic, from Jefferson's Monticello (the particular intermediaries used in arriving at the form are irrelevant to its ideological significance) to the full-scale temple-houses of the 1820s in New England and New York (figures 7.1, 7.2).

Of course, despite strictures against mixing, all sorts of modifications had to be made to Classical Revival styles, for many reasons. Once the Greeks fought their war of independence against Turkey, Greek architecture became all the rage, and only the most erudite purists forebore to mix Greek and Roman. Thomas Walter in the 1830s might model Nicholas Biddle's Andalusia on the Parthenon in Athens, but ordinary builders cheerfully mixed up Greek and Roman, even builders as educated as Ithiel Town, in fact (figure 7.3). Windows had to be cut in (neither Roman nor Greek temples had any; their light came only from front doorways), chimneys added, fireplaces devised, and small wings (often tiny temples in themselves) added to provide necessary enlargements and family living spaces. Incorporate confusions of Roman, Greek, and Italianate Tuscan columns, Roman and Renaissance domes, and the odd dash of Egyptian exotica—here a pylon doubling as a window frame, there a cavetto cornice gracing a front door—and the result in larger houses was a charmingly inventive naïveté, corresponding nicely to those naïve early American paintings of the day, with their neat certainties of line and color and idea (to be seen in the National Gallery's Garbisch collection, the Abby Aldrich Rockefeller collection at Williamsburg, and elsewhere). Smaller houses exhibited a truly creative vernacular style that became a direct ancestor of many Comfortable Houses (figures 7.4, 7.5, 7.6; and compare figures 4.18, 4.31, 4.32).

7.1 House designed by the firm of Town and Davis, ca. 1825 in Middletown, Connecticut (demolished). Intended to recall the Roman temple to Augustus at Nîmes (Maison Carrée).

7.2 Thomas Jefferson's Monticello at Charlottesville, Virginia, as completed in the first decade of the nineteenth century. Intended to recall the Pantheon in Rome. (IMG:NAL)

7.3 Bowers house, Northampton, Massachusetts, built ca. 1825 to designs by Ithiel Town (demolished).

7.4 Basilica type Classical Revival vernacular house, on Plymouth Road outside Ann Arbor, Michigan. Built ca. 1845, demolished ca. 1970. (IMG:NAL)

7.5 Classical Revival vernacular house in Sackett's Harbor, New York, built ca. 1820. The portico is reduced to a thin pilaster arcade, almost Federal in quality. The style is very common throughout upstate New York, with occasional examples in Canada, including the well-known Barnum house in Grafton, Ontario. (IMG:NAL)

7.6 Classical Revival vernacular house near Tecumseh, Michigan. Wing retains portico; main house retains only eaves-return and portico proportions. (IMG:NAL)

The Appeal of Classical Revival Styles

"The Greek mania here is at its height, as you infer from the fact that everything is a Greek temple from the privies in the back court, through the various grades of prison, theatre, church, custom-house, and state-house." So wrote *The Architectural Magazine's* New York correspondent to London in December 1834. In the decade 1825–35 enthusiasm for Greek styles was boundless; Greek largely supplanted Roman Revival for every sort of building. Of course foreigners laughed at it. But in those days Americans were confident that what foreigners laughed at today they would imitate tomorrow. They were the wave of the future, their government was a model for mankind, and Classical Revival architecture was the symbol of their success. Did not the anthem "My Country 'Tis of Thee," written to provide new and appropriate words to the old tune of "God Save the King," say outright "I love . . . thy templed hills"? What other land had templed hills?—temples that were not ancient ruins, but homes of a proud, free citizenry?

After 1850 that image tarnished, and in the Civil War it darkened so much that Americans began to feel inferior to Europeans. Or more exactly, the cultural elite, the pacesetters did—and do, to this day. But this colonial mentality spread only very slowly through the middle and lower classes. To this day as you go through the countryside you will see flags proudly flying beside tiny shacks; you will see mailboxes supported by cut-out figures of Uncle Sam; you will see billboards demanding "Get US out of the UN" in the spirit of George Washington. And to this day you will see all sorts of obvious descendants of Classical Revival house forms built in post-Victorian times to meet the most common popular taste. They are survivals, really, inheritors of the great hopeful spirit of the early Republic.[1]

Revivals and Survivals of Classical Revival (National Democratic) Styles

Academic Classical Revival—the deliberate, systematic, disciplined use of Roman and Greek forms for associative values and visual effects—was most effective in public buildings of the years 1890–1930 (where it often went under the name of Beaux-Arts or City Beautiful; see figure 1.1). Only occasionally did Academic architects design anything at all resembling the Greek and Roman temple-house of the early Republic; houses in high-style Academic Roman or Greek Revival are not only comparatively rare, but almost always conflated, in varying degrees, with Colonial elements (figures 7.7, 7.8). The principal reason is that use of architecture for deliberate historical allusions in general, and reproduction of a temple-house to signal the seat of the virtuous citizen of a reincarnated ancient republic in particular, had gone hopelessly out of fashion among the educated. Advances in scholarship and egalitarian democracy had spoiled the early Republic's naïve notion of Roman virtue; that Roman and Greek societies both rested on slave labor was troublesome now, as it had not been then, and the idea of screaming eagles carrying democratic blessings to the benighted was not unanimously admired now either. True, there was a flurry of Anglo–American imperialism in the 1890–1930 period, epitomized in the Spanish–American war and imaged in great Academic Roman Revival town halls and courthouses, but its appeal was transient.

On the mail-order and spec level the situation was a little different. One can find examples—admittedly not many, but enough—of actual temple-houses in the early Republic's manner, both standing and in catalogs (figures 7.9, 7.10, 7.11). The temple-house form lent itself to multifamily dwellings (the portico becoming a one- or two-story porch) and in this form is quite common (see figures 4.32, 4.33, 6.28). Mail-order versions of Classical Revival vernacular types survived into the first decade of the twentieth century, though not long thereafter (figure 7.12).

7.7 Pierson house, Pittsford, New York, ca. 1920. Academic Roman Revival portico on main house is reasonably correct, but the wing, despite ground-floor columns, has eighteenth-century English Colonial proportions. (IMG:NAL)

7.8 E. R. Motch house on South Park Boulevard in Shaker Heights, Ohio, 1924. Academic Greek Revival and Academic High-Georgian Revival elements are hopelessly mixed up. Charles Schneider, architect. (Photo by Eric Johannesen)

7.9 Temple-house model offered in John Henry Newson's *Homes of Character*, 1910. Though obviously a temple-house, it is here called "An Extreme Colonial Type" which, the caption says, "appeals to many who admire a plain and stately exterior."

Design No. 5007

Size: Width, 30 feet; Length, 36 feet

Blue prints consist of foundation plan; floor plan; front, rear, two side elevations; wall sections and all necessary interior details. Specifications consist of twenty-two pages of typewritten matter.

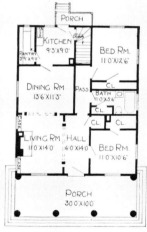

Floor Plan

PRICE

of Blue Prints, together with a complete set of typewritten specifications

ONLY

$8.00

We mail Plans and Specifications the same day order is received.

7.10 Design 5007 in *Radford's Artistic Bungalows* of 1908, a small Doric temple-house, has a curiously Post-Modern look.

7.11 Classical temple-house built by a Dr. Malmgren in 1906 in Phoenix, Oregon. Dr. Malmgren came from upper New York state, a great heartland of the Classical Revival temple-house, which may have influenced his choice of dwelling. The pseudo-Palladian gable window is a characteristic mail-order design signature. (IMG:NAL)

7.12 Aladdin's Michigan model, from 1912 catalog. One of Aladdin's first designs, obviously inspired by Classical Revival vernacular traditions in Aladdin's home state.

A L A D D I N   D W E L L I N G S

THE MICHIGAN

ERE is a model six-room dwelling which offers unusual value for the price. The interior rooms are arranged for convenience, ventilation, and plenty of light. The vestibule opens direct into either the living room or dining room. The up stairs bed rooms are well lighted, each having a closet. A good-sized porch with attractive turned pillars affords plenty of room for sitting out and enjoying the pleasant weather.

SPECIFICATIONS

Size, 24 x 24 ft. Price, $839. Cash Discount, 5%. Net Price, $797.05. See Terms.
All lumber selected Yellow Pine, Red Cedar, and Huron Pine.
Height of ceiling, 9 ft. first floor; 8 ft. second floor.
Sill, 6 x 8 in.
Studding, 2 x 4 in. Rafters and ceiling joists, 2 x 4 in.
Joists, 2 x 8 in. down and 2 x 8 in. up stairs.
Joists, ceiling joist and studding placed every 16 in.
Flooring, 1-inch matched, 3 inches wide. Sheathing lumber.
Roof, 1-inch lumber, overlaid with shingles.

Patent plaster board or lath and plaster.
Base board and all interior finish clear Yellow Pine.
Windows, 30 x 32 in., two sliding sash, double-strength glass.
Doors, outside, 2 ft. 8 in. x 6 ft. 8 in.; inside, 2 ft. 8 in. x 6 ft. 8 in.; front door, three-quarter length glass.
Front and rear steps.
All hardware, locks, hinges, knobs, nails, and paint for two coats inside and outside.
Complete instructions and illustrations for erecting.

First Floor Plan, The Michigan

Second Floor Plan, The Michigan

Examples of the use of Classical details abound on bungalows, foursquares, and homestead temple-houses; obviously, the middle- and lower-middle-class clientele of mail-order builders liked these allusions (figures 7.13, 7.14, 7.15). On the lowest social levels, small homestead temple-houses and foursquares, ornamental details are sparse enough that one can hardly speak of their having a "style" proper; nonetheless there is a kind of subliminal Classical style about them that is worth consideration.

As noted earlier, whenever you find aggregations of small, separate two- or three-room temple-houses, you have probably found a company town. Such houses were overwhelming favorites for housing employees, not entirely or necessarily by company fiat, either. Time and again it turns out that employees wanted this kind of house. The reason cannot be entirely utilitarian practicality, nor is it some strange coincidence. There has to have been some kind of unconscious predilection for them, an atavistic recollection or impulsive feeling that such houses "looked right" somehow. Obviously neither company officials nor workers were conscious of the association of temple-houses with the virtues and convictions of the early Republic. But there could have been some preference instilled by the "rightness" of the landscape one grew up in.

Furthermore, these temple-houses display a consistent taste for symmetry and balance that the pre-Classical Revival Colonial homestead did not. This taste is manifested very strongly in the humblest mail-order, ready-cut houses; to their clientele it obviously "looked right" and was a sales plus. It also appears with dramatic consistency in self-built homes (figure 7.16). There are many examples of dwellings obviously built by their owners and inhabitants without the aid of any plan at all, but which somehow ended up determinedly symmetrical and balanced. The taste you can recognize yet again in the way additions are still made to small lower- and lower-middle-class houses; where in theory a room

could be tacked on the back and a porch left open for summer breezes, in practice the porch gets glassed or walled in to form a front room that balances the back.[2]

Could such a taste be no more than some accidental or inevitable consequence of rectangular symmetrical structures being easier to build than asymmetrical ones? No, because mail-order builders offered lots of easy-to-build models in vestigial medieval or Picturesque styles that were asymmetric, and they never came close to rivaling vestigial Classical Revival in popularity—even in summer cottages, where you might expect something picturesque to prevail (figure 7.17). Truly, Classical Revival, image and carrier of high idealistic democracy, has been the quintessentially American style for the majority of the continent's population over many generations.

7.13 Even on this tiny workingman's temple-house, from Aladdin's 1912 catalog, columns of Roman Doric style are provided.

7.15 In the 1920s recognizable Classical Revival features persisted in small mail-order houses like Montgomery Ward's Avondale of 1927.

7.14 Radford's design 5077 features sturdy Roman Doric columns on a workingman's temple-house (*Radford's Attractive Artistic Bungalows,* 1908). To this day, whole streets in industrial towns like Louisville, Kentucky, or Gary, Indiana, are lined with houses like this.

7.16 House in Orrick, California, almost certainly built by owner and occupant. Folk traditions of symmetry are so dominant that superficially such a structure presents a resemblance to vernacular versions of the "appended portico" Classical Revival substyle.

7.17 Summer cottages advertised in Aladdin's 1919 catalog. Such transient structures were among prefabricators' first offerings. To some extent their forms may derive from some subliminal recollection of Colonial homestead forms; but mainly what directs them is an instinctive folk sense for symmetry.

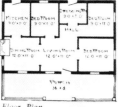

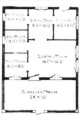

Summer Cottages

The Luna

See prices on inside of front cover.

ABUNDANT space in this trim little summer cottage. Well screened porch of good size. Three sleeping rooms, living room, dining room and kitchen on inside. You will note that it can be set on a very narrow lot. Gives splendid satisfaction. See General Specifications, page 114, for further information. See Terms on page 2.

*Floor Plan
The Luna*

See prices on inside of front cover.

A COSY summer home. Plenty of space on front porch—can be used for open-air dining room or sleeping room. Three bedrooms, dining room, living room and kitchen on inside. Plenty of light and air—an abundance of space. Is really one of the neatest cottages imaginable. See general summer cottage specifications, page 114 and Terms on page 2.

The Seaford

*Floor Plan
The Seaford*

See prices on inside of front cover.

A BIG summer cottage at a small price. Note the 36-ft. porch running all the way across the front of the building. Another one of our pioneer designs. Always makes a good impression and saves a good deal of money. See General Specifications, page 114, and Terms on page 2.

*Floor Plan
The Shasta*

See prices on inside of front cover.

THE Drayton sells for a low price. Two bedrooms can be arranged by combining living room and dining room. See General Specifications on page 114 and Terms on page 2.

See prices on inside of front cover

THIS building is designed for settler's house or hunter's lodge. It is built just like other houses, strong and substantial. Height of side wall, 7 ft. 6 in. No lath and plaster are furnished with this house at the price quoted. Size, 12 x 16 ft. See Terms on Page 2.

8

Medieval Revival
Styles

The Original Gothic Revival Styles

Gothic Revival churches appeared in the United States as early as the 1810s. Gothic Revival houses did not appear in any numbers much before the 1840s, however, and even then the style never came near rivaling in popularity Classical Revival or the later Italianate and Second Empire picturesque styles. With good reason: in the United States a faint air of subversion and eccentricity always hung over the Gothic Revival. It was a peculiarly British style. By the second half of the eighteenth century fashionable English milords had begun to build ancestor galleries in Gothic, if their mansions did not already have one, as a kind of image of deep ancestral roots. By the 1780s whole castles with Gothic crenellations and narrow diamond-mullioned windows were in evidence. In 1805 Parliament voted substantial funds to restore Westminster Abbey as a national monument; it is no mere coincidence that this was the year of Trafalgar, a turning point in the long wars with revolutionary France. Revolutionary France, like revolutionary America, conceived of itself as reincarnating the virtuous republics of antiquity. As in America, purged Classical styles were adopted to proclaim this conviction. Britain needed a style to image continuity—continuity of the monarchy against revolutionary republics, continuity of laws against wholesale innovations, continuity of institutions. Gothic castles and cathedrals provided just what was required. So in 1815 began the remodeling of Windsor Castle into Gothic form; its round, battlemented keep and diamond-mullioned bay windows were imitated by many a loyal British subject overseas. In the 1830s Westminster Old Palace, seat of Parliament for hundreds of years, burned in a spectacular fire. Its

replacement was in the same style as the old, providing a perfect visual metaphor of continuity of government. So developed the Imperial Gothic of dozens of legislative and judicial buildings in the overseas dominions and India during the nineteenth century. In Canada, the Gothic farmhouse or city row house with Gothic trim became as much a mark of loyal British subjects as temple-house variants were marks of loyalty to America.

All the efforts of romantic promoters of Gothic in America, like Andrew Jackson Downing, could not change those associations. Two American state capitols were built in Gothic Revival style, but both of them imaged potential subversion—one at Milledgeville, Georgia, another at Baton Rouge, both a decade or so before the Civil War broke out. The only way Gothic could be promoted effectively in America was on aesthetic grounds, as a picturesque image of home (figure 8.1). Even then, Gothic had relatively limited success. From its beginnings in America, Gothic was considered a "churchy" style to a degree it never was in Britain. Furthermore, Gothic was associated with other styles that smacked of eccentricity or worse—Chinese, Moorish, Elizabethan, and so on. Only as a romantic love of the picturesque—buildings and furniture that evoked a picture of pastness—became overwhelming, from about 1845 onward, could medieval styles become in any sense truly popular in America. But by approximately 1860 so many picturesque styles were developing that medieval ones became merely contributing elements to the general High-Victorian Picturesque style, as may be seen in the Connecticut State Capitol at Hartford, or Harvard's Memorial Hall, both designed in the 1870s (and often seen, too, as images of ideological confusion just after the Civil War).

8.1 The home as picturesque image, in a wood engraving ca. 1855. Sylvan setting, spangled with statues and sundials, embowered by trees—the style has to be Gothic: arches pointed, chimneys twisted and molded, windows diamond mullioned, gable pinnacled and eaved with boards shaped like the borders of medieval illuminations.

The Appeal of Revived Medieval Styles in Post-Victorian Times

Academic insistence on correctness began extricating the Gothic Revival style proper from its Picturesque trappings during the late 1880s. But its associations with eccentricity persisted. Post-Victorian Academic Gothic was no more a mainstream style than pre-Civil War Gothic Revival had been. Here and there tall buildings appeared in Gothic style, of which Cass Gilbert's Woolworth Building was the most famous (New York, 1913; see figure 1.3), but the associations were vaguely with height and aspirations rather than with anything specifically medieval. For Academic Gothic courthouses or capitols, you could search far and fruitlessly.

With churches, houses, and collegiate buildings it was different. In these areas, what had been the disadvan-

tage of Gothic Revival became a strong point: British associations. A "cathedral of learning" soared upward in Pittsburgh in the mid-1920s, and throughout the whole 1890–1930 period Yale and Princeton sprouted Gothic quadrangles, all aspiring to emulate Oxford and Cambridge. Greatest exemplar of the style was Ralph Adams Cram, who came from one of those good New England families whose need for reassuring roots produced dedicated Anglophiles in general, and, in his case, such numerous and disparate Academic Gothic protestations of Anglophilism as the United States Military Academy at West Point, the Princeton University Chapel, St. John the Divine Episcopal Cathedral in New York, the Swedenborgian Cathedral at Bryn Athyn, and a partial restoration of the crumbling church tower at Jamestown for the 1907 tercentenary celebrations. This same appeal to pro-British sentiments and Old Country roots, endemic to the post-Victorian age, was a principal source for what popularity medieval revival styles enjoyed.

Few, however, shared Cram's enthusiasm for Gothic as such, and not even he extended it to domestic building. Public opinion in the 1890–1930 years was simply too sophisticated to accept those quaint, spiky houses with pointed windows, spindly pinnacles, crotchety crocketts, and attenuated board-and-batten walls that had so enchanted their romantic grandparents. What most appealed to the post-Victorian generation were the domestic styles of the waning Middle Ages and early Renaissance in England—subsumed generally under the name Tudor. They admired Tudor craftsmanship; they admired what they perceived to be its honest expression of structures and materials; they admired the visual qualities of fieldstone and burnt brick and dark wood so variously combined by Tudor builders.

Revived Medieval Styles in Post-Victorian Building

Gothic

Gothic *per se* was rare in post-Victorian building. In high-style architecture some overtly Gothic elements appear—here a crenellated tower or an ogee arch, there a set of lancet windows or a castellated parapet—but invariably set within a context of Tudor and Elizabethan details, of half-timber patterns, tall twisted chimneys, diamond-mullioned casements, even the odd Renaissance pediment or quoin (figure 8.2).

Gothic was equally rare in mail-order building. There is an occasional survivor or descendant of an A. J. Davis or a Wheeler design from mid-century in a catalog—a pointed window, a medieval-looking window sill, a survival of that board-and-batten effect so characteristic of houses designed to project an image of Gothic verticality, beloved of Downing (figures 8.3, 8.4, 8.5). But in mail-order building the principal representative of medieval revival styles was a mixture of Tudor, Elizabethan, and Jacobean, which might well be called by the kind of ponderously cute name it so well deserves, Tudorbethean.

8.2 The home as picturesque image: front elevation of design 1070 in *MacLagan's Suburban Homes*, 1910. The picturesque elements are recognizable—diamond-mullioned windows, steep gable, crenellations. But all these elements are subjected to the discipline of Academic practice, whereby architects tried to put themselves in the shoes of a late medieval/early Renaissance builder and get it all "to the right period," not to invent something new (which the picturesque Gothic cottage essentially is).

8.3 An 1867 "House on a Farm" design by Gervase Wheeler. The four little pointed arches on each of the flanking chimneys is a unique note.

8.4 Design 117 in *Radford's Artistic Homes* of ca. 1907 featured vestigial Gothic Revival elements—mildly pointed gables (four of them), colored glass windows, and one entire diamond-shaped window (as if to make up for diamond-shaped mullions).

8.5 Design 7019-B in *Radford's Artistic Bungalows* of 1908 had as its principal design feature a vestigial survival of that board-and-batten effect so characteristic of Gothic Revival efforts to promote verticality.

Tudor

Academic architects claimed to make distinctions among three high styles that collectively spanned the Tudor period: Tudor proper, Elizabethan, and Jacobean. (Technically, Elizabethan is Tudor, because Elizabeth I was the daughter of Henry VIII; Jacobean is, properly, Stuart, since James I's patronymic was Stuart. The three reigns have been seen as a cultural unit.) The distinctive feature of Tudor proper was supposed to be a wall pattern resulting from half-timber construction (figure 8.6): darkened oak timbers whose interstices were filled with whitened nogging (rubble of various sorts, stuccoed, plastered, or whitewashed). Besides this decisive signal, Tudor could also be recognized by prominent, massive chimneys treated with varying degrees of decorative elaboration (channelled brick, twisted whorls, for example); prominent high-peaked roofs often deliberately given a sagging appearance by insertion of wedge-shaped blocks at the ends of roof trees; at least one story overhanging another; and windows composed of small panes separated by leaded mullions in diamond patterns (figure 8.7).

8.6 House designed in 1924 for Shaker Heights, Ohio, by architect Bloodgood Tuttle. Here the distinctive Tudor half-timber patterning is correctly based on structure. (Drawing by Patricia Forgac)

8.7 House designed in 1911 for the Oak Bay suburb of Victoria, British Columbia, by architect Samuel Maclure. Skillful cross-axial planning, imaginative combinations of elements, and subtle proportions belie the pejorative appellation of "stockbroker Tudor" sometimes given this style. (IMG:NAL)

Elizabethan was, according to one guide book, similar to Tudor except for having "less stone-work and a less fort-like appearance," whatever that might mean in practice (figure 8.8). Jacobean had many of the same features but was supposed to be distinguished by one peculiarity—a scalloped gable. Although Jacobean came late enough for some North American examples of the original to exist (Drax Hall in Barbados, Bacon's Castle in Virginia [figure 8.9]) and for the style to qualify as North American, relatively few examples exist in suburban houses. Jacobean gables, like the Dutch stepped gable, most commonly appeared on city row houses (figure 8.10).

8.9 The Arthur Allen house (Bacon's Castle) in Surrey County, Virginia, ca. 1655, showing the famous Jacobean gabled end. (IMG:NAL)

8.8 House on Austin Avenue in New Haven, Connecticut, in what could best be described as Elizabethan style, ca. 1925. (IMG:NAL)

8.10 Jacobean gables on row houses in the 2000 block of F Street N.W., Washington, D.C., ca. 1910. (IMG:NAL)

English Country ("Period")

In addition to these three, Academic architects also claimed to distinguish another generalized medieval revival style: the English Country House, or Cotswold Cottage style (the latter name popularized by Henry Ford's bringing a specimen from the Cotswolds to Greenfield Village, stone by stone, beam by beam, in 1915). It too partook of the general Tudor/Jacobean menu, but was to be identified especially by its roof, made of thatch (real or simulated) and designed with at least one steeply sloping eave (figure 8.11). Houses of this style have sometimes been designated "period houses." Originally that term had useful connotations; it referred to a characteristically Academic insistence on architects "getting into the shoes of a designer of the period," whether the period in question was medieval, Roman, or Rococo. But since in practice "period" has come to signify something vaguely medieval and little else, the tag now seems redundant.

8.11 Cotswold Cottage style suburban house in West Orange, New Jersey, ca. 1925. (IMG:NAL)

Medieval Revival Usages

Even on the Academic level these generalized medieval revival styles were often confused, despite all well-meaning efforts at separative definition. Of other levels it could be said that confusion was normal. Near-architects found Tudor half-timbered effects easily reproducible with reasonable accuracy. Henry Wilson's Tudor Bungalow of ca. 1910 is an example (figure 8.12), though there is something inherently incongruous about the idea of a Tudor bungalow itself. On the mail-order level, half-timbering tended to become simply a decorative device. Thus the Tudor patterns on Ward's Parkway of 1927 reproduce structural effects as far as they go; but they don't go to the ground (figure 8.13). By contrast, the pattern in design 559 in *Radford's Artistic Homes* of ca. 1908 certainly goes to the ground but corresponds to no structural reality (figure 8.14). With increasing frequency from the 1890–1930 years to the present, Tudor patterning became a business of black boards nailed on to white gables.

Other "Tudorbethean" elements were similarly conflated and confused on this level, reduced, often, to an odd hint or allusion—a bit of simulated thatch, a touch of half-timber, something resembling Cotswoldy chimney pots or sort-of-sweeping eaves, a sprinkling of near-overhangs, diamond mullions popping up once in a while, and the whole mixed up with "Colonial" gambrels and posts. "Jacobean" gables appear now and then, and in profusion when they do; one Radford design had no less than four on the same house (figure 8.15).

It is easy to make fun of such efforts. They recall Major-General Stanley's remorse, in the *Pirates of Penzance,* at sullying the "unstained escutcheons" of his ancestors. Frederick reminds him that he only bought the castle last year and its plaster is barely dry, which prompts the famous line, "I don't know whose ancestors they were, but I know whose ancestors they are." What needs to be kept in mind is that mail-order "Tudorbethean" had much the same social function as famous Academic mansions of the same period, like the Biltmore in Asheville—to satisfy that need for roots which is endemic to all peoples and all societies at all times, even one (or perhaps, especially one) as upwardly mobile as twentieth-century America.

8.12 A Tudor style bungalow, design 484 in Henry L. Wilson, *The Bungalow Book,* 1913.

8.13 Montgomery Ward's Parkway model, with gables and porch in Tudor style, 1927.

8.14 Design 559 in *Radford's Artistic Homes,* ca. 1908. Signed "C. W. Ashby, architect."

8.15 Design 8206 in *Radford's Cement Houses,* 1908. Four Jacobean gables, effects of Tudor half-timbering and board and batten, plus some Prairie school urns and low horizontal eaves.

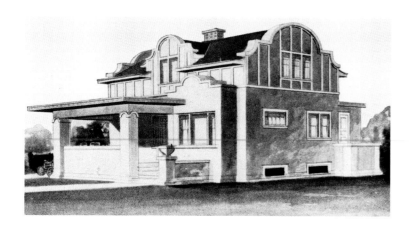

9

Picturesque Styles

The Original Picturesque Styles

In conventional architectural history, the years 1840–1885 were dominated by a succession of Picturesque styles. From approximately 1830, a trend toward ever-greater ornamentation set in, which by the end of the 1840s had so covered Classical Revival architecture with ornament and shapes drawn from Italian Renaissance and Italian rural vernacular building that it constituted a new style, the Italianate (figure 9.1). From around 1860, accumulation of yet more Italian plus French Renaissance ornament, especially French mansard roofs, turned Italianate into the French Second Empire style (see figures 5.22, 5.24). Still more heapings of ornamental detail from anywhere and everywhere, still more irregularities in plan and silhouette and shape, and French Second Empire became High-Victorian Picturesque, climaxing around 1870–1880. The Carson house at Eureka is archetypal (figure 2.1). Willful is the word for it. Legend maintains that Carson commissioned it to alleviate unemployment among woodworkers in the Eureka area and that he deliberately employed in it specimens of every native and imported wood he dealt in; that is, it was a monument to his total freedom to do what he wanted. Certainly it is a compendium of climactic picturesqueness: overall effects of complete asymmetry, an eye-catching mass of irregularities; an Italianate house, basically, attenuated to extreme verticality but with Second Empire towers capped by pseudo-mansards and cones; Gothic-like pinnacles; doors and windows framed by bulging and bending pilasters, and columns drawn vaguely from Renaissance, classical, and medieval sources; verandah,

9.1 Core of the Italianate house was usually a gussied-up version of the Georgian mansion, with more vertical emphasis in window proportions and a ground plan more nearly approaching a square. The essential Picturesque distinction is profusion of functionally useless ornament; that is, decoration for which no practical, ideational, or symbolic need is apparent: eaves with prominently scrolled and cut brackets that do not actually support anything (the brackets could in fact be ordered precut and added after the house was erected); a tower with tiny cupola or belvedere never used for living or working; chimneys with prominent horizontal ledges; wraparound verandahs; double and triple round-headed windows.

chimneys, balconies, turrets, gables all shaped for eye-catching effect; walls alternately swathed in shingles or sheathed in painted wood and tiles; doors artfully disguised, so there seems no orienting axis to interrupt the mass irregularity . . . and so on.

Thereafter a reaction set in, manifested first in the Queen Anne and Richardsonian Romanesque styles that flourished from the 1870s through the 1890s. So strong was the appeal of Picturesque, however, that even these attempts to reform it look lavish to our eyes (figures 9.2, 9.3).

9.2 Design by Frank Freeman for a house in Richardsonian Romanesque style, built in 1889 on Riverside Drive at 108th Street in New York City. (From *A History of Real Estate, Building, and Architecture in New York City,* 1898)

9.3 George F. Barber's design 37 in Queen Anne style from his 1890 catalog, built in 1892 in Drain, Oregon. Such elaborate prefabrications could require as many as 300 crates to ship. Comparison with figure 9.2 shows the basic compatibility of the two styles. Both are unified around a square core with pyramidal roof (an ancestor of the foursquare); both emphasize wide arches, fenestration in ranges, turrets, gables, and solid chimney blocks. Above all, both have consistent unified effects, the one of massiveness, the other of lightness, appropriate to their materials.

Appeal of the Picturesque and Reactions Against It

The original appeal of Picturesque styles was that romantic idealization of the past, soothing to a century of rapid change and futuristic leaps, which had fueled the earlier Classical and Gothic Revivals. But their overwhelming appeal from mid-century on was due to the stunning visual metaphors of great wealth and sudden success that they could create. How Picturesque styles so worked in and for society is easier to understand now than at any time in the past fifty years. For they are composed of a series of what Post-Modernists call "quotations" from the past.

Picturesque styles have no direct literary references, as Greek or Roman or Gothic Revivals had. They evoke no particular associations, in the way that even Italianate or French Second Empire did—with "romantic Italy," with "French culture," or whatever. They have the same kind of function as ornaments on a stage set, to evoke a mood. That mood is "confidence"—and it is a staged, rather than genuine, confidence. Whereas the Roman Revival temple-house proclaimed, "here lives a virtuous citizen of the reincarnated Roman republic," the High-Victorian Picturesque house proclaimed: "here lives a wealthy and successful citizen." Its ornament announced what the Republic could offer its citizens: freedom via accumulated capital. Not the truth, but a big bankroll, shall make you free. And being free you can build whatever you like. Of course you can also dispense with any restrictions on zoning, and so forth.

A reaction against this kind of irredentist individualism set in simultaneously with the climax of the High-Victorian Picturesque. It took three distinct, though often interrelated, forms: modifying eclecticism in the direction of greater uniformity and ultimately academic correctness as to source; emphasis on fundamentals of architecture, such as structure and materials; abolishing ornament altogether as unscientific and counter to the spirit of the age.

Richardsonian Romanesque and Queen Anne

Richardsonian Romanesque and Queen Anne both began in the late 1860s as attempts to modify the extremes of picturesqueness by moving away from indiscriminate mixing of stylistic detail toward blends of styles perceived as historically compatible (figures 9.2, 9.3). To a modern eye both styles still seem loaded with ornament, but the principal difference between them is that in North America Richardsonian Romanesque featured massive stonework while Queen Anne was lighter and predominantly of wood (although brick was originally the favored material, and many brick Queen Annes do exist). Contemporaries had difficulties with their definition, too. T. D. G. of Carson, Iowa, wrote to the editors of *Carpentry and Building* in 1880:

Would you be kind enough to illustrate through the column of your journal the characteristics of the "Queen Anne," "Elizabethan" and "Eastlake" styles of architecture. Volume I of your journal treats the subject briefly, but I cannot distinguish the different styles from what I find there.

"It is quite impossible," the editor replies, "to say nowadays where one style begins and another ends."

At present they are rather names than styles, and architects use them without any very clear idea of their meaning, in a great many cases. Any attempt at classification would, we fear, be misleading. . . . At present our architects are so much in the habit of calling an eccentric design by any name that is likely to please the owner, that until something like a style has been developed out of all this confusion, it will be difficult to discuss intelligently the meaning of the various names in common use.[1]

That sounds familiar. Sometimes shorter answers were given. To a query by a *Carpentry and Building* reader of 1886—"Would a house with two gables be in the Queen Anne style, or to entitle it to this name must it have twenty gables or more? What is necessary to entitle a building to the name of Queen Anne?"—the editors replied, "We give up."[2] (Shortly thereafter *Carpentry and Building* gave up also.)

It was precisely to the awareness of architectural chaos as revealed by such correspondence that Richardsonian Romanesque and Queen Anne owed their appeal. What Montgomery Schuyler, best known in architectural history as H. H. Richardson's great champion, said about Queen Anne could just as well apply to Richardsonian Romanesque:

"Queen Anne" is a comprehensive name which has been made to cover a multitude of incongruities, including, indeed, the bulk of recent work which otherwise defies classification, and there is a convenient vagueness about the term which fits it for that use. But it is rather noteworthy that the effect of what is most specifically known as Queen Anne is to restrain the exuberances of design.[3]

Indeed the appeal of Queen Anne to educated architects rested in large measure on the claim by its English creator, R. Norman Shaw, to have restricted his ornamental elements to features from English architecture of the time of Queen Anne—Palladian windows, bulls-eye windows, quoins, shingles from "vernacular colonial" architecture—just as Richardson's contemporary reputation rested in large measure on confining *his* designs to compatible medieval features. There was in both styles an awareness of unified design that was lacking before. Highly textured areas were balanced against relatively smooth surfaces. This quality might not be immediately apparent to us, but critics at the time, accustomed to extravaganzas like the Carson house, were so struck by it as to talk of the beginning of a new American architecture. So W. P. P. Longfellow, summarizing and predicting "The Course of American Architecture" in *The New Princeton Review* in 1887, perceived the new architecture of his time as "an art of *ensemble,* of broad effects, wherein by far the most important consideration is the relation of the different factors of the design to the whole, and the unity of expression which they produce" (2:2, p. 208).

Progressive Styles: Prairie and Craftsman

The second reaction to excessively individualistic picturesqueness saw its antidote in a return to architectural primacies: structure and materials. Express these basics fully and honestly, and ornament will fall into its natural place, adorning but not dictating. Ultimately this impulse, like the urge toward restraint and correctness, was academic too: its rules of art were to be drawn from art itself. But full realization of that academic consequence lay in the far future. For the moment, the impulse was moral. It was no accident that spokesmen for this movement, like Gustav Stickley and Frank Lloyd Wright, were younger contemporaries of Woodrow Wilson, sharing a distinctively pre-1920s brand of high idealism; styles like Arts and Crafts and Prairie were, if you please, what Woodrow Wilson might have done had he gone into shaping home environments rather than the world. Elsewhere we noted a curious resemblance between a Currier and Ives print of Washington's birthplace and Gustav Stickley's Craftsman Farms buildings in Parsippany outside Morris Plains, New Jersey (see figures 6.13, 6.14). The influence, if any, was more likely to be moral and formal—an association with Washingtonian virtue, rather than the particular forms of that homestead, were what Stickley would have hoped to reproduce. Wright too believed that architecture had some ability to inculcate virtue; his Fellows and apprenticeship system had more than a little inspiration in common with Stickley's apprenticeship school at Craftsman Farms. So too the Prairie style could well be described as a more sophisticated and elitist version of Stickley's Craftsman. It put comparable emphasis on honest expression of structure and materials, but was far more stylistically self-conscious: conspicuously horizontal, with low spreading eaves and window strips and low walls; flattened parapets and flower urns; and many erudite touches of Japanese, Art Nouveau, Art Deco, Pre-Columbian ornament.

Modernismus

Third of the reactions to High-Victorian Picturesque was, of course, Modernism. Modernists were not interested in modifying the Picturesque; they wanted to abolish it. And they went about that task with all the moral fervor of their generation. Something like the Carson house was not just bad design, it was wicked, depraved. And so, of course, was the social and economic system that produced such a monstrosity. So the International Style, first of the Modern styles, proclaimed its purity of intent and form by mirror images of High-Victorian Picturesque. The opposite of an image of wickedness must be an image of salvation. So, instead of masses of applied ornament, none! Instead of bristling verticality, sleek horizontals! Instead of a massy pile, a light assemblage of surface bandings borne on stilts! Instead of jumbling curves and ovoids to delight the eye, cruelly impersonal straight lines (figure 9.4). And so on through all the successive Modernist substyles; lurking behind each new image of light was the darkness of Picturesque eclecticism and high capitalism.

What was the effect of all this on near-architecture and mail-order design?

Picturesque Styles in the Comfortable House

It is natural to suppose that in the 1890–1930 years mail-order near-architects were clinging doggedly to Picturesque styles, pleasing a philistine clientele unable to appreciate the new Academic, Arts and Crafts, and Modern architecture. When Modernists took over the cultural establishment after World War II, popular/commercial arts refused to accept their doctrines, even though every school and tastemaking medium in the country disseminated them. Colonial and Tudor and even Gothic Revival stubbornly refused to obey Modernist predictions and injunctions to disappear forthwith and forever. But nothing of that sort happened in the 1890–1930 years. True, there were Picturesque survivals.

9.4 Only a few blocks from the Carson house in Eureka stands the Parkside Manor Apartment, built ca. 1937 in what David Gebhard called "moderne" style. Not quite Modern—it has an urn-like window box that could be called ornamental—it is still a stark, in every sense of the word, and stern riposte to Carson's frivolous capitalist extravaganza. (IMG:NAL)

A taste for bracketing was apparent on all levels (figure 9.5), and there were even reminiscences—and more than reminiscences—of Italianate cube houses (see figure 4.17) in Aladdin's Standard or Virginia models from the 1919 catalog (figure 9.6). The copy emphasizes precisely the feature that caused Italianate in its own time to be called "bracketed style":

Notice the architectural detail under the eaves, porch and dormer. . . . The scrolled brackets which are especially machined for the Standard add a finished touch to the sweeping eaves. Possibly you have noticed that this has been carried out on all eaves—dormer and porch included. . . . Hip roof, heavy boxing and scrolled brackets, tapering porch columns and full-length spindles all form a delightful contrast to the ordinary.

Mansard roofs can also be found and presumably, therefore, a surviving taste for French Second Empire stylings (figure 9.7).

There are occasional examples of Richardsonian Romanesque, as, for example, a row of houses by the old New York Central tracks in Amsterdam, New York, built of cinder block to resemble stony effects and incorporating a small turret and verandahs, and bay and quasi-Palladian windows (figure 9.8).

Queen Anne, of course, throve on into the 1910s (figure 9.9). As late as 1895 the August issue of *Art Interchange*, one of the early popular, as distinct from scholarly, architectural periodicals, carried an article on cottages by Hobart A. Walker which declared:

When a person is at a loss for a suitable name by which to convey an idea of the beauty and charm of his home, it is "Queen Anne." Of course, when there is "love in a cottage," that cottage can be none other than "Queen Anne." When the ubiquitous speculating builder wishes to lure an intended victim he baits his hook with "beautiful Queen Anne cottage. All modern improvements" (p. 50).

After 1900 Queen Anne began succumbing to the drift toward stylistic unification and correctness and toward reformed—that is, less and less—ornament.

9.5 Workingman's temple-house with Italianate brackets, from Bennett Better-Built Ready-Cut Homes catalog, 1925.

9.6 Aladdin Standard model, from 1919 catalog, was a foursquare in Italianate style.

9.7 Design for a house with French Second Empire mansard roof, offered by architects Clark and Walcott, in *The Books of a Thousand Homes*, 1923.

9.8 Two of five houses in modified Richardsonian Romanesque style built in Amsterdam, New York, beside the New York Central tracks. (IMG:NAL)

9.9 "The brick house at 253 West Idaho Street," described in Don Hibbard's *Architecture in Weiser Idaho* as "a stellar example of the Queen Anne style in Weiser . . . designed by Tourtellotte & Company for Herman Haas in 1900. . . . Such details as the porch's turned balustrade, the delightful Palladian window in the front gable, and the turret's beautifully garlanded frieze justify the *Weiser Signal's* labelling this building 'one of the architectural triumphs of Idaho.' "

In addition to these "regular" Picturesque styles, there are numerous mail-order and near-architect designs that could be called Picturesque Eclectic Survival. It is not just that their stylistic quotations and shapes are confused somewhat—otherwise you could call a majority of mail-order designs before the 1920s Picturesque Eclectic Survival. It is that no one stylistic reference is consistent or dominant. Three broad categories are discernible: designs in which diverse forms are mixed up for Picturesque effect (figures 9.10, 9.11, 9.12); designs whose formal style is quite recognizable—bungalow, suburban cottage, foursquare—but whose ornamental detail is all mixed up (figures 9.13, 9.14, 9.15); and, finally, designs in which both forms and ornamental detail are mixed up for Picturesque effect (figures 9.16, 9.17, 9.18).

But by the 1920s such vestigial ornament had become comparatively rare. Not only was Academic restraint on ornament manifest, whereby even mail-order designs were usually limited to a single stylistic format, but mail-order designs also commonly featured versions of "progressive" styles like Craftsman and Prairie.

9.10 *Radford's Artistic Homes* design 544 is given Picturesque character by a mixture of eaves—straight, gambrel, arched, hood, pent—in a variety of horizontal and diagonal slants.

9.11 A variety of eave forms makes this bungalow in Lavale, Maryland, of ca. 1923, Picturesque. (IMG:NAL)

9.12 Montgomery Ward's Sheridan model (1927 catalog) offers a Picturesque array of gables, chimneys, and uprights.

9.13 The Benjamin Shambaugh house, 219 North Clinton Street, Iowa City, designed in 1898 and finished in 1901. There is no doubt about what style of homestead this is: an early foursquare. It is the style of ornament that is doubtful: Classical columns, Colonial balustrade, Shingle walls, Italianate brackets are all here, plus Rococo shellwork and pointed arches in the hip-roof dormer. Such a mixture could only be called Picturesque Eclectic Survival. (Photo courtesy State Historical Society of Iowa)

9.14 Close-up of front dormer of Shambaugh house, Iowa City. (Photo by Janelle Luppen, University of Iowa Foundation)

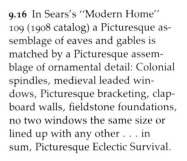

9.16 In Sears's "Modern Home" 109 (1908 catalog) a Picturesque assemblage of eaves and gables is matched by a Picturesque assemblage of ornamental detail: Colonial spindles, medieval leaded windows, Picturesque bracketing, clapboard walls, fieldstone foundations, no two windows the same size or lined up with any other . . . in sum, Picturesque Eclectic Survival.

9.15 What puts Radford's cottage design 5089 into a Picturesque Eclectic Survival category is its extraordinary mixture of ornamental elements drawn from a wide variety of past styles: Palladian window and Tudor half-timbering, Colonial pilasters with board-and-batten effects, two different kinds of bay windows, and so on.

9.17 Concrete house on the main street of Norwood, Ontario, ca. 1920. What a demonstration of independence to build such a thing in such a conservative place as a small town in Ontario! Spanish Colonial may have been the stylistic intent (tiled hoods over the windows, for example) with a touch of Pueblo (projecting beam ends on porch), but both forms and ornament are so mixed and nondescript as to be categorizable only as Picturesque Eclectic Survival. (IMG:NAL)

9.18 Somewhere behind this house from the 1920s in Washington, Georgia, lurks a foursquare, but it is well concealed beneath a Picturesque Eclectic Survival jumble of diverse shapes and ornamental forms—Craftsman-like beam ends, Federal-like fanlights, round Italianate arches, and what appear to be stunted Jacobean gables. (IMG:NAL)

9.19 Craftsman interior, designed by Gustav Stickley.

The popularity of Craftsman is not surprising; it was, after all, intended to be a style for the masses. Stickley, a self-taught designer and writer, disseminated through his *Craftsman* magazine, published between 1901 and 1916, his passionate beliefs that an honest home made honest people, that an honest home let its materials and structure be frankly and freely expressed, that the most honest home of all was one built by its occupant. He therefore provided plans and specifications not only for houses but also for furniture to be assembled by the homeowner as well, since character is formed along with art. Stickley's influence went far beyond immediate use of his magazine; *Craftsman* designs were probably pirated more than any others.[4]

Pure Craftsman style was a bit stark for contemporary taste (figure 9.19); as John Freeman once observed, it "fairly bristled with maleness."[5] Therefore in mail-order building it was nearly always mixed with other styles; but it was common, even through the 1920s, long after both firm and magazine had gone bankrupt (1917). Craftsman elements were very distinctive. Many of them were picturesque in visual effect but consistent with

9.20 Small bungalow in Craftsman style, Victoria, British Columbia. (IMG:NAL)

"honest" expression of materials and structure (figure 9.20). Obliquely-cut rafters that project ostentatiously are characteristically Craftsman; so are wooden elements like curved roofs or exotic piled capitals, which derive from or were thought to derive from Japanese traditional architecture. Pergolas are very characteristic; one might almost say, wherever you see a pergola, a Craftsman style house cannot be far away. Often those pergolas have the short, canted columns that are another signal of Craftsman. Textural and ornamental use of stonework is often associated with Craftsman, in variegated colors and shapes rather than the regular rough-hewn sandstone associated with Richardsonian Romanesque. Clinker brick is likewise characteristically Craftsman, as is stucco, often enough mixed with rough sand or bits of glass to emphasize texture. There was a distinctive Craftsman sort of fireplace, the metaphorical hearth of the home.

All these features, needless to say, can be found in a refined and elitist form in Frank Lloyd Wright's architecture, and in Prairie school generally. Indeed, much of it

is Prairie. Not least of the surprises in studying the Comfortable House is how many specimens of Prairie there are on the popular level. In any town you care to examine, you can find the low, spreading eaves, low walls functioning as property barriers, windows arranged in strips of two to four or more, and semi-geometric ornament that mark Prairie (figures 9.21, 9.22, 9.23, 9.24); and they came out of mail-order building catalogs or were the work of local contractors.

Legend has it, of course, that the great Prairie style was destroyed by soulless Philistines, Babbitts, Mencken's Booboisie. Study of popular/commercial building suggests that the legend needs revision. The reason that Wright's kind of Prairie house did not flourish on more than an upper-middle-class level was that he did not really design suburban houses. He designed for ample country acres and affluence. When given carte-blanche, as at the Coonley house, Wright produced not so much a Prairie house as a Prairie villa of a nineteenth-century sort, complete with rural accessories like stables and chicken coops and cow sheds and paddocks, not to

9.21 The Chicago House Wrecking Company's design 154C in its 1908 *Book of Plans* is a foursquare with Prairie features.

9.22 The Spokane model in Aladdin's 1919 catalog was a Prairie style foursquare.

The Spokane

See prices on inside of front cover.

THERE'S something about the Spokane, one of ALADDIN'S newest designs that seems to radiate warmth and coziness the minute you look at it. Whether it is the simplicity of design, the broad and spacious front piazza, the half siding, half stucco walls, the broad, sloping square roof—something seems assuring of the sunshine and gladness that must reign in this home.

A wide archway opens into the big living room and as you pass through this a huge fireplace, symbolical of beauty and comfort meets your eyes. With three windows in front, a big one flanked by two small ones, and two on the side, the living room has an abundance of light.

Through swinging French doors you pass on into the dining room and here again the designer has provided for plenty of light and sunshine as a glance at the floor plans will show. On your way to the kitchen you pass through a good sized pantry.

Good sized kitchen, well lighted, the "home workshop" of the Spokane will please the scrutinizing housewife. A rear porch of ample size is directly off the kitchen.

The floor plan of the second story is the equal of the first floor as a study of it will reveal.

Now turn to pages 12 and 13 and read the specifications. For price refer to the inside of front cover and the terms can be seen on page 2.

9.23 Big bungalow with some Craftsman and Prairie features, in Grass Valley, California. (IMG:NAL)

9.24 *Radford's Bungalows* design 5039 has consistent Prairie style features. Compared to Wright and his school, its relative proportions are ineffective, but as a suburban house it would work better because it is designed to fit on to a narrow lot, with pergola parallel to the deep lot axis.

mention an extensive wooded park with gardner's cottage and walled gardens, something far closer to Downing's Hudson Valley estates than to any Chicago suburb. What, in fact, does his preliminary design recall (figure 9.25)? A kind of High-Victorian villa laid on its side, all bristling and bustling with protrusions and recessions, nooks and crannies, rooflines variegated and walls colorfully tiled, plants and shrubs trailing all around o'er creeping arcades and spreading verandahs. Wright felt that the Coonley house was "the most successful of my houses from my standpoint"; but as Norris Smith noted:

Whether or not the house proved satisfactory to the Coonleys we do not know; but then perhaps it was not built for them at all. It was a splendid image, created by its architect to declare his intuitive understanding of what it means for a free man [Coonley had a considerable private income in years when the income tax as yet took no bite] to possess a social space in a spacious and beneficent world.

Isn't that very much the image the Newsomes create for William Carson in Eureka? (I'm not talking about aesthetic quality, but social function, of course.)

9.25 Wright's preliminary design for the Coonley house, Riverside Illinois, ca. 1908. (From N. K. Smith, *Frank Lloyd Wright*, Englewood Cliffs, 1969)

Did Wright then deserve that jeer about "the greatest architect of the nineteenth century"? Not at all. He was modifying and disciplining in a very modern way the kind of High-Picturesque chaos represented by Carson's house, not reproducing it; it is just that he was not as ideologically opposed to the American system as the European Moderns were. He had no particular aversion to people getting rich; indeed, he had an instinctive affinity for wealth and culture as against poverty of spirit. It is therefore true to say that American suburbs were not necessarily philistine havens just because they weren't lined with Wrightian mansions. Wright's mansions just didn't belong there, and his laments about being able to rebuild America if just given a chance were essentially posturings; he did not, in fact, build for the "mobocracy." He let ready-cut and mail-order builders do that; and they displayed a remarkably high level of taste for their time and place (figure 9.26).

Those Picturesque styles found in mail-order design represented not defiance of reigning taste, only cultural lag; what happened in high architecture was reflected and repeated in mail-order building five, ten, twenty years later (depending on place). Mail-order designs were of course simpler, cheaper, and less erudite, but they did follow high-style leads. There were the same impulses to coordinate and harmonize and restrain, the same tendency to greater historical correctness, on a smaller, cheaper scale and later in time.

What this means, very simply, is that in the post-Victorian period North American culture was still whole. There was not the gulf between fine arts and popular arts that broke open when Modernism took over. Mail-order and Academic and organic architects all occupied the same world, spoke the same language, had an accepted set of common values. It is or should be axiomatic that we study the past in order to learn from it; here is something to be learned from a study of the Comfortable House, 1890–1930.

9.26 Design 8215 in *Radford's Artistic Homes* of ca. 1910 lacks Wright's characteristic proportional touch and feel for materials, but otherwise seems quite similar—until you look at the plan and realize that this, too, is definitely designed for a narrow suburban lot and not, as the elevation suggests, for some spaciously elegant or rural setting.

Design No. 8215

Size: Width, 25 feet; Length, 48 feet 6 inches

Blue prints consist of basement plan; roof plan; first and second floor plans; front, rear, two side elevations; wall sections and all necessary interior details. Specifications consist of about twenty pages of typewritten matter.

PRICE

of Blue Prints, together with a complete set of typewritten specifications

ONLY FIFTEEN DOLLARS

We mail Plans and Specifications the same day order is received.

First Floor Plan

Second Floor Plan

10

The Unified Cultural
Matrix of Architects,
Near-Architects, and
Non-Architects in
Post-Victorian America

Common Stylistic Principles

Styles of popular mail-order building cannot be analyzed without reference to high-style architecture. No matter how much spitting and sniping went on between architects and builders, they worked from common principles. The styles of popular building derived from high-style precedent via professional and popular magazines; the latter especially multiplied fantastically in this period. Such borrowings could not happen, of course, unless there was the kind of fundamental agreement about basics that had united high and low building in common endeavor for centuries past. And it did exist.

It is typical of the post-Victorian age that public and domestic building were closely interrelated; that the Van Sweringens should simultaneously develop suburban Shaker Heights and downtown Cleveland; that the philosopher George Santayana should devise a theory whereby the "American Will" inhabited the skyscraper, but "the American intellect inhabits the colonial mansions." A common set of principles informed both and, to a surprising degree, on all levels:

1. retention of ornament, which distinguishes them both from Modern styles;

2. a generous scale, which distinguishes them both from Romantic styles, which are almost always on a much smaller scale;

3. decorative restraint and a tendency to use only one eclectic style per building, which distinguishes them both from Picturesque styles;

4. "associationism" of a vague and general sort, despite learnedly accurate eclectic detail.

Obviously these qualities are not found to the same degree in popular/commercial mail-order building during the period, not because they were deliberately rejected, but for reasons of economy and cultural lag. Otherwise there is no disagreement or divergence.

Mail-order architecture did not retain quite as much ornament as Academic Colonial or Gothic or Tudor. Economy was the obvious reason. Where economy was not a factor, as in the expression of the nature of hand-crafted materials (stucco, for example) as a kind of ornament, mail-order builders were no different from professional architects. Such supererogatory—non-physically functional—ornament is antithetical to the fundamental principles of Modernism, be it said. On this issue professionals and mail-order builders were on the same side. (One absolutely could not imagine Le Corbusier or Gropius admiring, much less designing, anything like the Montgomery Ward warehouse in Chicago, with concrete cast into typical Prairie ornamental patterns; but one could imagine Radford doing something like it!)

They agreed about scale, too. Both architect-designed and mail-order buildings had a generous scale that distinguished them from the much smaller scales of preceding revival styles. Great windows, often glazed by single panes of those dimensions made possible by new technology, were common in houses of all sorts. Ceilings of mansions and suburban tract houses alike were higher than their preceding counterparts. Fireplaces were bigger. Verandahs were equally high ceilinged, with substantial columns, solid-looking pillars. Heavy plate rails, massive coffered doors—these were found not only in the mansions of the rich, but also, in appropriately cheaper versions, in the mail-order homes of the poor. Generous scale is characteristic of this age regardless of the absolute size of the buildings; the relative scale of bungalows could be as generous as major monuments.

Decorative restraint and the tendency to restrict eclecticism to one style per building were more pronounced among professional architects than among speculative builders. But that is simply because designers of popular/commercial architecture, and (more importantly) their clients, were closer to Picturesque taste than the architectural academies were. Again, it is relative. A mail-order Colonial design of the 1920s differs as much in simplicity and restraint from a Queen Anne as Academic Georgian of the 1920s does from Richardsonian Romanesque.

For vague associationism, there is little to choose between high and popular/commercial styles at any level. The old kind of symbolism, the old concept of architecture as visual metaphor, was fading fast from all minds. "Roots," "home," "security," "the Good and Virtuous Life," these kinds of concepts appear in writings about mansions in Newport as well as mail-order houses in Newton. Whereas in the early Republic the "American" connotations of Classical architecture were precise and specific—Roman republican virtue, Greek democratic liberty, and so on—post-Victorians understood the "American" implications of Imperial Roman railroad stations or Louis XVI mansions in a far more general way, as manifestations of the wealth, power, and cultural achievements possible under the American system of government. Post-Victorians of all kinds could see Americanism embodied impartially in such diverse forms as rough, rambling, shingled Cape Cod cottages; the plain brick walls and chaste rows of dormers on Georgian college dormitories; or grandiose Roman porticos and marble walls because fifty years of intervening scholarship enabled them to see each of these styles in the perspective of given times and conditions in American history, to understand them as general manifestations of the American past rather than specific statements about the American character.

As for academic correctness of detail, obviously that is what people went to architectural schools to learn, and mail-order designers had not learned it as precisely as professional architects, though in fact there is a surprising amount of accurate detailing at all levels.

Liberal Pluralism

In *My Life in Architecture* Ralph Adams Cram declared:

Gothic is no isolated style with its own individual laws wrought out of nothing for its own original ends. The *forms* of beauty vary from age to age; the creative and controlling laws are ever the same, and it is because they were recognized and obeyed in Trinity [Boston, by Richardson] in the McKim Library [Boston Public] and in St. Augustine [Ponce de Leon Hotel by Carrère and Hastings] that they are all good.[1]

Cram, it may be reasonably postulated, did not have the Aladdin Company's designers in mind when he wrote this, or Sears's, or the Keith Architectural Company of Minneapolis; but the same point would apply to their work as well. If people like Cram could have brought themselves to realize how such views could be extended, they might have introduced the principle of variability into artistic judgments—what is good art for one class or one sort of individual is not necessarily good art for another; nor indeed is there any reason why the same person need apply identical standards of excellence in art at all times and places.

Then we might have been in a better position to avoid and evade Modernism's rigid orthodoxies—but that is pure speculation, one of the great might-have-beens of the post-Victorian era. Even as it was, the total body of building in this age was a great cultural expression of liberal democratic capitalism, of a society on the surface pluralistic but at core a solid body of common conviction and agreement about fundamentals.

Those suburbs full of bungalows and foursquares, Dutch Colonials and Georgians and Prairies—surely they were the very image of "every person born alive is either a little Liberal or a little Conservative." Seen casually or superficially, such suburbs displayed the wildest variety—magnificent homes for the rich, prefabricated bungalows for the poor; some professing to revive Classical Revivals and something of the gentilities of the early Republic, others reviving colonial frontier simplicities or colonial aristocratic pretensions, still others naturally expressing materials in ways dimly or directly recalling the doctrines of Morris or Walt Whitman. In some mansions lived professed believers in Darwinian and Spencerian survival of the fittest through economic competition, in others fervent pacifists or populists or democratic egalitarians. Chaotic, strife-ridden? Only to outward appearances. All these people, like all the substyles of their houses, held in common a core of consensual principles. Just as Craftsman architects might switch to Classical Revival styles, or the same designer might do Mediterranean one week and elitist Arts and Crafts the next with no real inconsistency, so in the politics of this age, one side may gain an ascendancy and make some laws to promote its interests for a few years, then the other takes over and promotes *its* interests for a while; but both have common goals in view. Just so in architecture; they commonly agreed upon the need for good taste and generous proportioning and restrained correctness, however much they differed about details. Like baseball—that truly democratic game, depending on skill and brains instead of physical accidents of height or weight—this society was governed by the accepted notion that sooner or later the other side would get another chance to bat, another inning to see what they could do; and its architecture expressed this kind of culture precisely. "During the twenties," wrote Jonathan Lane,

despite the fact that many architects were relying upon methods of planning in use before 1900 while others were employing new ideas of great importance for the future, there was no apparent division of the profession into conservatives and progressives.[2]

He then quotes an architect from the 1927 *Architectural Record:*

I wish people would accept the present method of construction for what it is, and be satisfied to call the result "modern." A modern style has as much right to exist as a Renaissance or Colonial. It does not necessarily mean anything cubistic or impressionistic. Like all other styles, it takes sound traditions wherever they can be found and adapts them to present day conditions.

Those were the days, my friend. Soon enough a new category, and a new attitude, will appear, expressing the convictions of people who want to play by a different set of rules; who intend, if and when they get an inning, to begin tearing the ball park down, metaphorically speaking. Practically speaking they mean, if they can, to ensure that all eclectic styles will be dumped into the "dustbin of history"; they intend to work in a new spirit for a new age, saying, with St. John at the Apocalypse, "Behold! I make all things new." Their efforts constitute a different stylistic category altogether.

Of course the 1890–1930 kind of liberal attitude was contingent on an assumption that there was prosperity enough to go around, an assumption that, by and large, seemed justified in those decades. The country's material resources still seemed to be nearly endless; who today could venture to advertise "we'll pay $1 for every knot you can find" in the lumber for a precut middle-class house! The Comfortable House's generous proportions reflected cheap heating fuel. Its spacious porches suggested an easy-going life-style and a notion that family life ought to be fun, which in many cases it was, especially for the middle classes in the 1920s. It must have been fun to be a "sheik" with slicked and shiny hair, and roadster polished to match; fun to be a "flapper" with hair bobbed short and skirts hiked even shorter; fun to dance the Charleston and the "Black Bottom," to play jazz and talk slang. And in this age there was no middle-class drug problem to speak of, little crime in the middle-class suburbs. And those suburbs were usually what sheiks and flappers alike had in long-range view: the very conventional goal of any ivy covered cottage— just Molly and me, and baby makes three, we're happy in My Blue Heaven.

Middle-Class Confidence

That what the Comfortable House expressed was obviously a middle- and upper-middle class culture did not bother people in post-Victorian times as much as it does us. In those days America was supposed to be a middle-class country. Nobody bothered much about "the others." Insofar as they were thought of, it was as a people who were trying to become middle- and upper-middle-class Americans as fast as possible—which, by and large, they were. Not only the body of post-Victorian building, but also post-Victorian architects and builders manifest this middle-class character.

Some architects were very rich; some were poor. But in any case to be an architect was to have a status in the community comparable to a doctor, or a lawyer, or a minister—in which professions there also were rich and *arriviste,* poor and dedicated. Architecture was a middle-class profession then, in contrast to the status which Modernists promoted for it, of artist-bohemian, in a class with painters and poets, patronized by radical-chic rich liberals. Obviously mail-order builders were middle-class men too, sturdy businessmen out to serve mankind and make a buck at the same time (not, by the way, always incongruous aspirations). When the Architects' Small House Service Bureau wanted to elevate taste, they promoted their service by appealing to increasing real-estate values—exactly like the Van Sweringens or Aladdin or Sears.

Controlled Technology

Architects and builders shared some more general attitudes as well. Toward technology, for instance. Both perceived, used, and understood technology in ways fundamentally different from European Modernists. Modernists glorified technology. They thought of it as the "spirit of their times," an imperious *Zeitgeist* that *must*—though exactly who or what authority issued this imperious edict, they never tried to explain—be obeyed.

In an age of steam and steel, of machines and oil, the Modernists said, humans should not live in structures made of saws and axes, but in the kind of structures the *Zeitgeist* demanded: railroad stations and factory interiors, not colonial cottages or Gothic castles. That Philip Johnson did not live in his Glass House but in a comfortable eighteenth-century farmhouse up the hill, that Giedion refused to move into his International style piloti'd and strip-windowed house at number 9 Donderthal in Zürich but continued in stolid bourgeois comfort in Biedermier style number 7, that Le Corbusier lived at 35, rue de Sèvres and . . . well, it's all immaterial anyway. The point is, post-Victorian American architects and mail-order builders alike had a quite different attitude to technology. They designed as if it were intended to be their servant, not their master. They used it to incorporate labor-saving devices and cost-saving economies into the Comfortable House—whether that house was a mansion on the hill or a homestead temple-house by the tracks. The kind of house that did flaunt technology—like William Carson's house in Eureka, with its arrant display of what woodcutting machines could do—they thought of as unspeakably vulgar.

The Social Function of a House

Above all, they agreed on what the social function of a house should be. Not a display case for great wealth, as their predecessors would have it. Not a Machine for Scientific Living, as their Modernist followers insisted. But a Comfortable House, an instrument for promoting stability in society at large and the good life for individuals in families; an instrument for meeting and satisfying the immemorial human longing for privacy and space to grow and develop. And, of course, to rise in society. That meant, among other things, to display Culture; whence a major social function of the historic styles, whether in the academically correct mansions of the wealthy or the scraps and tags of historic styles on economy-line mail-order models.

The Comfortable House's social function operated on all levels. It served middle-class homeowners who had risen from the ranks of laborers and who had finished high school where their parents only just managed the lower grades, just as well as it served the Harvard man whose father, like Bernard Berenson's, trundled a push-cart around Boston streets. For the extreme social mobility characteristic of America in the 1820s through the 1870s was now more an exception than the rule. Typical figures of this age were not the rags-to-vast-riches climbers, nor homesteaders on the Great Plains or in Oregon (Oklahoma was the last great frontier), but those middle-class urban dwellers whose lives were chronicled in the comic strips (Maggie and Jiggs, Toots and Casper, Blondie and Dagwood, and the clan in Gasoline Alley). These were people who had risen from lower- or working-class origins not to great wealth but to modest stability and respectability; and stability and respectability were the qualities they wanted to express in the discipline and restraint of Academic principles in every area of building. So the catalog-built suburban houses shared the same social function as Vizcaya, Longwood, or Biltmore—all in their way were instruments for promoting a more disciplined social order (or a society with more disciplined awareness of culture), all served as expressions of a stable conservative period in American culture.

Streets of suburban houses from the 1890s, the 1910s, 1920s, or 1930s are obvious expressions of a change in public mood which made the unrestrained individuality of the preceding decades—so well expressed and promoted by Picturesque styles—no longer generally acceptable. Just as income tax laws could now be put on the books where earlier attempts had failed (because back in the 1870s or earlier people still cherished the notion that somehow everybody can get rich and such laws would eventually hit them, while now they were resigned to such ideas being fantasies), so now crazy displays of wealth like the Carson houses in Eureka, set side-by-side with poor shacks, were felt to be in bad taste; the gap between images of wealth and spectres of poverty narrowed, as the gap between the very rich and the lower-middle class narrowed too.

That laws of good taste were applied to the buildings of the rich and the poor alike, were employed by major architects and humble spec builders alike, made the domestic building of this age an instrument for promoting the ideal of "freedom and justice for all." It was of this, surely, that Evelyn Watson was thinking when she declared that the bungalow was "stamping our architecture with an adaptability and adjustment that is as ingenious as the American himself."[3] To her, bungalows were images of democracy on its way to fulfillment, to "a time when the houses of the rich will be recognized to have the same fundamental lines as the houses of the poor." She was perceptive. That was the general goal sought—and it was as nearly reached as human conditions would ever allow, in the Comfortable House.

No country in the history of the world ever proclaimed that *all* its citizens had a right to comfortable housing—not just to housing, but a comfortable home. No other country ever proclaimed that all its citizens had a right to homes of their own if they wanted one. An age which came so close to realizing such goals must be counted as a major chapter in the history of architecture, not just in the United States, but in the world.

Notes

Introduction

1.

From an article by Edward L. Merritt, Architect, *The Bungalow Magazine,* March 1914.

2.

Occasionally some awareness of dwindling resources appears on the popular level, as when we read in the introduction to Radford's *Cement Houses* (1909):

America is fast losing the forest primeval. One needs only to take a short trip through northern Michigan, Wisconsin, or any of the other states, to realize the truth of this statement. Where once stood vast forests of pine, hundreds of miles in extent, now not one tree remains. The forests of the south are fast being denuded, and it will not be long before the mountains of the West will be bare.

So what is Radford's solution? Build concrete houses! Not, actually, as dumb as it sounds; but salesmanship, not prescience, is what is in evidence here.

3.

Philip Alexander Bruce, *Economic History of Virginia in the Seventeenth Century* (New York: Macmillan, 1896; Johnson Reprint, 1966). His observations about the impermanence of early American building have been abundantly confirmed by archaeology over the last twenty years.

4.

John Brinckerhoff Jackson, *Discovering the Vernacular Landscape* (New Haven: Yale University Press, 1984), 100–101.

5.

One of the unsatisfactory alternatives is described by Gilbert Herbert in *The Dream of the Factory-Made House: Walter Gropius and Konrad Wachsmann* (Cambridge: The MIT Press, 1984).

Chapter 1

1.

Quoted in Karl Löwith, *Meaning in History* (Chicago: University of Chicago Press, 1949), 100.

2.

Ralph Adams Cram, *My Life in Architecture* (Boston, 1936), 79.

3.

Quoted in Wendy Caplan, "R. T. H. Halsey," *Winterthur Portfolio* 17:1 (1982), 17. For other useful documentation and quotes on fear of "New Americans" from "Old Americans," see Jan Cohn, *The Palace or the Poorhouse* (East Lansing: Michican State University Press, 1979), 155–160.

4.

On utopias, see further my *Prophetic Allegory: Popeye and the American Dream* (Watkins Glen, NY: American Life Foundation, 1983).

5.

See Jack Green, "Search for Identity," *Journal of Social History* 3:4 (1970).

6.

Richard Hofstadter, *The American Political Tradition* (New York, 1948), 162.

7.

Barry Schwartz, "George Washington and the Whig Concept of Heroic Leadership," *American Sociological Review* (1983), 145–177.

8.

George W. Nelson, "The Individual House," in Talbot Hamlin (ed.), *Forms and Functions in Twentieth-Century Architecture* (New York, 1963), 201.

9.

As William Rhoads reminds us in "The Colonial Revival and American Nationalism," *Journal of the Society of Architectural Historians* 35:4 (1976), and his book *The Colonial Revival* (New York: Garland Press, 1978).

10.

Rhoads, *Colonial Revival*, 82.

11.

Caplan, "R. T. H. Halsey," 54.

12.

Rhoads, *Colonial Revival*, 35.

13.

Joy Wheeler Dow, *American Renaissance: A Review of Domestic Architecture* (New York: William Comstock, 1904), comparing Plate VII representing "American Renaissance" (identified in text as "the old house on Benefit Street in Providence") and its "100% Anglo-Saxon home atmosphere," with Plate VIII, a specimen of "The Newly Invented Architecture" (not identified—it looks like some follower of Wright's working with some Spanish Colonial details) analyzed as "Moresque Spain 10%, Moresque Algiers 10%, Moresque California Mission 10%, Indian 5%, Newly Reclaimed Land 10%, Chinese ornament 5%, Modern Invention 50%, Anglo-Saxon atmosphere 00%." Dow's book well exemplifies the hysterical reaction to social change among some old-line Americans in this time; that any American might have Spanish ancestors or roots simply never occurs to him.

14.

Dow, *American Renaissance*, "Ethics," 19.

15.

Quoted in Rhoads, *Colonial Revival*, 85.

16.

Herbert Croly, "English Renaissance at Its Best: The House of James Parmelee," *Architectural Record* (1914), 154.

17.

Alan Gowans, "The Mansions of Alloway's Creek," *RACAR* 3:2 (1976), 55–72; reprinted with emendations in D. Upton and J. Vlach, *Common Places: Readings in Material Culture* (Athens, GA: University of Georgia Press, 1985).

18.
A. J. Downing, *The Architecture of Country Houses* (1850; reprinted Da Capo Press, New York, 1968).

19.
Dow, *American Renaissance*, 167: "We call Biltmore [the Vanderbilt mansion in Asheville built to R. M. Hunt's designs in the 1890s] French Renaissance now; it will be American Renaissance later on."

20.
Downing, *Country Houses*, 79.

21.
Warren Harding's speech is recorded in Henry Atterbury Smith, *The Book of a Thousand Homes* I (1923), 279.

22.
Norris Kelly Smith, *Frank Lloyd Wright: A Study in Architectural Content* (New York, 1969; reprinted American Life Foundation, Watkins Glen, NY, 1978).

23.
Frank Lloyd Wright, On Architecture, edited by Frederick Gutheim (New York, 1941), 62.

Chapter 2

1.
Classic recent studies of suburban development include Harold R. Mayer and R. C. Wade, *Chicago: Growth of a Metropolis City* (Chicago: University of Chicago Press, 1969); Sam Bass Warner, *Streetcar Suburbs* (Cambridge: Harvard University Press, 1974); Eric Johanneson, *Cleveland Architecture 1876–1976* (Cleveland, 1979).

2.
How decidedly center city was the place to be through most of Western history is brought out especially well in Lynn White's *Medieval Technology and Social Change* (Oxford: Clarendon Press, 1962); once improved horse harnesses and consequent enlargement of wagons (from the twelfth century onward) made it possible for peasants to get into market regularly, they chose, when possible, to live in towns and commute out to their fields, rather than the ancient practice of living on the land and visiting the town only on rare occasions, such as for safety from invading armies.

3.
Warner, *Streetcar Suburbs*, is especially good in making distinctions (*passim*) between "developments" and "planned communities." Typically, an entrepreneur bought a farm or two, divided it into lots, usually but not always installed sewers and sidewalks, then sold the lots either directly to prospective homeowners or to small businessmen or contractors who would erect houses for speculative sale. Planning was not explicit in such "development of land," but was inherent in the system of pricing all houses in a given area in the same range and in the way neighborhoods were defined by schools (municipalities built the schools; neighborhoods found definition by the school districts in which given homeowners found themselves). Deliberately preplanned suburbs were decidedly an exception in this era.

4.
Over the last couple of decades the contrast has more commonly been made between the mansion and the tenement; a good example is Jan Cohn, *The Palace or the Poorhouse: The American House as Cultural Symbol* (East Lansing: Michigan State University Press, 1979), especially chapters 5 and 6, pp. 115–174. Her excellent discussion of the contrast between mansion and tenement lacks a third, extenuating dimension that more attention to the most successful resolution of this problem, suburban housing, might have provided.

5.
Helen M. and Robert S. Lynd, *Middletown: A Study in Contemporary American Culture* (New York: Harcourt Brace, 1929).

6.
Quoted in Barbara Rubin, "A Chronology of Architecture in Los Angeles," *Annals of the Association of American Geographers* 4 (1977).

7.
Victor Gruen, *Centers for the Urban Environment* (New York, 1973).

8.
The appended bibliography on catalogs gives some idea of how extensive was the trade literature dealing with appliances and interior appointments.

9.
This quote is a central theme in Reyner Banham's *Los Angeles: The Architecture of Four Ecologies* (London: The Penguin Press, 1971); the whole book is, in a sense, a refutation of it.

10.
Warner, *Streetcar Suburbs*, 37.

11.
Christopher Tunnard and Boris Pushkarev, *Man-Made America: Chaos or Control* (New Haven: Yale University Press, 1963).

12.
In F. A. Hayek, *Capitalism and the Historians* (Chicago, 1954).

13.
Johanneson, *Cleveland Architecture*, 184.

Chapter 3

1.
Bertram Goodhue, "The Modern Architectural Problem," *Craftsman* 8 (June 1905), 332–333.

2.
Nathan Silver, *Lost New York* (New York, 1967), 9.

3.
Norris Kelly Smith, *Frank Lloyd Wright: A Study in Architectural Content* (New York, 1969), 110.

4.
William B. Rhoads, *The Colonial Revival* (New York: Garland Press, 1978), 338.

5.
Smith, *Frank Lloyd Wright,* 88.

6.
Ibid., 89–90.

7.
Charles Reilly, *McKim, Mead and White* (London, Benn, 1924), 10.

8.
Smith, *Frank Lloyd Wright,* 119.

9.
"Near-architect" is a useful term much used in the early 1900s.

10.
This warning appears on the second (inner title) page of every Aladdin catalog, for instance, and variants of it in other builders'.

11.
In the 1850s 70,000 copies a month were printed; in 1869 the magazine boasted it had half a million readers. George L. Hersey, "Godey's Choice," *Journal of the Society of Architectural Historians* 18:3 (1959), 104.

12.
Godey's Magazine 38 (1849), 71, quoted by Hersey.

13.
H. W. Cleaveland, W. Backus, and S. D. Backus, *Village and Farm Cottages* (New York, 1856), 7. This work was reprinted in 1981 by the American Life Foundation, Watkins Glen, NY, with a very useful introduction by David Schuyler. (Numerous other builders' guides have been reprinted by this foundation.)

14.
The "war" between Shoppell and the Pallisers is extensively described, and admirably illustrated by extant buildings taken from their respective plans, in James L. Garvin, "Mail order house plans and American Victorian architecture," *Winterthur Portfolio* 16:4 (1981), 309–334.

15.
Quoted in Rhoads, *Colonial Revival,* 102.

16.
A good many still stand. For random example, three are mentioned in Michael Tomlan's *Walking Tour of Canandaigua* [NY] (Watkins Glen, NY: American Life Foundation, 1978). In 1956 Marion D. Ross cited two in "Architecture in Oregon, 1845–1895," *Oregon Historical Quarterly* 52:1 (1956), 56–57: the C. D. Drain house in Drain and the Jerry

Nunan house in Jacksonville, for which H. F. Wood was builder. But, characteristically for that time, Ross did not realize they were mass-prefabricated: "It is improbable that the architect, Mr. Barber, actually came to either Drain or Jacksonville, and it appears all the more remarkable that the local builders were so well able to execute his fantastic designs." See further on Barber in Patricia Poore, "Pattern Book Architecture," *The Old-House Journal* (1980) 184–186, and Garvin, "Mail order house plans," 334.

17.
According to Alfred Bruce and Harold Sandbank, *History of Prefabrication* (New York: Pierce Foundation, 1943; reprinted Arno Press, 1972). Though often cited, this book is not altogether reliable, having been produced hurriedly to promote prefabs for wartime purposes.

18.
This same advertisement and picture appear with only minor variations in Aladdin catalogs from 1912 through the 1920s.

19.
Communication from W. J. Sovereign to the author, September 1982.

20.
See H. L. Cohn, ed., *1922 Montgomery Ward Catalog* (New York, 1969).

21.
In *Goldenseal* magazine, published by West Virginia Department of Culture and History, 8:2 (Spring 1982).

22.
Quoted in Rubin, "Chronology of Architecture in Los Angeles," 528 and 531, from Robert Jones, "The Architects' Small House Service Bureau," *Architectural Forum* 44 (1926), 208; and Charles Kyson, "Fashions in Architecture," *California Southland* (August 1928), 30.

23.
Quoted in Rhoads, *Colonial Revival,* 210.

24.
Arthur Bridgman Clark, "Some Very Bad Designs," *Art Principles in House, Furniture, and Village Building* (Stanford: Stanford University Press, 1921), 41–48, and elsewhere through the book. Clark actually epitomizes the ASHSB's and HOSI's problem later: his basic theme is that everybody should live in fine, architect-designed houses and all would be well.

25.
"Architects' Small House Service Bureau of Minnesota, Inc.," *Journal of the American Institute of Architects* 9 (1921), 134–40; see also Robert Jones, "The Architects' Small House Service Bureau," *Architectural Forum* 44 (1926), 201–216; Thomas Harvey, "Mail Order Architecture in the Twenties," *Landscape* 25:3 (1981), 1–9.

26.
Your Future Home (St. Paul, MN: Weyerhauser Company, 1923), 10.

27.
Quoted in Rubin, "Chronology of Architecture in Los Angeles," 527 and 528, from Kyson, "Fashions in Architecture," and Leigh French, "The Small House and Candor in Designing," *Architectural Forum* 44 (1926).

28.
Howard Atterbury Smith, *The Book of a Thousand Homes* (New York, 1921), 13.

29.
Quoted in Harvey, "Mail Order Architecture," 5.

30.
Octagon 2:2 (1930), 22.

31.
Ibid.

Chapter 4

1.
Henry Glassie, "Folk Art," in *Folklore Today: Festschrift for Richard M. Dorson,* edited by L. Degh, H. Glassie, F. J. Oinas (Bloomington, IN, 1976).

2.
Reyner Banham, *Los Angeles: Architecture of Four Ecologies* (New York, 1971), 72; Vincent Scully, *American Architecture and Urbanism* (New York, 1973); Harold Kirker, *California's Architectural Frontier* (Santa Barbara, 1973). The original attribution seems to derive from a short article by L. Morgan Yost, "Greene and Greene of Pasadena," *Journal of the Society of Architectural Historians* 9:1 (1950) 11–19.

3.
Barbara Rubin, "A Chronology of Architecture in Los Angeles," *Annals of the Association of American Geographers* 4 (1977), 522.

4.
Robert Winter, *The California Bungalow* (Los Angeles, 1980), 19.

5.
Arthur C. David, "An Architect of Bungalows in California," *Architectural Record* (October 1906), 67.

6.
Ibid., 68.

7.
Anthony King, "The Art of Bungalows," *Architectural Association Quarterly* (1973).

8.
Henry Saylor, *Bungalows* (New York, 1913), 144.

9.
This origin is cited in "The Origin of the Bungalow," *Country Life in America* 19:2 (1911), 309, and taken for granted in most contemporary writings (e.g., Ethel Merman, *Typical California Bungalows* [Los Angeles, 1914] and Henry Wilson, *The Bungalow Book* [Chicago, 1910]). See also Harold Kirker, *California's Architectural Frontier*, 128: "The characteristics that made the bungalow practical in India and Ceylon, maximum circulation of air achieved by means of raised foundations and wide verandahs, assured its success in California." But the primitive Asian bungalow immediately was elaborated upon, both in size and by addition of tags of ornament from historical styles—Spanish and English Colonial, Arts and Crafts, even Swiss châlets and Japanese temples. Of course this happened in India too; for examples, see Janet Pott, *Old Bungalows in Bangalore, South India* (London, published by the author, 1977).

10.
If Henry Saylor is to be trusted; cf. *Bungalows*, 152: "It will be generally admitted, I believe, that the bungalow as a distinct type of architecture is far better suited to employment for the temporary home, the shooting-lodge and the week-end retreat in the woods or along the shore, than it is to use for permanent homes in suburban communities. There is at least a suggestion of following after a mere fad in the building of row upon row of bungalows along a suburban street." But he then adds, "In all probability this fad, like others, will die out"—with California cities and towns already full of just such bungalow-lined suburban streets!

11.
Clay Lancaster, "The American Bungalow," *Art Bulletin* 40:3 (1958), 243–244.

12.
Mabel Chilson, "Historical Aspects of the Bungalow," *Keith's Magazine* 24:12 (December 1910), 369.

13.
Mabel Chilson, "What is a Genuine Bungalow?" *Keith's Magazine* 35 (April 1916), 38.

14.
Ibid., 39.

15.
Andrew Jackson Downing, *Architecture of Country Houses* (New York, 1850; reprinted New York: Da Capo, 1968), 112.

16.
Cary Carson, Norman F. Barka, William M. Kelso, Garry Wheeler Stone, and Dell Upton, "Impermanent Architecture in the Southern American Colonies," *Winterthur Portfolio* 16:2–3 (1981), 135–196. Seldom are terms like "seminal" and "revolutionary" so well deserved as for this extraordinary piece of scholarship.

17.
I take the term "national rebuilding" from Carson, et al., "Impermanent Architecture," 162 (the original term comes from W. G. Hoskins, "The Rebuilding of Rural England 1570–1640," *Past and Present* 4:11 (1953), 44–59): "Throughout the Chesapeake region the replacement of

homestead housing was slow to start and then was attenuated and prolonged for more than a century until finally it was subsumed in the first truly nationwide rebuilding of the early nineteenth century. Only at that point, say the period 1820–50, would trend lines for New England and the Old South finally converge." In some ways the suburban expansion of 1890–1930 might be considered another nationwide rebuilding—that is, replacing urban housing with suburban.

18.
Carson, et al., "Impermanent Architecture," 144. Mass-prefabricated houses 1890–1930 even resembled "beginners' homesteads" in having optional chimney arrangements; characteristically, "ordinary beginners'" houses on the first frontier had no chimney.

19.
Ibid., 140.

Chapter 5

1.
Quoted in William B. Rhoads, *The Colonial Revival* (New York: Garland Press, 1978), 118.

2.
H. W. Cleaveland, W. Backus, and S. D. Backus, *Village and Farm Cottages* (New York, 1856), 65.

3.
Quote from official city hall brochure.

4.
Earl Pomeroy, *In Search of the Golden West* (New York: Knopf, 1957), 37.

5.
S. Story, *To the Golden Land, Sketches of a Trip to Southern California* (London: Scott, 1889); J. W. Hanson, *The American Italy* (Chicago, 1896); R. Hicks, *Southern California, or The Land of the Afternoon* (Springfield, MA: Springfield Printing and Binding Company, 1898).

6.
Matlack Price, "'Mediterranean' Architecture in Florida," *Architectural Forum* (1926), 89.

7.
Joe Hendrickson, *The Tournament of Roses* (Los Angeles: Brooke House, 1971).

8.
Jules Huret, *En Amérique, de San Francisco au Canada* (Paris, 1907), 22.

9.
For a more extensive treatment of Spanish Colonial substyles, see my article, "Post-Victorian Domestic Architecture: The Spanish Colonial Revival Style," *Old House Journal* 10:10 (1982), 198–202.

10.
David Gebhard, "The Spanish Colonial Revival in Southern California," *Journal of the Society of Architectural Historians* 26 (1967), 142.

11.
French is a style almost never mentioned in catalogs and guides aimed at a middle- to lower-middle-class market. Cf. W. J. Keith, *Historic Architecture for the Home Builder* (Minneapolis: The Keith Co., 1905).

12.
Reginald Blomfield's *History of French Architecture from the Reign of Charles VIII to the death of Mazarin* (London, 1911) was a standard in architecture schools and the offices of "the better-class" architects until the Bauhaus Blitz.

13.
As a source of period detail generally, Sir Banister Fletcher's *History of Architecture on the Comparative Method* remained unrivaled throughout this period. First published in London in 1896, it has gone through eighteen editions since, and another, though much rewritten, edition is underway.

14.
Hugh Morrison, *Early American Architecture* (New York, 1952), 70.

15.
Fiske Kimball, *Domestic Architecture of the American Colonies and of the Early Republic* (Philadelphia, 1922), 98.

16.
Rhoads, *Colonial Revival*, 39.

17.
Ibid., 42. Yet even the Stanley Flagg house has a porch with obviously English Colonial columns.

18.
Quoted in ibid., 43.

19.
Philadelphia Inquirer, 13 December 1981.

Chapter 6

1.
See the discussion in my *Images of American Living* (Philadelphia/New York, 1964), 74.

2.
Ernest Allen Connally, "The Cape Cod Cottage: an Introductory Study" *Journal of the Society of Architectural Historians* 11:2 (1960).

3.
First identified by H. C. Forman in *The Architecture of the Old South* (Cambridge: Harvard University Press, 1934).

4.

See, for example, Cary Carson, et al., ''Impermanent Architecture in the Southern Colonies,'' *Winterthur Portfolio* 16:2–3 (1981), 160 n82.

5.

See my ''Mansions of Alloway's Creek,'' in D. Upton and J. Vlach (eds.), *Common Places: Readings in Material Culture* (Athens, GA: University of Georgia Press, 1985).

6.

Fred Kniffen, ''Folk Housing: Key to Diffusion,'' *Annals of the Association of American Geographers* 55:4 (1965).

7.

Henry Glassie, *Patterns in the Material Folk Culture of the Eastern United States* (Philadelphia: University of Pennsylvania Press, 1968), 78.

8.

Also by the number of times an exotic feature like the inset pilasters was copied; it even got into the *Book of a Thousand Homes* (see the adaptation by Henry H. Dean as Plan 263).

9.

On Imperial British styles, see my review of Mark Girouard's *Return to Camelot* and Robert Grant Irving's *Indian Summer* in *Architectura* (1983), 80–83; also my forthcoming ''Paradigmatic Social Function in Anglican Church Architecture of the Fifteen Colonies,'' in *Studies in the History of Art* (Washington, D.C.: Center for Advanced Study in the Visual Arts, 1986).

10.

Quoted in William B. Rhoads, *The Colonial Revival* (New York: Garland Press, 1978), 107.

11.

Quoted in ibid., 130.

12.

''A House that has the Quality of an Old Homestead, built by Laura Coombs Hills at Newburyport,'' *Craftsman* 14:4 (1908), 388.

13.

Vincent Scully, *The Shingle Style* (New Haven: Yale University Press, 1955); reissued in 1976 as *The Shingle Style and the Stick Style.*

14.

I have explored implications of this subject at exhaustive, even exhausting, length in *The Unchanging Arts* (Philadelphia: Lippincott, 1971) and *Learning to See: Historical Perspectives on Modern Popular/Commercial Arts* (Bowling Green: Popular Press, 1981).

15.

William B. Rhoads, ''The Colonial Revival and American Nationalism,'' *Journal of the Society of Architectural Historians* 35:4 (1976).

Chapter 7

1.

On survival of Classical Revival sentiment on the popular level, a major contribution has been made by Wilbur Zelinsky's two articles, ''Classical Town Names in the United States,'' *Geographical Review* 57 (1967), 435–495, and ''Nationalism in the American Place-Name Cover,'' *Names* 31:1 (1938), 1–28.

2.

On symmetry in folk consciousness, a major essay is Henry Glassie's definition of folk art in *Folklore Today: Festschrift for Richard M. Dorson,* edited by L. Degh, H. Glassie, F. J. Oinas (Bloomington, IN, 1976).

Chapter 9

1.

Carpentry and Building 2:8 (1880), 156, quoted in Sadayoshi Omoto, ''The Queen Anne Style and Architectural Criticism,'' *Journal of the Society of Architectural Historians* 23:1 (1964), 30 n9.

2.

Carpentry and Building 8:5 (1886), 90, quoted in ibid., 34 n34.

3.

Quote from Montgomery Schuyler in W. Jordy and R. Coe (eds.), *American Architecture and Other Writings by Montgomery Schuyler* (Cambridge, Harvard University Press, 1961). Original source: ''Recent Building in New York,'' *The Harper's New Monthly Magazine* 67:9 (1883), 558.

4.

Robert Winter gives an instance in *Bungalows* (1981) where a Stickley design was copied exactly in Cheney's *Artistic Bungalows* of 1910, with the sole addition of one figure in the inglenook.

5.

John C. Freeman, *Forgotten Rebel* (Watkins Glen, NY: Century House Press, 1966), 17.

Chapter 10

1.

Ralph Adams Cram, *My Life in Architecture* (Boston, 1936), 42.

2.

Jonathan Lane, ''The Period House in the Nineteen-Twenties,'' *Journal of the Society of Architectural Historians* 20:4 (1961), 174.

3.

Quoted by Mabel Chilson, ''Historical Aspects of the Bungalow,'' *Keith's Magazine* 24 (December 1910), 369.

Bibliography

Compiled by Lamia Doumato

A Selected List of Home Builders Guides and Catalogs

Aladdin Company. *Aladdin Homes "Built in a Day".* Bay City, Michigan, ca. 1910.

Aladdin Company. *Aladdin Houses "Built in a Day".* Bay City, 1914.

Aladdin Company. *Aladdin Homes—Some Interesting Facts About Aladdin Service for 1922.* Bay City, 1922.

Aladdin Company, *Aladdin Readi-Cut Homes.* Bay City, n.d.

Aladdin Company, *Catalog No. 32–33.* Bay City, 1920–21.

Aladdin Company, *Instructions for the Erection of Your Aladdin Home.* Bay City, 1921.

Aladdin Company. *What Do Aladdin Owners Think of Thier Aladdin Homes?* Bay City, n.d.

American Steel & Wire Company. *Stucco Houses.* n.p., 1921

Architects' Small House Service Bureau of the United States. *The Small Home.* 12 vols. Minneapolis, 1922–32.

Architects' Small House Service Bureau of the United States. *Small Homes of Architectural Distinction.* Minneapolis, 1927.

Architects' Small House Service Bureau. *Your Future Home.* St. Paul: Weyerhauser Forest Products, 1923.

Architectural Designing Company. *Plans and Designs of Bungalows, Modern Homes, Churches, Schools, etc.* Spokane, Washington, 1912.

Atlas Portland Cement Company. *Building a Bungalow.* New York/Chicago, 1915.

Atlas Portland Cement Company. *Concrete Garages: The Fireproof Home for the Automobile.* New York, 1923.

Atlas Portland Cement Company. *Concrete Houses and Cottages.* 2 vols. New York, 1909.

Atlas Portland Cement Company. *The Stucco House.* New York, n.d.

Baker, Zephaniah. *Modern House Builder.* Boston, 1857.

Barber, George F. *The Cottage Souvenir.* Knoxville, 1892.

Barber, George F. *Modern Dwellings.* Knoxville, 1905.

Bennett, Ray H. Lumber Company. *Bennett Homes.* North Tonawanda, New York, 1922. Later versions of this catalog appeared in 1924 and in 1930.

Bennett, Ray H. Lumber Company. *Bennett Better-Built Ready-Cut Homes.* North Tonawanda, 1926.

Bennett, Ray H. Lumber Company. *Bennett Homes: Catalog No. 18.* North Tonawanda, 1920.

Bicknell, A. J. & Company. *Bicknell's Cottage and Villa Architecture.* New York, 1878.

Bicknell, A. J. & Company. *Bicknell's Village Builder.* New York, 1872. A revised edition of the same title was published in New York in 1878.

Bicknell, A. J. & Company. *Bicknell's Village Builder: Bicknell's Victorian Buildings.* New York: Dover Books, 1979.

Bicknell, A. J. & Company. *Detail, Cottage and Constructive Architecture.* New York, 1875.

Bicknell, A. J. & Company. *Supplement to Bicknell's Village Builder, Containing Eighteen Modern Designs for Country and Suburban Houses of Moderate Cost, With Elevations, Plans, Sections and a Variety of Details, All Drawn to Scale, Also, A Full Set of Specifications With Approved Form of Contract and Estimates of Cost.* New York, 1871.

Bossert, Louis, and sons. *Bossert Rebuilt Homes, "Not Even a Nail to Buy," Bungalows, Garages, Boat and Play Houses, Churches, Schools, Banks, Real Estate Offices, Barracks and Both Permanent and Emergency Buildings of All Kinds.* Brooklyn, 1915.

Building Brick Association of America. *A House of Brick of Moderate Cost.* Boston, 1910.

Bungalowcraft Company, *Bungalowcraft.* Los Angeles, 1922.

Bungalowcraft Company, *Homes of the Moment.* Los Angeles, 1929.

Bungalowcraft Company, *The New Spanish Bungalow.* Los Angeles, 1912. Catalogs of same title published in 1926 and 1931.

Carpenter, James H. *The Complete House Builder: Containing Fifty Plans and Specifications of Dwellings, Barns, Churches, Public Buildings, Etc.* Chicago, 1890.

Carr, Aute Lee. *A Practical Guide to Prefabricated Houses.* New York, 1947.

Cheney, Clyde J. *Artistic Bungalows.* Los Angeles, ca. 1912.

Chicago House Wrecking Company. *Catalog No. 157.* Chicago, 1909.

Chicago House Wrecking Company. *A Book of Plans.* Chicago, 1910.

Chivers, Herbert C. *Artistic Homes.* St. Louis, 1910.

Cleaveland, Henry W.; Backus, W.; and Backus, S. D. *Village and Farm Cottages: The Requirements of American Village Homes, with Designs for Such Houses.* New York, 1856.

Comstock, William T. (comp.). *American Cottages Containing Original Designs of Medium and Low Cost Cottages, Seaside and Country Houses. . . .* New York, 1883.

Comstock, William T. *Specimen Book of One Hundred Architectural Designs.* New York, 1878.

Comstock, William P. and Schermerhorn, C. E., *Bungalows, Camps, and Mountain Houses.* New York, 1908. Second edition, 1915; third edition, 1924.

Craftsman Bungalow Company. *Craftsman Bungalows*. Seattle, 1912. Other editions 1913, 1914, 1916, 1917, 1919, 1920.

Dalzell, Kenneth W. and Hammel, E. F. *Homes of a Moderate Size: A Collection of Photographs and Plans*. New York, 1921.

Davis, Alexander Jackson. *The Architecture of Country Houses*. New York, 1850.

Davis, Alexander Jackson. *Cottage Residences*. New York and London, 1842.

Davis, Alexander Jackson. *Rural Residences*. New York, 1837.

DeLuxe Building Company. *Draughtsman Bungalows*. Los Angeles, 1912.

DeLuxe Building Company. *"Plan Kraft" Homes*. Los Angeles, 1912. Other editions 1913, 1919.

Downing, Andrew Jackson. *The Architecture of Country Houses*. New York, 1851.

Downing, Andrew Jackson. *Cottage Residences*. New York, 1873.

Dwyer, Charles P. *The Economic Cottage Builder or Cottages for Men of Small Means*. Buffalo, 1856.

Fenner Manufacturing Company. *Fenner Small Homes*. Portland, Oregon, ca. 1916.

Fowler, Orson Squire. *A Home for All*. New York, 1857.

Garlinghouse, Lewis Fayette. *Bungalow Homes*. Topeka, Kansas, 1920.

Garnsey, George O. *American Homes*. Chicago, 1888.

Gordon-van Tine Company. *Building Material: Fall Catalog*. Davenport, Iowa, 1915.

Gordon-van Tine Company. *Grand Millwork Catalog for Homebuilders*. Davenport, Iowa, 1911.

Harris Brothers Company. *Catalog No. 187*. Chicago, 1923.

Harris Brothers Company. *Harris Homes, Building Materials, and Garages*. Creskill, New Jersey, 1929.

Harris Brothers Company. *Presto-Up Patented Bolt-Together House, Garages, Barns, etc.* Chicago, 1919.

Harris Brothers Company. *Up-in-a-Day Presto-Up. . . . Sectional Buildings, The Wonder Buildings of the Age*. Chicago, 1918.

Harrison, Percival T. *Bungalow Residences*. London, 1906.

Hodgson [E. F.] Company. *Hodgson Portable Houses*. Boston, 1912.

Hodgson [E. F.] Company. *Hodgson Houses*. Boston, 1935.

Hodgson [E. F.] Company. *Hodgson Houses: Camps and Equipment*. Dover, Massachusetts, 1936.

Hodgson [E. F.] Company. *Houses as Constructed by Hodgson*. Boston, 1928.

Hodgson, Ernest Franklin. *Wigwam Portable Homes*. Dover, 1908.

Hodgson, Frederick T. *Modern Carpentry*. Riverside, Illinois, 1902.

Hodgson, Frederick T. *Practical Bungalows*. Chicago, 1906. Other editions 1912, 1916.

Holly, H. Hudson. *Modern Dwellings in Town and Country Adapted to American Wants and Climate*. New York, 1878.

Hopkins, David S. *Cottage Portfolio*. New York, 1886.

Hopkins, David S. *Houses and Cottages*. Grand Rapids, 1889.

Jacques, D. H. *The House: A Manual of Rural Architecture, With Numerous Original Plans*. New York, 1886.

Jenkins, Henry C. *Healthy Houses Adapted to American Conditions*. New York, 1879.

Keeley, Cecil J. *A Book of Bungalows and Modern Homes*. New York, 1928.

Keith's Twenty Wonder Houses. M. L. Keith Company, Minneapolis, 1919. Summarizes a number of earlier catalogs and designs in *Keith's Magazine of Home Building*, 1899–.

King, David W. *Homes for Home Builders*. New York, 1886.

King, David W. *Modern Cottages*. Syracuse, 1886.

King, David W. *Portfolio of Cottages*. Syracuse, n.d.

Lakey, Charles D. *Lakey's Village and Country Houses*. New York, 1875.

Leffel, James and Co. *Leffel's House Plans*. New York, 1884.

Leuchars, Robert B. *Practical Treatise on Construction, Heating, and Ventilating of Hot Houses*. Boston, 1851.

The Liberty Company. *Liberty Ready-Cut Homes*. Bay City, Michigan, n.d., ca. 1918.

Lindsley & Drummond. *Lindsley & Drummond, Manufacturers of Portable and Ready-Made Houses. Catalog*. Chicago, 1885.

Lindstrom and Almars. *Cottages and Semi-Bungalows*. Minneapolis, 1925.

Lindstrom and Almars. *Duplex and Apartment Houses*. Minneapolis, ca. 1920. Also has plans for small banks, and a Christian Science church.

Lindstrom and Almars. *From Mansion to Bungalow*. Minneapolis, n.d.

Los Angeles Investment Company. *Practical Bungalows of Southern California*. Los Angeles, 1910. Second edition, 1911; third edition, 1912.

Los Angeles Investment Company. *Modern Homes of California.* Los Angeles, 1913.

MacLagan, P. J. *MacLagan's Suburban Homes.* Newark, 1910.

Mason, George C. *The Old House Altered.* New York, 1878.

Menkin, Henry (ed.). *Bungalowcraft.* Los Angeles, 1908.

Menkin, Henry. *California Bungalow Homes.* Los Angeles, 1911.

Mershon & Morley. *M&M Gold Bond Portable Houses and Garages.* Saginaw, Michigan, ca. 1915.

Montgomery Ward & Company. *Building Materials.* New York, 1914.

Montgomery Ward & Company. *Building Materials.* Chicago, 1925.

Montgomery Ward & Company. *Building Materials Shipped Direct from Factory to You.* Chicago, 1929.

Montgomery Ward & Company. *Coverall Paint.* Chicago, 1917. Another catalog of the same title was issued in 1918.

Montgomery Ward & Company. *Economy in Plumbing and Heating.* Chicago, 1918.

Montgomery Ward & Company. *For the Home Beautiful.* Chicago, 1933.

Montgomery Ward & Company. *Heating the Home.* Chicago, 1917.

Montgomery Ward & Company. *Paint.* Chicago, 1915.

Montgomery Ward & Company. *Paint Protects Your Buildings, Increases Their Value, Prolongs Their Life.* Chicago, 1919.

Montgomery Ward & Company. *Ward's Complete Catalog of Plumbing, Heating, Building Materials.* Chicago, 1933.

Montgomery Ward & Company. *Wardway Homes.* Chicago, Kansas City, St. Paul, Baltimore, Oakland, Portland, Fort Worth, 1927. Variants of this catalog appeared throughout this time period.

National Architects' Union. *Artistic One-Storey Houses.* New York and Philadelphia, 1893.

National Architects' Union. *Modern Homes.* Philadelphia, 1889.

National Architects' Union. *Modern Rural Homes.* 3 vols. Philadelphia, 1885–91.

National Architects' Union. *Picturesque Houses for Forest and Shore.* Philadelphia, 1891.

National Architects' Union. *Sensible Low-Cost Houses.* 3 vols. New York, 1895.

National Builder. *Complete Plans for Eighteen Houses of from four to six Rooms, Drawn Especially for the National Builder by the Regional Bureaus of the Architects Small House Service of the U.S.* Chicago, 1923.

National Fire Proofing Company. *A Book of House Designs.* Boston, 1910.

National Fire Proofing Company. *The Natco Bungalow for Four Thousand Dollars.* Boston, 1913.

National Fire Proofing Company. *The Natco House for Six Thousand Dollars.* Boston, 1912.

Newsom, John Henry. *Homes of Character: A Plan Book.* [San Francisco?] ca. 1913.

Palliser and Palliser Co. *New Cottage Homes.* Bridgeport, Connecticut, 1887.

Palliser and Palliser Co. *Palliser's American Cottage Homes.* Bridgeport, 1887.

Palliser and Palliser Co. *Palliser's Model Homes for the People.* Bridgeport, 1876.

Pederson, Jens. *Beautiful Homes and Plans.* St. Paul, 1919.

Porter, J. W. *Modern Cottage Homes.* Monmouth, Illinois, 1894.

Radford Architectural Company. *Architectural Details for Every Type of Building.* Chicago, 1921.

Radford Architectural Company. *Our Farm and Building Book.* Chicago, 1914.

Radford Architectural Company. *The Radford American Homes.* Riverside, Illinois, 1903.

Radford Architectural Company, *Radford's Artistic Bungalows, Unique Collection of 208 Designs, Best Modern Ideas in Bungalow Architecture.* Chicago, 1908.

Radford Architectural Company. *Radford's Artistic Homes, 250 designs, the largest single book of house designs ever published . . . every effort has been made by a corps of experienced licensed architects to provide for the most economical home construction.* Chicago, 1908.

Radford Architectural Company. *Radford's Bungalows.* New York, 1908.

Radford Architectural Company. *Radford Cement Homes.* Chicago, 1909.

Radford, William A. *Cement Houses and How to Build Them: perspective views and floor plans of concrete-block and cement-plaster houses.* Radford Architectural Company, Chicago, 1909.

Radford, William A. *How To Read Plans and Take off Bills of Material.* Chicago, 1925.

Radford, William A. *Radford's Modern Homes.* Chicago, 1909.

Radford, William A. *Radford's Portfolio of Plans.* Chicago, 1909.

Reed, Samuel B. *Cottage Houses for Village and Country Homes.* New York, 1883.

Reed, Samuel B. *Dwellings for Village and Country.* New York, 1885.

Reed, Samuel B. *House Plans for Everybody.* New York, 1878.

Reid, David B. *Ventilation in American Dwellings.* New York, 1858.

Riddell, John. *Architectural Designs for Model Country Residences.* Philadelphia, 1861.

Ritch, John W. *The American Architect: Comprising Original Designs of Cheap Country and Village Residences.* 2 vols. New York, 1848–49.

Robinson, C. H. *A Home of Your Own: Catalogue of "Mill-Made" and "Framed Up" Bungalows and Houses.* Providence, 1900.

Romaine, Lawrence B. *A Guide to American Trade Catalogs, 1744–1900.* New York, 1960.

Saint Paul Home Plans Book Company. *The Book of Bungalows.* St. Paul, ca. 1915.

Saint Paul Home Plans Book Company. *The Book of Commercial Homes.* St. Paul, ca. 1918.

Saxton, Glenn L., Architect. *The Plan Book of American Dwellings.* Minneapolis, 1914.

Saylor, Henry H. *Bungalows.* New York, 1913.

Saylor, Henry H. *Distinctive Homes of Moderate Cost.* New York: McBride, Nast and Co., 1913.

Saylor, Henry H. *Inexpensive Homes of Individuality.* New York: McBride, Nast and Co., 1912.

Sears, Roebuck & Company. *Book of Modern Homes and Building Plans.* Chicago, 1908, and later years.

Sears, Roebuck & Company. *Building Material, Millwork and Roofing.* Philadelphia, 1926.

Sears, Roebuck & Company. *Catalogue of Cement Block Machines.* Chicago, 1907.

Sears, Roebuck & Company. *1897 Sears Roebuck Catalogue.* New York: Chelsea House Publishers, 1968.

Sears, Roebuck & Company. *Honor-bilt Modern Homes.* Chicago/Philadelphia, 1922, and later years.

Sears, Roebuck & Company. *Instructions for Installing Modern Plumbing Systems.* Chicago, 1922.

Sears, Roebuck & Company. *Modern Plumbing and Heating Systems.* Chicago, 1924.

Sears, Roebuck & Company. *1908 Catalogue No. 117.* Chicago: Gun Digest Co., 1969.

Sears, Roebuck & Company. *1909 Catalog.* New York: Ventura Books, 1979.

Sears, Roebuck & Company. *The 1902 Edition of the Sears Roebuck Catalogue.* New York: Bounty Books, 1969.

Sears, Roebuck & Company. *Wallpaper, Certified Fadeproof.* Chicago, 1931.

Shoppell, Robert W. *Artistic Modern Houses of Low Cost.* New York, 1881.

Shoppell, Robert W. *How to Build A House.* New York, 1881.

Shoppell, Robert W. *Modern Houses: Beautiful Homes.* 2 vols. New York, 1887.

Shoppell, Robert W. *Shoppell's Building Plans for Modern Low-Cost Houses.* New York, 1884.

Shoppell, Robert W. *Shoppell's Model Houses.* New York, 1980.

Sidney, J. C. *American Cottage and Villa Architecture.* New York, 1850.

Skillings, David Nelson. *D. N. Skilling's and D. B. Flint's Illustrated Catalogue of Portable Sectional Buildings. Patented November 19, 1861.* Boston, 1862.

Sloan, Samuel. *American Houses: A Variety of Original Designs for Rural Buildings.* Philadelphia, 1861.

Sloan, Samuel. *The Model Architect: A Series of Designs for Cottages, Villas, Suburban Residences.* 2 vols. Philadelphia, 1852.

Sloan, Samuel. *Sloan's Homestead Architecture: Containing Forty Designs for Villas, Cottages, and Farm Houses.* Philadelphia, 1861.

Smith, Herbert Atterbury. *The Books of a Thousand Homes.* New York, 1921.

Southern Architectural Bureau. *One Hundred Plans Showing the Manner in Which Beauty, Comfort, Hospitality, Distinction Are Combined with Economy in Homes of the South Adaptable for Construction Anywhere.* Shreveport, 1922.

Springfield Manufacturing Company. *Portable Homes.* Springfield, Massachusetts, 1913.

Stevens, John C. *Examples of American Domestic Architecture,* New York, 1889.

Stickley, Gustav. *Craftsman Homes: Architecture and Furnishings of the American Arts and Crafts Movement.* 1909; New York: Dover Books, 1979.

Stickley, Gustav. *More Craftsman Homes.* New York, 1912.

Tabor, Clarence H. *Modern Homes.* Chicago, 1889.

Thomas, T., Jr. *The Workingman's Cottage Architecture.* New York, 1848.

Todd, Sereno E. *Todd's Country Homes and How to Save Money.* Hartford, 1870.

Trendall, E. W. *Original Designs for Cottages and Villas . . . Adapted to the environs of the Metropolis and Large Towns, Consisting of Plans, Elevations, and Estimates of Each Design with Appropriate Details.* London, 1831.

Tuthill, William B. *The Suburban Cottage: Its Design and Construction.* New York, 1885.

Vaux, Calvert. *Villas and Cottages: A Series of Designs Prepared for Execution in the United States.* New York, 1857.

Walker Bin Company. *Walker Bin's Book of Homes.* Penn Yan, New York, 1922.

Webber Lumber & Supply Company. *The Home: From Cellar to Shingles.* Fitchburg, Massachusetts, 1927.

Wheeler, Gervase. *Homes for the People in Suburb and Country: The Villa, The Mansion, The Cottage.* New York, 1868.

Wheeler, Gervase. *Rural Homes: Or Sketches of Houses Suited to American Country Life.* New York, 1851.

Wheeler, Gervase. *Rural Homes . . . with Original Plans.* New York, 1867.

White, Alfred T. *Improved Dwellings for the Laboring Classes.* New York, 1877.

Wilson, Henry L. *The Bungalow Book* (also known as *The Wilson Bungalow*). Chicago, 1910.

Wilson, Henry L. *The Bungalow Book.* New York, 1923.

Woodward, George E. *Woodward's Cottages and Farm Houses.* New York, 1867.

Woodward, George E. *Woodward's Country Houses.* New York, 1886.

Woodward, George E. and Thompson, Edward G. *Woodward's National Architect: Design Plans and Details.* New York, 1869.

Woolett, William M. *Old Homes Made New.* New York, 1878.

Woolett, William M. *Villas and Cottages.* New York, 1876.

Wyckhoff Lumber & Manufacturing Company. *Cornell Portable Houses.* Ithaca, ca. 1910.

Wyman, Morrill. *A Practical Treatise on Domestic Architecture.* Boston, 1846.

"Ye Planry" Building Company. *"Ye Planry" Bungalows.* Los Angeles, 1908. Other editions 1909, 1910, 1911.

Yoho and Merritt. *Colonial Homes, A Collection of the Latest Designs featuring the new Colonial Bungalow.* Seattle, 1921.

Books

Abraham, Pol. *Architecture préfabriqué.* Paris: Dunod, 1946.

Adams, Mary E. *The Lockwood-Mathews Mansion.* Norwalk, Connecticut: The Lockwood-Mathews Mansion Museum, 1969.

Allen, Frank P. *Artistic Dwellings.* Grand Rapids: Frank P. Allen, 1893.

Allen, Frank L. *Only Yesterday: An Informal History of the Nineteen Twenties.* New York: Harper and Bros., 1931.

American Home. *American Home Book of House Plans.* Garden City, New York: American Home, 1934.

American Shelter: An Illustrated Encyclopedia of the American Home. Woodstock: Overlook Press, 1981.

Ames, Kenneth. *Beyond Necessity: Art in the Folk Tradition.* New York: W. W. Norton, 1977.

Anderson, Charles F. *Anderson's American Villa Architecture: With an Essay on Architecture.* New York: G. P. Putnam's Sons, 1853.

Architects Emergency Committee. *Great Georgian Houses of America.* Vol. 1 New York: Kalkhoff Press, 1933; vol. 2 New York: Scribners, 1937.

Arnot, David Henry. *Gothic Architecture Applied to Modern Residence.* New York: D. Appleton and Co., 1849.

Atterbury, Grosvenor. *The Economic Production of Workingmen's Homes.* New York: n.p., 1930.

Atwood, Daniel. *Country and Suburban Houses.* New York: Orange, Judd, and Co., 1871.

Atwood, Daniel. *Modern American Homesteads.* New York: A. J. Bicknell and Co., 1876.

Baker, Z. *Modern House Builder from the Log Cabin and Cottage to the Mansion.* Boston: Higgins, Bradley, & Dayton, 1857.

Baldrige, Letita. *Home.* New York: Viking Press, 1972.

Banham, Reyner. *Los Angeles: The Architecture of Four Ecologies.* New York: Allen Lane, 1971.

Beecher, Catherine E. and Stowe, Harriet Beecher. *The American Woman's Home.* New York: J. B. Ford and Co., 1869.

Bettman, Otto L. *The Good Old Days—They Were Terrible!* New York: Random House, 1974.

Bloomfield, Reginald. *A History of French Renaissance Architecture.* 2 vols. London: G. Bell and Sons, 1911.

Blumenson, John. *Identifying American Architecture: A Pictorial Guide to Styles and Terms, 1600–1945.* Nashville: American Association for State and Local History, 1977.

Boorstin, Daniel. *The Americans: The National Experience.* New York: Vintage, 1965.

Bremer, Frederika. *The Homes of the New World: Impressions of America.* New York: Harper and Bros., 1853.

Brooks, H. Allen. *The Prairie School.* Toronto: University of Toronto Press, 1972.

Bruce, Alfred and Sandbank, Harold. *A History of Prefabrication.* New York: John B. Pierce Foundation, 1943. Reprinted by Arno Press, New York, 1972.

Brumbagh, G. Edwin. *Colonial Architecture of the Pennsylvania Germans.* Norristown: Norristown Herald, 1933.

Bullock, John. *The American Cottage Builder: Designs, Plans, and Specifications for Homes for the People.* New York: Stringer and Townsend, 1854.

Calvert, Frank (ed.). *Homes and Gardens of the Pacific Coast.* Los Angeles and Seattle: C. Laughlin, [1905].

Carr, A. L. *A Practical Guide to Prefabricated Houses.* New York: Harper, 1947.

Cavalier, Julian. *American Castles.* South Brunswick, New Jersey: A. S. Barnes, 1973.

Central States Research. *The Story of the Factory-Made Houses.* Columbus, Indiana: Acme Mimeograph Service, 1946.

Chandler, Joseph Everett. *The Colonial House.* New York: McBride, 1916.

Clark, Arthur Bridgman. *Art Principles in House, Furniture, and Village Building.* Stanford: Stanford University Press, 1921.

Clute, Eugene. *The Treatment of Interiors.* New York: Pencil Points, 1926.

Cohen, H. L. (ed.). *1922 Montgomery Ward Catalogue.* New York, 1969.

Cole, Katherine H. *Houses By Mail: A Field Guide to Mail Order Houses from Sears Roebuck and Co.* Washington, D.C.: Preservation Press, ca. 1986.

Cooper, James Fenimore. *Home as Found.* New York: Stringer and Townsend, 1852.

Cornfield, William H. *Dwelling Houses: Their Sanitary Construction.* New York: D. Van Nostrand, 1880.

Cram, Ralph Adams. *My Life in Architecture.* Boston: Little, Brown, & Co., 1936.

Croff, G. B. *Progressive American Architecture.* New York, 1875.

Current, Karen and Current, William R. *Greene and Greene: Architects in the Residential Style.* Fort Worth: Amon Carter Museum of Western Art, 1974.

Davidson, Marshall B. *The American Heritage History of Notable American Houses.* New York: American Heritage Pub. Co., 1971.

Desmond, Henry Ward and Croly, Herbert. *Stately Homes in America.* New York: D. Appleton and Co., 1903.

Dow, Joy Wheeler. *American Renaissance: A Review of Domestic Architecture.* New York: William T. Comstock, 1904.

Dow, Joy Wheeler (ed.). *The Book of a Hundred Houses: A Collection of Pictures, Plans, and Suggestions for Householders.* Chicago, 1902.

Drake, Samuel Adams. *Our Colonial Homes.* Boston: Lothrop, Lee & Shepard Pub. Co., 1894.

Drexler, Arthur (ed.). *The Architecture of the Ecole des Beaux-Arts.* New York: Museum of Modern Art, 1977.

Drury, John. *The Heritage of Early American Houses.* New York: Coward, McCann, 1969.

Dulles, Foster Rhea. *The Imperial Years.* Ann Arbor: University of Michigan Press, 1956.

Dustman, U. M. *Dustman's Book of Plans and Building Construction for General Contractors and Home Builders.* Freeport, Illinois: Charles C. Thompson Co., 1909 and 1910.

Eaton, Leonard K. *Two Chicago Architects and their Clients: Frank Lloyd Wright and Howard Van Doren Shaw.* Cambridge: The MIT Press, 1969.

Eberlein, Harold D. *Early Architecture of Pennsylvania.* New York: Architectural Record, n.d.

Eberlein, Harold D. *Portrait of a Colonial City, Philadelphia, 1670–1838.* Philadelphia and New York: J. B. Lippincott, 1939.

Edwardes, Michael. *British India, 1772–1947.* London: Sidgwick & Jackson, 1967.

Egleston, Nathaniel H. *The Home and Its Surroundings.* New York, 1884.

Elliott, Charles W. *The Book of American Interiors from Existing Houses with Preliminary Essays and Letterpress Descriptions.* Boston: James R. Osgood, 1876.

Elliott, Charles W. *Cottages and Cottage Life.* Cincinnati: H. W. Derby and Co., 1848.

Embury, Aymar. *The Dutch Colonial House.* New York: McBride, Nast and Co., 1913.

Field, M. *Rural Architecture or Designs for Villas, Cottages.* New York: Miller and Co., 1957.

Fitzpatrick, John Clement. *Some Historic Houses.* New York: Macmillan, 1939.

Fitzsimons, Jack. *Bungalow Bliss.* Kells: Kells Art Studies, 1972.

Foley, Mary Mix. *The American House.* New York: Harper and Row, 1980.

Ford, James and Ford, Katherine. *The Modern House in America.* New York: Architectural Book Publishing, 1940.

Ford, Katherine Morrow. *The American House Today.* New York: Reinhold Publishing Corp., 1951.

Forman, Henry C. *The Architecture of the Old South.* Cambridge: Harvard University Press, 1948.

Forman, Henry C. *Jamestown and St. Mary's: Buried Cities of Romance.* Baltimore: n.p., 1938.

Fuller, Albert W. *Artistic Homes in City and Country.* Boston: James R. Osgood, 1882. Published in a revised and expanded edition by Ticknor and Co., Boston, 1886.

Gardner, Eugene C. *Home Interiors.* Boston: J. R. Osgood, 1878.

Gardner, Eugene C. *Homes and All About Them.* Boston: J. R. Osgood, 1885.

Gardner, Eugene C. *Homes and How to Make Them.* Boston: J. R. Osgood, 1874.

Gardner, Eugene C. *The House That Jill Built After Jack's Had Proved A Failure.* New York: Ford, Howard and Hulbert, 1882.

Gardner, Eugene C. *Illustrated Homes: A Series of Papers Describing Real Houses and Real People.* Boston: James R. Osgood and Co., 1875.

Gault, Lila. *The House Next Door: Seattle's Neighborhood Architecture.* Seattle: Pacific Search Press, 1981.

Gebhard, David. *The Architecture of Gregory Ain.* Santa Barbara: Peregrine Smith, 1980.

Gebhard, David, et al. *Samuel and Joseph Cather Newsom: Victorian Architectural Imagery in California.* Santa Barbara: Peregrine Smith, 1979.

Gibson, Louis H. *Beautiful Houses: A Study in House-Building.* New York: Thomas Y. Crowell, 1895.

Gibson, Louis H. *Convenient Houses, with Fifty Plans for the Housekeeper.* New York: Thomas Y. Crowell, 1889.

Gill, Brendon. *Summer Places.* New York: Methuen, 1978.

Glassie, Henry. *Folk Culture of the Eastern United States.* Philadelphia: University of Pennsylvania Press, 1968.

Glassie, Henry; Degh, Linda; and Oinas, Felix J. *Folklore Today: Festschrift for Richard M. Dorson.* Bloomington, Indiana: Research Center for Language and Semiotic Studies, 1976.

Gloag, John. *House Out of Factory.* London: G. Allen and Unwin, 1946.

Goforth, William D. *Old Colonial Architectural Details in and Around Philadelphia.* New York: W. Hilburn, 1890.

Goodykoontz, Colin B. *Home Missions on the American Frontier.* Caldwell, Idaho: The Caxton Printers, 1939.

Goodnow, Ruby R. *The Honest House.* New York: Century, 1914.

Gould, Lucius D. *The American House Carpenter's and Joiner's Assistant.* New York: Daniel Burgess and Co., 1853.

Gould, Mary E. *The Early American House: Household Life in America, 1620–1850.* New York: Charles E. Tuttle Co., 1965.

Gowans, Alan. *Building Canada: An Architectural History of Canadian Life.* Toronto: Oxford University Press, 1966.

Gowans, Alan. *Images of American Living: Four Centuries of Architecture and Furniture in the United States.* Philadelphia and New York: J. B. Lippincott, 1964.

Gowans, Alan. *Learning to See: Historical Perspectives on Modern Popular Commercial Arts.* Bowling Green, Ohio: Popular Arts Press, 1982.

Gowans, Alan. *The Unchanging Arts.* Philadelphia and New York: J. B. Lippincott, 1971.

Graff, R. K.; Matern, R. A.; and Williams, H. L. *The Prefabricated House: A Practical Guide for the Prospective Buyer.* Garden City, New York: Doubleday, 1947.

Great Georgian Houses of America. 2 vols. New York: Kalkhoff Press for the benefit of the Architects Emergency Committee, 1933–37.

Grow, Lawrence. *Old House Plans: Two Centuries of American Domestic Architecture.* New York: Main St. Press, 1978.

Gruen, Victor. *Centers for the Urban Environment.* New York: Van Nostrand Reinhold Co., 1973.

Gutheim, Frederick. *One Hundred Years of Architecture in America, 1857–1957.* New York: Reinhold Pub., 1957.

Hale, Edward Everett. *Workingmen's Homes.* Boston: J. R. Osgood and Co., 1874.

Hall, Ben M. *The Best Remaining Seats: The Story of the Golden Age of the Movie Palace.* New York: C. N. Potter, 1961.

Hamlin, Talbot (ed.). *Forms and Functions in Twentieth-Century Architecture.* New York: Columbia University Press, 1963.

Hamlin, Winthrop A. *Low Cost Cottage Construction in America.* Cambridge: Harvard University Press, 1917.

Hammond, George W. *A Mill-Built Dwelling House.* Boston: Parkhill, 1892.

Hammond, John M. *Colonial Mansions of Maryland and Delaware.* Philadelphia: J. B. Lippincott, 1914.

Handlin, David P. *The American Home: Architecture and Society, 1815–1915.* Boston: Little, Brown and Co., 1979.

Harrison, Percival. *Bungalow Residences*. London: Lockwood and Sons, 1909.

Hartshorne, Henry. *Our Homes*. Philadelphia: P. Blakiston, 1880.

Hatfield, Robert G. *The American House Carpenter*. New York and London: Wiley and Putnam, 1844.

Haweis, Mary E. *Beautiful Houses*. New York: Scribner and Welford, 1882.

Hayek, F. A. (ed.). *Capitalism and the Historians*. Chicago: University of Chicago Press, 1954.

Hersey, George L. *High Victorian Gothic: A Study in Associationism*. Baltimore: John Hopkins University Press, 1972.

Hill, Amelia Leavitt. *Redeeming Old Houses*. New York: Henry Holt and Company, 1923.

History of Real Estate, Building, and Architecture in New York City during the last quarter of a century. New York: Real Estate Record Association, 1898. Reprinted by Arno Press, New York, 1967.

Hitchcock, Henry Russell. *American Architectural Books*. Minneapolis: University of Minnesota Press, 1962.

Hoffman, Donald and Condit, Carl. *Frank Lloyd Wright's Fallingwater: The House and Its History*. New York: Dover, 1978.

Hofstadter, Richard. *American Political Tradition and the Men Who Made It*. New York: Vintage Books, 1948.

Hofstadter, Richard. *Rendez-vous with Destiny*. New York: Vintage Books, 1965.

Holst, H. V. von. *Modern American Homes*. Chicago: American Technical Society, 1914.

Homes of American Authors, Comprising Anecdotal, Personal and Descriptive Sketches. New York: D. Appleton and Co., 1852.

Homes of American Statesmen, with Anecdotal, Personal and Descriptive Sketches. New York: G. Putnam and Son, 1854.

Hubbell, Lucy Embury. *The Book of Little Houses*. Garden City, New York: Doubleday and Co., 1916.

Hunter, Robinson Paul and Reichardt, Walter L. *Residential Architecture in Southern California*. Los Angeles: A.I.A., 1939

Hussey, Elisha C. *Home Building*. New York: Leader and Van Hoesen, 1876.

Hussey, Elisha C. *Houseplanning at Home*. St. Louis: C. B. Woodward and Co., 1894.

Hussey, Elisha C. *Hussey's National Cottage Architecture: Or Homes for Everyone, Chiefly Low-Priced Buildings for Towns, Suburbs and Country*. New York: George E. Woodward, 1847.

Isham, Norman M. *Early American Houses*. Topsfield, Massachusetts: Walpole Society, 1928.

Isham, Norman M. *A Glossary of Colonial Architectural Terms*. New York: Walpole Society, 1939. Reprinted by American Life Foundation in Watkins Glenn, New York, 1976, with an additional bibliographic essay entitled "Quest of the Colonial: A Bibliography of Books on the Colonial Revival 1880–1930" by John Freeman.

Jackson, John B. *The Necessity for Ruins*. Amherst: University of Massachusetts Press, 1980.

Jakle, John, et al. *American Common Houses: A Selected Bibliography of Vernacular Architecture*. Monticello, Illinois: Vance Bibliographies, 1981.

James, George Wharton. *In and Out of the Old Missions of California*. Boston: Little, Brown and Co., 1905.

Johanneson, Eric. *Cleveland Architecture, 1876–1976*. Cleveland: Western Reserve Historical Society, 1979.

Johl, Karen. *Timeless Treasures: San Diego's Victorian Heritage*. San Diego: Rand Editions, 1982.

Johnson, William K. *Modern Homes*. Chicago: n.p., 1894.

Jones, Howard Mumford. *The Age of Energy*. New York: Viking Press, 1970.

Keefe, Charles S. (ed.). *The American House*. New York: U.P.C. Book Co., 1933.

Keeler, Charles. *The Simple Home*. New York: P. Elder and Co., 1904. Reprinted Santa Barbara, 1979.

Keith, Walter Jewett. *Historic Architecture for the Home Builder*. Minneapolis: The Keith Co., 1905.

Kellar, Harbert A. (ed.). *Solon Robinson, Pioneer and Agriculturist*. Indianapolis: Indianapolis Historical Society, 1936.

Kelly, J. Frederick. *Early Domestic Architecture of Connecticut*. New Haven: Yale University Press for the Connecticut Tercentary Commission, 1935.

Kidney, Walter C. *The Architecture of Choice: Eclecticism in America 1880–1930*. New York: Braziller, 1974.

Kimball, Sidney Fiske. *Domestic Architecture of the American Colonies and of the Early Republic*. New York: Dover Publishers, 1966.

Kimball, Sidney Fiske. *Thomas Jefferson*. (Monticello Papers no. 1). New York, 1924.

King, Anthony D. *The Bungalow*. London: Routledge and Kegan Paul, 1984.

Kirker, Harold. *California's Architectural Frontier*. San Marino: Huntington Library, 1960.

Koch, Robert. *Louis C. Tiffany*. New York: Museum of Contemporary Crafts, 1964.

Kornwolf, James D. *A History of American Dwellings*. New York: Rand McNally, 1967.

Lamb, Martha J. (ed.). *The Homes of America*. New York: D. Appleton, 1879.

Lancaster, Clay. *The Japanese Influence in America*. New York: W. E. Rawls, 1963.

Lancaster, Clay. *The American Bungalow, 1880's–1920's*. New York: Abbeville Press, 1985.

Lathrop, Elsie L. *Historic Houses of Early America*. New York: Robert McBride and Co., 1927.

Leicht, Alfred F. *A Few Sketches of Picturesque Suburban Homes*. New York: n.p., 1892.

Leland, E. H. *Farm Homes In-doors and Out-doors*. New York: Orange Judd Co., 1881.

LeMoyne, L. V. *Country Residences in Europe and America*. New York: Doubleday and Co., 1908.

Leonidoff, Georges Pierre; Guindon, Vianney; and Gagnon, Paul. *Comment Restaurer une Maison Traditionnelle*. (Collection Civilisation du Québec, 12, série architecture). Québec: Ministère des Affaires Culturelles, 1973.

Lessard, Michel and Marquis, Huguette. *Encyclopédie de la Maison Québecoise*. Montréal: Les Editions de l'Homme, 1972.

Lessard, Michel and Villandre, Gilles. *La Maison Traditionnelle au Québec*. Montréal: Les Editions de l'Homme, 1974.

Lindstrom and Almars, Minneapolis. *From Mansion to Bungalow*. Minneapolis, n.d.

Löwith, Karl. *Meaning in History*. Chicago: University of Chicago Press, 1957.

Lynd, Robert Staughton and Lynd, Helen M. *Middletown: A Study in Contemporary American Culture*. New York: n.p., 1930.

Lynd, Robert Staughton and Lynd, Helen M. *Middletown in Transition*. New York: Harcourt, Brace and World, 1937.

Lynes, Russell. *The Tastemakers: The Shaping of American Popular Taste*. New York: Dover, 1980.

McAlester, Virginia and McAlester, Lee. *Field Guide to American Houses*. New York: Knopf, 1984.

McCall's Magazine. *The American Woman's Home of Tomorrow*. New York: McCall Corp., 1945.

McKennee, Oscar W. *Prefabs on Parade*. New York: Housing Institute, 1948.

McKinnon, Sarah M. *Traditional Rural Architecture in Quebec: 1600–1800*. (Centre for Urban and Community Studies Report 9). Toronto: University of Toronto Press, 1977.

Major, Howard. *The Domestic Architecture of the Early American Republic, The Greek Revival*. Philadelphia: Lippincott, 1926.

Mass, John. *The Victorian Home in America*. New York: Hawthorn Books, 1972.

Mayer, Harold M. and Wade, Richard C. *Chicago: Growth of a Metropolis*. Chicago: University of Chicago Press, 1969.

Mills, Weymer Jay. *Historic Houses of New Jersey*. Philadelphia: J. B. Lippincott, 1902.

Moore, Charles and Smith, Kathryn (eds.). *Home Sweet Home: American Domestic Vernacular Architecture*. Los Angeles: Craft and Folk Art Museum, 1983.

Morrill, Milton Dana. *The Morrill Moulded Concrete Houses*. New York: Morrill, 1917.

Mumford, Lewis. *The City in History*. New York: Harcourt, Brace and World, 1961.

Murmann, Eugene. *Typical California Bungalows*. Los Angeles: Eugene Murmann, 1913.

National Builder. *Catalogue of Building Designs Originally Presented in the Monthly Issues of the National Builder*. Chicago: Porter, Taylor and Co., 1899.

National Fire Proofing Co. *Fireproof Construction for Houses and Other Buildings at Moderate Costs*. Chicago: National Fire Proofing Co., 1909.

Newcomb, Rexford. *The Colonial and Federal House*. Philadelphia: J. B. Lippincott Co., 1933.

Newcomb, Rexford. *Spanish Colonial Architecture in the United States*. New York: J. J. Augustin, 1937.

Newson, Thomas McLean (ed.). *The Independent Farmer and Fireside Companion*. St. Paul, 1879.

Nicholson, Arnold. *American Houses in History*. New York: Viking Press, 1965.

Oakey, Alexander F. *Building A Home*. New York: D. Appleton and Co., 1881.

Ogilvie, George W. *Architecture Simplified or How to Build a House*. Chicago: George W. Ogilvie, 1885.

Old House Journal Buyer's Guide. Brooklyn: Old House Journal Corp., 1976.

Ordish, George. *The Living American House.* New York: Morrow, 1981.

Ormsbee, Agnes Bailey. *The House Comfortable.* New York: Harper and Bros., 1892.

Osborne, Charles Francis. *Notes on the Art of House Planning.* New York: W. T. Comstock, 1888.

Pfeiffer, Carl. *American Mansions and Cottages.* Boston: Ticknor and Co., 1889.

Pickering, Ernest. *The Houses of America, as They Have Expressed the Lives of Pure People for Three Centuries.* New York: Crowell, 1951.

Plummer, Peter W. *The Carpenters' and Builders' Guide: Being a Hand-book for Workmen, also a Manual of Reference for Contractors, Builders, etc.* Portland: Hoyt, Fogg, and Donham, 1879.

Pomeroy, Earl. *In Search of the Golden West.* New York: Knopf, 1957.

Pott, Janet. *Old Bungalows in Bangalore, South India.* London: Mrs. J. Pott, 1977.

Power, Ethel B. *The Smaller American House.* Boston: Little, Brown, 1927.

Pratt, Richard. *A Treasury of Early American Houses.* New York: Whittlesey House, 1949.

Price, Bruce. *A Large Country House.* New York: William T. Comstock, 1887.

Ranlett, William H. *The Architect: A Series of Original Designs for Domestic and Ornamental Cottages and Villas. . . .* 2 vols. New York: William H. Graham, 1847–49.

Reed, Henry Hope. *The Golden City.* New York: W. W. Norton, 1959.

Richardson, Charles J. *House Building: From a Cottage to a Mansion.* New York: G. Putnam's Sons, 1873.

Rifkind, Carol. *A Field Guide to American Architecture.* New York: New American Library, 1980.

Robinson, Dean H. *Book of Small Home Designs.* Detroit: Home Planning Co., 1948.

Robinson, Ethel F. and Robinson, Thomas P. *Houses in America.* New York: Viking Press, 1936.

Rogers, Meyric Reynold. *American Interior Design: The Traditions and Development of Domestic Design from Colonial Times to the Present.* New York: W. W. Norton, 1947.

Romaine, Lawrence B. *A Guide to American Trade Catalogs, 1744–1900.* New York, 1960.

Saylor, Henry H. *Bungalows.* New York: McBride, Nast and Co., 1913.

Schuyler, David. *Cleaveland and Backus' Village and Farm Cottages.* Watkins Glenn, New York: American Life Foundation, 1981.

Scott, Mellier. *American City Planning Since 1890.* Berkeley: University of California Press, 1969.

Scully, Vincent. *American Architecture and Urbanism.* New York: Praeger, 1969.

Scully, Vincent. *The Shingle Style.* New Haven: Yale University Press, 1955.

Sedgwick, Catharine. *Home.* Boston: J. Munroe, 1835.

Sexton, Randolph W. *Spanish Influence on American Architecture and Decoration.* New York: Brentano's, 1927.

Sheldon, G. W. *Artistic Country Seats.* New York: D. Appleton and Co., 1886.

Shepp, James W. and Shepp, Daniel B. *Shepp's World's Fair Photographed.* Chicago and Philadelphia: Globe Bible Pub. Co., 1893.

Sherwin-Williams Co. *Your Home and Its Decoration.* Cleveland: Sherwin Williams Co., 1910.

Short, R. *Proper Homes and How to Have Them.* New York: n.p., 1887.

Shurtleff, Harold R. *The Log Cabin Myth.* Cambridge: Harvard University Press, 1939.

Silver, Nathan. *Lost New York.* New York: Weathervane Books, 1967.

Sloan, Maurice M. *The Concrete House and Its Construction.* Philadelphia: Association of American Portland Cement Manufacturers, 1912.

Smith, Frank L. *A Cosy Home: How It Was Built.* Boston: T. O. Metcalf and Co., 1887.

Smith, Frank L., *Suburban Homes.* Boston: Wood, Harmon and Co., 1890.

Smith, Norris K. *Frank Lloyd Wright: A Study in Architectural Content.* Englewood Cliffs, New Jersey: Prentice Hall, 1969. Reprinted Watkins Glenn, American Life Foundation, 1977.

Staats, H. Philip. *Calfifornia Architecture in Santa Barbara.* New York: Architectural Book Pub. Co., 1929.

Stern, Robert A. M. (ed.). *The Anglo-American Suburb.* New York: Architectural League, 1981.

Strand, Janan. *A Greene and Greene Guide.* Pasadena: The Castle Press, 1974.

Sturgis, Russell and Frothingham, A. L. *A History of Architecture.* 4 vols. Garden City, New York: Doubleday, Page and Co., 1915–17.

Sturgis, Russell. *Homes in City and Country.* New York: Charles Scribners Sons, 1893.

Stutchbury, Howard E. *The Architecture of Colen Campbell.* Cambridge: Harvard University Press, 1967.

Sullivan, Mark. *Our Times, 1900–1925.* New York: C. Scribners Sons, 1926.

Sweeney, John. *Grandeur on the Appoquinimink.* Newark: University of Delaware Press, 1959.

Sylvester, William A. *Modern House Carpenter's Companion and Builder's Guide.* Boston: A. Williams and Co., 1882.

Thompson, Robert E. *The Development of the House.* Philadelphia: University of Pennsylvania Press, 1885.

Tunnard, Christopher and Pushkarev, Boris. *Man Made America: Chaos or Control.* New York: Harmony Books, 1981.

Varney, Almon Clothier. *Our Homes and Their Adornments.* Detroit: J. C. Chilton and Co., 1882.

Walker, Lester. *American Shelter: An Ilustrated Encyclopaedia of the American Home.* Woodstock, New York: Overlook Press, 1981.

Ware, John F. W. *Home Life.* Boston: W. V. Spencer, 1864.

Warner, Sam Bass. *Streetcar Suburbs: The Process of Growth in Boston 1870–1900.* Cambridge: Harvard University Press, 1962.

Waterman, Thomas Tileston. *The Dwellings of Colonial America.* Chapel Hill: University of North Carolina Press, 1950.

Weslager, C. A. *The Log Cabin in America: From Pioneer Days to the Present.* New Brunswick: Rutgers University Press, 1969.

Whiffen, Marcus. *American Architecture Since 1780: A Guide to the Styles.* Cambridge: The MIT Press, 1969.

White Pine Series of Architectural Monographs. Vols. 1–14. New York, 1915–28.

White, Charles, Jr. *The Bungalow Book.* New York: Macmillan Co., 1929.

White, Charles, Jr. *Successful Houses and How to Build Them.* New York: Macmillan Co., 1912.

White, Lynn, Jr. *Medieval Technology and Social Change.* New York: Oxford University Press, 1962.

Wilson, Henry L. *The Bungalow Book.* Chicago: Wilson, 1910.

Winter, Robert. *The California Bungalow.* Los Angeles: Hennessey and Ingalls, 1980.

Wright, Frank Lloyd. *The National House.* New York: Horizon Press, 1954.

Wright, Gwendolyn, et al. *Moralism and the Model Home: Domestic Architecture and Cultural Conflict in Chicago 1873–1913.* Chicago: University of Chicago Press, 1980.

Periodical Articles and Essays

"Adoption of Pueblo Architecture in the University of New Mexico." *Architect's and Builder's Magazine* 41 (April 1909): 282–85.

"An American Dream House." *Domus* 610 (October 1980): 42–43.

"The American Ideal Home." *Architects Journal* 92 (August 22, 1940): 143–45.

"American Modern Architecture." *House Beautiful* 80 (September 1938): 22–25.

"America's New Dream House is Illegal." *American Builder* 99 (September 1966): 59–66.

"American Small House: Exhibit at the Museum of Modern Art." *Architects Journal* 102 (August 30, 1945): 155–59.

"American Small Houses Lead the World's." *American Architect* 116 (September 24, 1919): 415–16.

Anshen, S. Robert. "The Postwar House and Its Materials." *Arts and Architecture* 62 (November 1945): 43, 56–58.

"The Architect and the $5,000 House." *Architectural Forum* 64 (April 1936): 248–357.

"The Artistic Development of the Standardized House." *American Architect* 117 (May 12, 1920) 571–78.

Atterbery, Jennifer E. "The Square Cabin: A Folk House Type in Idaho." *Idaho Yesterdays* 26/3 (1982): 25–31.

Benjamin, Muriel. "Octagonal Houses: An Experiment in American Design." *American Art and Antiques* 2/3 (1979): 98–105.

Benton, Arthur. "The California Mission and Its Influence Upon Pacific Coast Architecture." *Architect and Engineer* 24 (February 1911): 35–75.

"The Best House of the Year." *Country Life in America* 26 (October 1914): 34–40.

Blake, Peter. "The Vanishing American House." *Zodiac* 1 (1957): 90–94.

Blumenson, John J. G. "'A Home for All': The Octagon in American Architecture." *Historic Preservation* 25/3 (1973): 30–35.

Brooks, Arthur C. "The Old Time House." *Art World* 3 (October 1917): 63–65.

"Building Types: Houses $7,500 and Under." *Architectural Record* 83 (March 1938): 133–63.

"Built in U.S.A.: Postwar Architecture." *Architectural Record* 113 (February 1953): 10–12.

"Built in U.S.A.: Postwar Architecture." *Progressive Architecture* 34 (February 1953): 172 + .

Burnham, Alan. "The New York Architecture of Richard Morris Hunt." *JSAH* 11 (May 1952): 9–14.

Bushman, Richard. "American High-Style and Vernacular Cultures," in Greene, Jack P. and Pole, J. R., eds., *Colonial British America: Essays in the New History of the Early Modern Era*. Baltimore: Johns Hopkins University Press, 1984.

"Case Study House for 1949." *Arts and Architecture* 66 (December 1949): 26–39.

Castle, Marian. "Give me a House I Can Hide in." *Michigan Society Monthly Bulletin* 26 (January 1952): 13, 15.

Chappell, Edward A. "Acculturation in the Shenandoah Valley: Rhenish Houses of the Massanutten Settlement." *Proceedings of the Philosophical Society* 124/1 (1980): 55–89.

Chase, Laura. "Eden in the Orange Groves: Bungalows and Courtyard Houses of Los Angeles." *Landscape* 25/3 (1981): 29–36.

Chilson, Mabel. "Historical Aspects of the Bungalow." *Keith's Magazine* 24 (December 1910): 369.

Clark, Clifford, E., Jr. "Domestic Architecture as an Index to Social History: The Romantic Revival and the Cult of Domesticity in America, 1840–1870." *Journal of Interdisciplinary History* 7/1 (1976): 33–56.

Colean, Miles. "The Miracle House Myth . . ." *House Beautiful* 86 (December 1944): 78–79.

Colean, Miles. "Your Dream House." *House Beautiful* 87 (November 1945): 138, 184–86.

"Contemporary Home Replaces Expensive Victorian Mansion." *New Pencil Points* 24 (October 1943): 36–45.

"The Contemporary Suburban Residence." *Architectural Record* 11 (January 1902): 69–81.

"Craftsman Summer Log Houses: The Entire Upper Story Arranged for Outdoor Sleeping." *Craftsman* 20 (1911): 506–11.

Cramer, Richard. "Images of Home." *AIA Journal* 34 (September 1960): 40–49.

Creese, Walter, "Fowler and the Domestic Octagon." *Art Bulletin* 28 (1946): 89–102.

Croly, Herbert D. "The California Country House." *Sunset* 18 (November 1906): 50–65.

Croly, Herbert D. "English Renaissance at Its Best: The House of James Parmelee." *Architectural Record* 36 (August 1914): 80–97.

David, Arthur C. "An Architect of Bungalows in California." *Architectural Record* 20 (October 1906): 306.

deKay, Charles. "Villas All Concrete." *Architectural Record* 17 (1905): 85–100.

"Design for a House." *California and Architecture* 61 (February 1944): 24–25.

Dresser, Peter van. "The Productive Home." *Free America* 3 (February 1939): 13.

Eaton, Leonard K. "The Architecture of the Ecole des Beaux-Arts." *Progressive Architecture* 6 (January 1979): 133–35.

"Economical Houses for the Southwest." *Architectural Record* 105 (November 1946): 88–89.

Edgerton, Samuel Y. "Heat and Style: 18th Century House Warming by Stoves." *JSAH* 20 (March 1961): 20–26.

"The Eight Thousand Pound House." *Architectural Forum* 84 (April 1946): 129–36.

Embury, Aymar. "The Country House." *Western Architect* 17 (1911): 52–54.

Evans, E. Raymond. "The Strip House in Tennessee Folk Architecture." *Tennessee Folklore Society Bulletin* 42/4 (1976): 163–66.

"Expansible Bungalow." *Architectural Forum* 85 (July 1948): 116–17.

"Expansible Row House." *Architectural Forum* 85 (July 1946): 106–8.

Fallon, J. T. "Domestic Architecture of the Early Nineteenth Century." *American Architect* 110 (1916): 139–44, 167–71.

Farrell, Richard T. "Advice to Farmers: The Content of Agricultural Newspapers, 1860–1910." *American Agriculturist* 51 (1977): 209–17.

Feldman, Edmund Burke. "Homes in America." *Arts and Architecture* 74 (October 1957): 22–23; (November 1957): 20–21, 34–35.

"Fifteen Good Halls and Stairways." *Ladies Home Journal* 16 (1899): 18.

Filler, Martin. "Charles Moore: House Vernacular." *Art in America* 68 (October 1980): 105–12.

Finley, Robert and Scott E. M. "Great Lakes to Gulf: Profile of Dispersed Building Type." *Geographical Review* 30 (1940): 412–19.

"The First Post War House." *House Beautiful* 88 (May 1946): 82–123.

"Five Distinctive Homes." *Architectural Record* 148 (November 1970): 109–20.

"Five Houses." *Architectural Record* 120 (November 1956): 161–86.

"For Houses—Open or Closed Planning." *Architectural Record* 115 (April 1954): 174–82.

"Four Homes of Tomorrow." *House and Garden* 74 (November 1938): 22–27, 38, 43.

Francaviglia, Richard. "Main Street U.S.A.: A Comparison-Contrast of Streetscapes in Disneyland and Walt Disney World." *Journal of Popular Culture* 15/1 (1981): 22ff.

"Freedom in House Design." *Architectural Record* 114 (December 1953); 154–59.

French, Leigh, Jr. "The Small House and Candor in Designing." *Architectural Forum* 44 (1926): 175.

Fusch, Richard and Ford, Larry R. "Architecture and the Geography of the American City." *Geographic Review* 73/3 (1983): 324–40.

Garvin, James L. "Mail-Order House Plans and American Victorian Architecture." *Winterthur Portfolio* 16 (Winter 1981): 309–34.

Gebhard, David. "Fifty Years of the American Home." *Landscape* 8 (Autumn 1958): 5–9.

Gebhard, David. "The Spanish Colonial Revival in Southern California." *JSAH* 26 (May 1967): 131–47.

Glassie, Henry. "Eighteenth Century Cultural Process in Delaware Valley Folk Building." *Winterthur Portfolio* 7 (1971): 29–57.

Glassie, Henry. "Vernacular Architecture." *Society of Architectural Historians Journal* 35 (December 1976): 294.

Goodhue, Bertram G. "The Modern Architectural Problem Discussed from the Professional Point of View." *Craftsman* 8 (1905): 325–35.

Gough, Marion. "Honeymoon Home." *House Beautiful* 88 (June 1946): 62–65.

Gowans, Alan. "Back to the Drawing Board: A review of Wolf von Eckhardt's new work." *Inquiry* 2 (December 11, 1978): 27–28.

Gowans, Alan. "The Mansions of Alloway's Creek." *RACAR* 3 (1976): 6f. Reprinted in Upton, Dell and Vlach, John, eds. *Commonplaces: Readings in American Vernacular Architecture.* Athens: University of Georgia Press, 1985.

Gowans, Alan. "The Plight of the Conservative: Charles Donagh Maginnis, Academic Architect." *Dictionary of American Biography, Supplement V* (1977): 462.

Gowans, Alan. "Post Victorian Domestic Architecture: The Spanish Colonial Revival Style." *Old House Journal* 10 (October 1982): 198–202.

Gowans, Alan. "Review of Robert Fishman's *Urban Utopias of the Twentieth Century.*" *Inquiry* 11 (July 1978): 26–27.

Gowans, Alan. "Review of Tom Wolfe's *From Bauhaus to Our House.*" *Inquiry* (December 7, 1981): 31.

Greene, Jack. "Search for Identity." *Journal of Social History* 111/3 (1970): 205 ff.

"A Group of Small Homes." *Architect and Engineer* 164 (February 1946): 14–15.

Grider, Sylvia A. "The Shotgun House in Oil Boomtowns of the Texas Panhandle." *Pioneer America* 7/2 (1975): 47–55.

Guthrie, Hugh. "Quest for the Colonial: A Bibliography of Books, 1880–1930." In Norman Morrison Isham, *Early American Houses.* Watkins Glenn, New York: American Life Foundation, 1968.

Halpin, Kay. "Sears Roebucks' Best-Kept Secret." *Historic Preservation* (September-October 1981): 24–29.

Hamlin, A. D. F. "The American Country House." *Architectural Record* 44 (October 1918): 274–379.

Hamlin, Talbot Faulkner. "Of Houses as Places to Live." *Pencil Points* 19 (August 1938): 487–94.

Hanchett, Thomas W. "Origins of the American Foursquare," in *Proceedings of the Vernacular Architecture Forum.* Annapolis, Maryland: Vernacular Architecture Society, 1982.

Harvey, Thomas. "Mail Order Architecture in the Twenties." *Landscape* 25/3 (1981): 1–9.

Hayes, William H. "Structural Requirements for Houses." *Architectural Record* 86 (July 1939): 79–92.

Heisner, Beverly. "Harriet Morrison Irwin's Hexagonal House: An Invention to Improve Domestic Dwellings." *North Carolina Historical Review* 58/2 (1981): 105–23.

"Hints for Home Decoration and Furnishing." *Art Amateur* 18 (1888): 119.

Holdsworth, Deryck. "House and Home in Vancouver: Images of West Coast Urbanism, 1886–1929." In Stetler, Gilbert A. and Artibise, Alan, F. J., eds., *The Canadian City: Essays in Urban History.* Toronto: McClelland and Stewart, 1977, pp. 186–211.

Holdsworth, Deryck. "Regional Distinctiveness in an Industrial Age: Some California Influences on British Columbia Housing." *American Review of Canadian Studies* 12/2 (1982): 64–81.

Holdsworth, Deryck and Ennals, Peter. Vernacular Architecture and the Cultural Landscape of the Marine Provinces: A Reconnaissance." *Acadiensis* 10/2 (1981): 86–106.

Hopkins, Una Nixon. "A Picturesque Court of Thirty Bungalows: A Community Idea for Women." *Ladies Home Journal* 30 (April 1913): 97–99.

Horwitz, Richard P. "Architecture and Culture: The Meaning of the Lowell Boarding House." *American Quarterly* 25/1 (1973): 64–82.

Hosmer, Charles B., Jr. "The Broadening View of the Historic Preservation Movement," in Quimby, Ian M., ed., *Material Culture and the Study of American Life.* New York: W. W. Norton and Co., 1978.

"House America Needs." *Ladies Home Journal* 78 (October 1961): 78.

"A House is a House is a House." *Architectural Record* 108 (November 1950): 131–54.

"Houses in U.S.A.: A Brief Review of the Development of Domestic Architecture in America, 1607–1946." *Architectural Forum* 86 (January 1947); 81–88; (March 1947): 97–104; (May 1947): 81–88.

"How Architect and Owner Create the Personal House." *House and Garden* 137 (January 1970): 64–75.

Howett, Catherine M. "Frank Lloyd Wright and American Residential Landscaping." *Landscape* 26/1 (1982): 33–40.

Howling, G. "The Contemporary American House." *Builder* 182 (June 13, 1952): 876–77.

Jackson, Alan. "A New American Phenomenon—Luxurious Smaller Houses." *Arts and Decoration* 43 (February 1936): 11–15.

Jones, C. R. "Orson Squire Fowler: Practical Phrenologist." *Old Time New England* 57/4 (1967): 103–10.

Kahn, Renee. "The Bungalow Style." *Old House Journal* (September 1977): 92–102.

Kahn, Renee. "The Dutch Colonial Revival Style." *Old House Journal* (May 1982): 99–102.

Kaplan, Wendy. "R. H. T. Halsey." *Winterthur Portfolio* 17 (Spring 1982): 43–53.

Kent, William. "Domestic Architecture of California." *Architectural Forum* 32 (1920): 95–100, 151–56.

Kiesler, Frederick J. "Notes on Architecture as Sculpture." *Art in America* 54 (May 1966): 57–68.

Kimball, Fiske. "The American Country House." *Architectural Record* 46 (October 1919): 291–400.

King, Anthony. "Art of Bungalows." *Architectural Association Quarterly* 5 (Autumn 1973): 4–26.

Kniffen, Fred B. "Folk Housing: Key to Diffusion." *Annals of the Association of American Geographers* 55 (1965): 549–77.

Labine, Clem and Poore, Patricia. "The Comfortable House: Post Victorian Domestic Architecture." *Old House Journal* (February 1982): 99–102.

Lancaster, Clay. "The American Bungalow." *Art Bulletin* 40 (September 1958): 253.

Lane, Jonathan. "The Period House in the Nineteen-Twenties." *JSAH* 20 (December 1961): 169–76.

Larned, E. S. "The Edison Concrete House." *Cement Age* 6 (1908): 268–81.

Lazear, M. H. "The Evolution of the Bungalow." *House Beautiful* 36 (June 1914): 194.

Lewis, Peirce. "Common Houses. Cultural Spoor." *Landscape* 12 (1971): 1–22.

"Livable New House That's Firmly Rooted in Rural America." *Better Homes and Gardens* 52 (October 1974): 18.

Longstreth, Richard. "Academic Eclecticism in American Architecture." *Winterthur Portfolio* 17 (Spring 1982): 55–82.

MacKinnon, Richard. "Company Housing in Wabana, Bell Island, Newfoundland." *Material History Bulletin* 14 (1982): 67–72.

Mattson, Richard. "The Bungalow Style." *Journal of Cultural Geography* 2 (1981): 75 ff.

Mayer, M. M. "Domestic Architecture of the Reign of Terror in the United States." *Society of Architectural Historians Journal* 7 (July 1948): 25–26.

"Mediterranean Architecture in Florida." *Country Life* 70 (October 1936): 25–28.

Mercer, Henry C. "The Origin of Log Houses." *Bucks County Historical Society Papers* 5 (1926): 568–83.

Michael, Ronald L. and Carlisle, Ronald C. "A Lof Settler's Fort/Home." *Pennsylvania Folklife* 25 (1976): 39–46.

Moe, John F. "Concepts of Shelter: The Folk Poetics of Space, Change and Continuity." *Journal of Popular Culture* 11/1 (1977): 219–53.

Moss, Roger. "Painting the American House, 1820–1920." *Old House Journal* 9 (April 1981): 71–75.

"Mother and Home." *Mother's Magazine* 19 (1851): 23–25.

Mumford, Lewis. "The House with an Interior." *House Beautiful* 95 (June 1953): 128–30, 188–91.

Mumford, Lewis. "Where did the Contemporary American House Come From?" *House Beautiful* 94 (October 1952): 200–1, 235–36, 240, 242, 245–46, 252, 255–57.

Neuman, David J. "The American Courtship of House and Car." *Journal of Popular Culture* 7/2 (1973): 434–45.

Newcomb, Rexford. "Brief History of Rural Architecture in the United States." *President's Conference on Home Building and Home Ownership* 7 (1932): 35–56.

Newton, Roger H. "Our Summer Resort Architecture: An American Phenomenon and Social Document." *Art Quarterly* 4 (1941): 297–321.

Noyes, Daniel P. "Aim to Make Home Permanent and Attractive." *Mother's Magazine* 19 (1851): 101–3.

Olsen, David. "The Contraspatial House." *Arts and Architecture* 65 (April 1948) 30–35.

Omoto, Sadayoshi. "The Queen Style and Architectural Criticism." *JSAH* 23 (March 1964): 29–37.

Osgood, Samuel. "The Home and the Flag." *Harper's New Monthly Magazine* 26 (1863): 644–70.

Parrington, V. L. "On the Lack of Privacy in American Village Homes." *House Beautiful* 13 (1903): 109–12.

Parsons, James. "Home Building and Furnishing Industries." In Clifford Zierer, ed., *California and the Southwest.* New York: Wiley, 1956, pp. 262–75.

Peet, Stephen D. "Ethnic Styles in American Architecture." *American Antiquarian* 24 (January 1902): 19–34, 59–76.

Peterson, Fred W. "Vernacular Building and Victorian Architecture: Mid-western American Farm Homes." *Journal of Interdisciplinary History* 12 (Winter 1982): 409–27.

"Plan and Design Bungalows." *Architectural Forum* 85 (July 1946): 101–5.

"Planning the Post War House." *Architectural Forum* 80 (March 1944): 79–84.

"Platform Houses." *Architectural Record* 120 (October 1956): 205–12.

Poore, Patricia. "Pattern Book Architecture." *Old House Journal* (1980): 183 f.

Poppeliers, John, et al. "What Style Is It?" *Historic Preservation* 28/3 (1976): 34–43; 28/4 (1976): 14–23; 29/1 (1977): 14–23.

"The Private House." *Progressive Architecture* 36 (May 1955): 89–121.

"The Quality House." *House and Home* 14 (November 1958): 80–163.

Quinan, Jack. "Asher Benjamin and American Architecture." *Journal of the Society of Architectural Historians* 38/3 (1979): 244–54.

Rhoads, William B. "The Colonial Revival and American Nationalism." *JSAH* 35 (December 1976): 239–54.

Ricci, James M. "The Bungalow: A History of the Most Predominant Style of Tampa Bay." *Tampa Bay History* (Fall–Winter 1979): 6–13.

"Rooms and Their Ornaments." *Mother's Magazine and Family Monitor* 21 (1853): 209–11.

Roth, Leland. "Three Industrial Towns by McKim, Mead, and White." *JSAH* 38 (December 1979): 317–47.

Rubin, Barbara. "A Chronology of Architecture in Los Angeles." *Annals of the Association of American Geographers* 4 (1977): 521–37.

Schwartz, Barry L. "George Washington and the Whig Concept of Heroic Leadership." *American Sociological Review* 48 (1983): 18–33.

Schwartz, Barry L. "The Social Context of Commemoration: A Study in Collective Memory." *Social Forces* 61/2 (1982): 374–402.

Scully, Vincent, Jr. "American Villas: Inventiveness in the American Suburb from Downing to Wright." *Architectural Review* 115 (March 1954): 168–79.

Schapiro, Meyer. "Style." In A. L. Krober, ed., *Anthropology Today.* Chicago: 1953, pp. 287–312.

"The Sound of America Hammering." *Time* 116 (July 28, 1980): 61.

Spencer, Robert C. "Planning the Home, A Chapter on Porches," *House Beautiful* 17 (1905): 26–27.

Steiner, Frances H. "Post-Victorian Domestic Architecture: The Prairie Style." *Old House Journal* 12 (January–February 1984): 14–18.

Stickley, Gustav. "Craftsman Concrete Bungalows, Showing Economy of Construction," *Craftsman* 21 (1912): 662–75.

Stone, May N. "The Plumbing Paradox: American Attitudes Toward Late Nineteenth Century Domestic Sanitary Arrangements." *Winterthur Portfolio* 14 (Autumn 1979); 283–309.

Stowe, Harriet Beecher. "House and Home Papers." *Atlantic Monthly* 14 (January–December 1864), entire issue devoted to this theme.

Sturgis, D. N. "The Modern American Residence." *Architectural Record* 16 (1904): 297–406.

"Successful Houses." *House Beautiful* 1 (1897): 64–69.

Symonds, William H. "Rectangular Houses: Beautiful and Practicable." *Suburban Life* 15 (1912): 118–19.

Taylor, G. Stanley. "Mediterranean Architecture for the American Home." *Arts and Decoration* 25 (August 1926): 34 f.

"The Tiffany House." *Architectural Record* 10 (1900): 191–202.

Tipple, John. "The Robber Barons in the Gilded Age." In H. W. Morgan, ed., *The Gilded Age: A Reappraisal.* Syracuse: Syracuse University Press, 1963.

Twombly, Robert C. "Saving the Family Middle Class Attraction to Wright's Prairie House, 1901–1909." *American Quarterly* 27/1 (1975): 57–72.

Upton, Dell. "The Power of Things: Recent Studies in American Vernacular Architecture." *American Quarterly* 35/3 (1983): 262–79.

Van Rensselaer, Mrs. Mariana. "American Country Dwellings." *Century Magazine* (May 1886): 3–20; (June 1886): 206–20; (July 1886): 421–34.

Van Rensselaer, Mrs. Mariana. "Recent Architecture in America V: City Dwellings." *Century Magazine* 31 (November 1885–April 1886): 548.

Vlach, John M. "The Shotgun House: An African Architectural Legacy." *Pioneer America* 8/1 (1976): 47–56.

Walsh, George E. "New Open Air Architecture." *House Beautiful* 24 (1908): 118–19.

Welsch, Roger L. "The Meaning of Folk Architecture: The Sod House Example." *Keystone Folklore* 21/2 (1976–1977): 34–49.

West, Harvey G. "Built in U.S.A.: Postwar Architecture." *Progressive Architecture* 34 (February 1953): 172 + .

"What Is a Bungalow?" *Arts and Decoration* 28 (October 1911): 487–88.

Wheeler, Candace. "The New Woman and Her Home Needs." *Christian Union* 43 (1895): 895.

Wheeler, Gervase. "Pecularities of Domestic Architecture in America." *RIBA Papers* (1867–1868): 117–28, 167–89.

Wiener, Paul Lester. "A Modern American Home." *London Studio* 10 (November 1935): 251–55.

Wight, Peter B. "California Bungalows." *Western Architect* 27 (October 1918): 97.

Wight, Peter B. "Bungalow Courts in California." *Western Architect* 28 (1919): 17–19.

Wilson, H. "Origin of the Bungalow." *Country Life in America* (February 1911).

Wilson, Richard G. "The Early Work of Charles F. McKim: Country House Commission." *Winterthur Portfolio* 14/3 (1979): 235–67.

Winkelman, Michael. "The Visible City: Jackson Heights." *Metropolis* (March 1982): 23 ff.

Woods, N. M. "Planning the Small House." *House Beautiful* 35 (1914): 148–50.

Zelinsky, Wilbur. "Classical Town Names in the United States: The Historical Geography of an American Idea." *Geographical Review* 57 (1967): 435–95.

Zelinsky, Wilbur. "Nationalism in the American Place-Name Cover." *Names* 31/1 (1938): 1–28.

Zukowsky, John R. "The English Chapter House and Some American Gothic Spaces." *Studies in Medievalism* 1/2 (1982): 43–49.

Theses

Frances, Ellen E. "Progressivism and the American House: Architecture as an Agent of Social Reform." M.A. Thesis, University of Oregon, 1982.

Holdsworth, Deryck. "House and Home in Vancouver: The Evolution of a West Coast Urban Landscape." Ph.D. Dissertation, University of British Columbia, 1981.

Jones, James B., Jr. "Domestic Architecture as a Material Culture Artifact: Its Uses in the Interpretation and Teaching of American History." D.A. Dissertation, Middle Tennessee State University, 1983.

Jucha, Robert John. "The Anatomy of a Streetcar Suburb: A Development and Architectural History of Pittsburgh's Shadyside District, 1860–1920." Ph.D. Dissertation, George Washington University, 1980.

Kehler, Joel R. "A House Divided: Domestic Architecture as American Romantic Subject and Symbol." Ph.D. Dissertation, Lehigh University, 1975.

Leonidoff, Georges Pierre. "Origine et Evolution des Principaux Types d'Architecture Rurale au Québec et le cas de Charlevoix." Ph.D. Dissertation, Université Laval, Québec, 1981.

McDannell, Mary Colleen. "The Home as Sacred Space in American Protestant and Catholic Popular Thought 1840 to 1900." Ph.D. Dissertation, Temple University, 1984.

McMurry, Sally Ann. "American Farm Families and Their Houses: Vernacular Design and Social Change in the Rural North, 1830–1900." Ph.D. Dissertation, Cornell University, 1984.

Matchak, Stephen. "Folk Houses of the Northeast." Ph.D. Dissertation, University of North Carolina at Chapel Hill, 1982.

Prendergast, Norma. "The Sense of Home: Nineteenth Century Domestic Architectural Reform." Ph.D. Dissertation, Cornell University, 1981.

Schimmelman, Janice G. "The Spirit of Gothic: The Gothic Revival House in Nineteenth Century America." Ph.D. Dissertation, University of Michigan, 1981.

Vernooy, David A. "The Bungalow." M. Arch. Thesis, University of Texas at Austin, 1978.

Index

General Index